Happy Birthday Margaret

We miss you and your girls...
Dolly, Mavis, and Bonnie

Chicken and Egg

Lots of Love,

Maki

Shella

George

September 2011

Chicken and Egg

A Memoir of Suburban Homesteading
with 125 Recipes

BY *Janice Cole*

PHOTOGRAPHS BY ALEX FARNUM

CHRONICLE BOOKS
SAN FRANCISCO

To Marty, without whom this book could never have happened.

Library of Congress Cataloging-in-Publication Data available.
ISBN 978-0-8118-7045-0

Manufactured in China.

Designed by **Anne Donnard**
Prop styling by **Christine Wolheim**
Food styling by **Erin Quon**

10 9 8 7 6 5 4 3 2 1

Chronicle Books LLC
680 Second Street
San Francisco, California 94107
www.chroniclebooks.com

Acknowledgments

To my sons, Andrew and Adam, who love good food as much as I do and are always willing to listen when I need someone to bounce ideas off. You've developed into great cooks in your own right, with refined palates that I trust. Thanks for listening and for all your help.

To Marty. Thank you for your encouragement, patience, support, and humor. You not only read numerous manuscript drafts and ate the results of countless recipe revisions; you also kept everything else in our lives going while I buried myself in my work. I am truly fortunate.

I'm especially grateful for my agent, Stacey Glick, who was the first to recognize the potential of this project and expertly guided me through the steps toward publication.

I'm also grateful for my editors, Bill LeBlond and Sarah Billingsley, at Chronicle Books for undertaking this project and offering their encouragement and wise words to make this book the best it can be. Doug Ogan, Anne Donnard, Ben Kasman, Peter Perez, David Hawk, and the rest of the staff at Chronicle also deserve a huge thank-you. You do a remarkable job and produce beautiful books. Thanks also to Deborah Kops, my copy editor, for her fine eye and excellent advice.

My gratitude goes out to Adam Cole and Taylor Selsback, who stepped in when I needed help and learned firsthand the rigors of recipe testing. They each developed into wonderful assistants and I couldn't have done it without them.

Thank you also to those of you who tested individual recipes for me: Andrew Cole, Cheryl Flandrena, Juline Flandrena, my mother Dolores Gromek, Mary Margaret Ness, and Cheryl Seefeldt. I owe you all. Thanks also go to Ruth Petran for her expertise. I also appreciate and want to thank my extended family and friends, who gave me encouragement, offered their help, understood when I had to decline invitations, and gratefully tasted yet another version of a recipe. You're the best.

Thank you Mary Michelle van Wijk for your expert advice regarding the New Zealand Pavlova, and Anneke Hills for sharing your special recipe. You've turned me into a fan of this luscious dessert.

I'd also like to thank the staff at *Cooking Club* magazine (formerly *Cooking Pleasures*). You've all taught me a lot about writing and putting out a publication, and I appreciate your support and friendship through the years.

Finally, I want to thank my hens, which have graciously allowed me into their world and helped build a bridge between chickens and humans. As anyone who has pets knows, all creatures are essentially more similar than they are different. We all want a safe, warm place to live; enough food; and love in our lives.

TABLE OF CONTENTS

INTRODUCTION

There's something about chickens. Their very image seems to produce a chuckle. Just mention that you have chickens or that you want them, and you'll be descended upon by someone wanting to know more. Chickens generate a response from everyone, from those who want a flock and need the specifics to those who think you're crazy.

My interest in chickens started over nine years ago. When I finally got a tiny backyard flock, five years later, it immediately proved to be as interesting and fun as I hoped it would be. Today my hens continue to influence me and inspire my cooking.

This book is meant to encourage you—not necessarily to raise your own chickens, unless that's your particular passion—to appreciate these birds and what they offer us. My hope is that as you begin to understand this species, you will consider the impact you can make when shopping for food and base your choices on how well the chickens are treated, whether they're raised for eggs, meat, or companionship.

The recipes in this book reflect the bounty provided by the entire chicken. I have therefore included recipes for meat as well as eggs. You may eat chicken or not, depending on your own personal food philosophy. This book is not about influencing this type of food choice.

The chapters are arranged seasonally because chickens are seasonal in their behavior. In the fall and winter, the number of eggs that chickens produce decreases, sometimes so dramatically that they don't lay at all for days or even weeks at a time. As a result, each egg is more precious, and we're more careful about how many we use. In the spring and summer, the increased daylight stimulates the chickens to produce lots of eggs, which we use with abandon.

How we cook the meat also changes by season. In the spring and summer, grilled chicken appears on our table along with salads and light sautés, while in the winter we long for soups, roasts, and hearty braises. The recipes showcase the vibrant flavors these birds can provide.

Ingredients

Eggs

All of the recipes in this book are based on large eggs. The U.S. Department of Agriculture (USDA) standard for a large egg in the shell is 2 ounces in weight. A large egg white measures 2 tablespoons, and the yolk measures 1 tablespoon, for a total of 3 tablespoons per large egg. That said, in a carton of eggs you will find some slightly larger and others slightly smaller because it is the total weight of a dozen eggs that determines the size.

SIZE OF EGG	OUNCES PER DOZEN	OUNCES PER EGG
Jumbo	30	$2\frac{1}{2}$
Extra-large	27	$2\frac{1}{4}$
Large	24	2
Medium	21	$1\frac{3}{4}$
Small	18	$1\frac{1}{2}$

Obviously, backyard hens produce eggs of varying sizes. When using your own eggs, especially for baking, weigh or measure the eggs before using.

Chicken

If asked what's for dinner, a majority of families across the United States would answer chicken. The amount of chicken Americans consume has more than doubled since 1970. But as processors have scrambled to keep up with the demand, the quality and taste of our chicken has declined. I hope this book will encourage you to search out well-raised chicken and prepare it creatively.

Whether whole or in pieces, chickens vary in size, especially if you buy pasture-raised or free-range hens. Most recipes indicate a range of cooking times, along with a doneness cue. You may need to adjust the time, based on the size of your bird. It's important to not overcook chicken, regardless of what type you buy. But be sure it's cooked through—the temperature at the thickest part of the meat should be at least 165°F.

The USDA has defined the following categories of chicken:

BROILER/FRYER: A young chicken, about 7 weeks old, weighing between $2\frac{1}{2}$ and $4\frac{1}{4}$ pounds. The majority of chickens sold are in this category. The recipes in this book all work with this category of chicken.

ROASTER: An older chicken, about 3 to 5 months, weighing 5 to 7 pounds. Roasters have a generous amount of meat.

CAPON: A 4- to 8-month-old castrated rooster weighing about 4 to 7 pounds, with plump, moist flesh.

STEWING HEN: A mature hen over 10 months old. The meat is less tender and requires slow moist-heat cooking, such as stewing or braising. It is almost impossible to find a stewing hen in a supermarket, but you may be able to find one at a farmers' market or an ethnic grocery store.

When you're shopping for chickens and eggs, labels can be confusing. Here's a guide to help you through the maze:

CAGE FREE: This USDA designation means the chickens have been raised without cages, and it usually means they can walk, spread their wings, scratch the ground, and nest. It does not mean they have any access to the outdoors.

FREE RANGE: This term, also regulated by the USDA, means the chicken has access to the outdoors, but there are no requirements on how much time is spent outside or what the conditions are.

HUMANE: This label is not covered by the USDA, but there are groups, such as Humane Farm Animal Care, that offer certified programs for chickens raised under humane conditions. They usually require that the birds be cage free, with more space than traditional facilities provide, and have access to the outdoors. They prohibit forced molting (to control laying), and require a natural diet with no animal by-products.

NATURAL: This term is meaningless because it is not regulated. All chickens are considered natural because they are not a processed food. However, even chickens labeled "natural" may contain natural additives such as seaweed extract (carageenan).

NO HORMONES OR ANTIBIOTICS ADDED: The USDA has ruled that no hormones can be given to chickens. It also forbids the routine use of antibiotics, but they may be given to treat ill chickens.

ORGANIC: Chickens and eggs with an "organic" label, which is regulated by the USDA, are kept cage free, with access to the outdoors. They cannot be given antibiotics, and their food must meet organic standards.

PASTURE RAISED: There are no USDA regulations for this term, but it usually implies the hens were allowed to forage on pasture and eat a natural diet of greens and bugs, supplemented by feed. I find these to be the best-tasting eggs and chicken, and studies have found them to be the most nutritious. You can purchase them at your local farmers' market or food co-op.

VEGETARIAN FED (OR GRAIN FED): Labels with these unregulated terms mean just what they say. Even though chickens are not natural vegetarians, "vegetarian fed" has gained widespread acceptance because it indicates the chickens were not given any feed containing chicken feathers, other chicken by-products, or pork or beef (unscrupulous, but not unheard-of practices).

Equipment

Pots and Pans

Good-quality cookware almost always makes a cook's job easier. I prefer pots and pans with a heavy core of aluminum on the bottom and sides, lined with a thin layer of stainless steel. That said, all of the recipes in this book will work well with whatever cookware you have in your kitchen, but lightweight pots and pans may require a little more vigilance.

An essential piece of equipment for many of the egg recipes in this book is a nonstick skillet. It's perfect for making cooking and cleanup a dream. Be sure your nonstick pots and pans are free of scratches and chips, however, to gain their full benefits. Nonstick cookware does have some drawbacks. It's usually not suitable for cooking over high heat and doesn't brown food as well as uncoated cookware.

Below are measurements for skillets and saucepans.

SKILLETS (MEASURED ACROSS THE TOP)	SAUCEPANS (MEASURED ACROSS THE TOP)
Small: 8 inches	Small: 1 to 2 quarts
Medium: 10 inches	Medium: 2 to 3 quarts
Large: 12 inches	Large: 3 to 4 quarts

Roasting and Baking Pans

It's important to choose the correct roasting pan for chicken, because most roasting pans are made for larger birds or cuts of meat. For perfect roasting, the chicken should be surrounded by the full heat of the oven, not shielded by the sides of the pan. If there are vegetables in the roasting pan, they should also get the full benefit of the oven heat. Too often roasting pans are deep, with 3-inch sides or higher, and the chicken barely rises above the top of the pan.

One of of my favorite pans for roasting a chicken, especially when it's surrounded by vegetables or other ingredients, is a large, rimmed baking sheet, which is also known as a half-size sheet pan or jelly-roll pan. The bottom half of a broiling pan or a roasting pan with low sides is also a good choice. A small, rimmed baking sheet, also known as a quarter-size sheet pan, is perfect for roasting chicken breasts, thighs, and other pieces.

RIMMED BAKING SHEETS
Large: 18 by 13 by 1 inches
Small: 13 by 9 by 1 inches

Techniques

Cooking Eggs

Many of the egg recipes in this book call for cooking the eggs until the whites are firm and the yolks are still soft. If you prefer firmer yolks, continue to cook the eggs for a slightly longer time.

Cooking Chicken

Pat the chicken dry thoroughly before cooking. Excess moisture will prevent browning and crisping.

Always heat the pan until hot before browning chicken. If the pan isn't hot enough, the chicken's juices will start to flow, and the meat will steam, rather than brown.

Do not crowd the pan. If necessary, brown or cook the chicken in several batches.

Always start with the top (the skin side) of the chicken breast down; it will brown better and have a nicer appearance.

Many of the recipes in this book call for cooked chicken meat. Feel free to use any left-over chicken you have available, or purchase a rotisserie chicken (preferably one that was humanely raised). To poach the chicken, see the Note on page 33. You can also sauté, roast, or grill the meat.

NUMBER OF BONELESS SKINLESS BREAST HALVES	WEIGHT	CUPS OF COOKED CHOPPED CHICKEN
1	6 ounces	1
2	12 ounces	2
3	18 ounces	3
4	1½ pounds	4

Grilling

If you have a gas grill, preheat it on high heat until the grill is hot. When ready to grill, reduce the burners to the grilling temperature recommended in the recipe. High heat is about 500°F on the grill thermometer, medium is about 350°F, medium-low is about 325°F, and low heat is about 300°F.

For a charcoal grill, light the coals and let them burn until covered with a thin layer of gray ash. Rake the coals over the bottom of the grill. To judge the temperature, hold your hand about 6 inches above the coals. For high heat, you should be able to keep your hand there for only 3 seconds before it feels uncomfortably hot. For medium heat, you should be able to last 7 seconds; for medium-low heat, about 10 seconds; and for low heat, about 12 seconds.

To oil the grill grate before you put on the chicken, wad some paper towels into a ball and dip lightly in oil. Use grilling tongs to wipe the grill grate lightly with the paper towels.

Measuring Flour

I measure flour by spooning it into a measuring cup and leveling it off without tapping. One cup of all-purpose flour weighs 4.4 ounces, and 1 cup of bread flour weighs 4.8 ounces.

CHAPTER · ONE
Why
CHICKENS?

Turkeys surrounded me when I received the phone call. Naked turkeys. I was at a photo studio miles from the office. The birds were lined up next to each other like beauty contestants as I closely examined their legs, thighs, and breasts. Only one bird could be chosen, and it had to be nearly perfect. The legs had to be slender and long, the breast high and well shaped, and the skin taut and blemish free. As I judged the shape of each bird (some had great breasts, others great legs, but which one had it all?), I couldn't help but notice the pale purplish tinge of the skin under the fluorescent lights. These turkeys looked like they were being prepped for the medical examiner's table instead of the dinner table. Reinforcing that image, I pulled on a pair of disposable gloves and got ready to slather the birds with a thick layer of shortening before popping them in the oven. It was the middle of a magazine photo shoot, and I was the food stylist. One of these turkeys was going to be featured on the cover of the fall issue of *Cooking Pleasures* magazine. On that gorgeous Minnesota day in May, five years ago, I didn't notice the weather. My eyes were focused on reading recipes and making Thanksgiving dinner. But before the phone rang, my mind was busy pondering the layoff rumors I'd heard through the company grapevine.

I've spent a good portion of my life trying to keep my glass filled full, but I readily admit that I subscribe more to a glass-half-empty view of life. So when the word went out that staff cutbacks were a real possibility, I expected the worst. Unfortunately, I was right. Everyone was sorry, it had nothing to do with me personally, it was just business. Right. I carefully kept my glass filled that evening—and for several weeks thereafter—with wine.

My editor in chief was wonderful and said all the right things when we met after the photo shoot. She didn't know how she was going to get along without me. She wanted to talk to upper management and try to get my job back as food stylist and food editor, but on a consulting basis. Would I be interested? I'd been in the food business a long time and had a number of paths I could follow. But I, along with the rest of our small staff, had been with *Cooking Pleasures* from the beginning. After eight years, I felt a deep connection to the group and what we were doing. The recipe-oriented magazine had grown to about half a million subscribers across the country, and we were all proud.

In the end, my boss was able to make an official proposal. But I had to think about whether I really wanted to revive the freelance career I had shelved to work at the magazine. Based on my editor's proposal, I would have at least one large client to begin with. I was tempted. On the other hand, like everyone else who has ever been laid off, I felt like shoving the offer in the company's face and shouting "Forget you!"

Eventually, I convinced myself that free-lance work would be the best of both worlds. I'd no longer have the daily two-hour-plus commute, in the summer I'd get to work in shorts and a tank top on the deck, and I'd have some money coming in to start with. I'd restart my freelance career, but then what? It seemed like there should be something more—something new, not just working for the same company, minus the benefits, and scrambling for extra work on the side.

I wish I could tell you that I decided to take the next year and travel the world, taking cooking classes on every continent. Or that I came into a windfall and bought a house in South America. Luckily my husband still had a good job, but we had two sons in college. I didn't have the option of doing something wild and extravagant and expensive. Still, I needed to make this change mean something. As I settled into my new/old role, I began thinking . . . about chickens!

My idea of raising chickens began a long time ago, almost as a joke. This was well before the current backyard chicken craze hit the country.

"I want chickens," I announced one day while my husband, Marty, was watching television. "Huh!" he mumbled. I went on to explain about how cute it would be to have a few chickens running around the backyard. "Um," he replied. I left it at that. A lot of our major decisions have similar beginnings.

Looking back, I'm not sure how serious I was when I first raised the idea of chickens. At the time, I still had a full-time job, the boys were living at home, and our lives were busy, verging on chaotic. But my chicken fantasy soon gained a life of its own. I became like the landowner in Woody Allen's movie *Love and Death* who carried a piece of turf in his pocket announcing to everyone "Someday I'm going to build on this land." Someday I was going to have chickens.

It's hard to pinpoint the exact moment I began fancying chickens, but it may have been immediately after my first taste of free-range organic eggs from the farmers' market. As a former restaurant chef, I've had my share of incredible food experiences. But those simply prepared eggs, only hours old, from chickens that had run in the sun and eaten natural food, was truly mind altering.

I still remember coming home from our local farmers' market and showing my two sons the beautiful green, tan, and dark-brown eggs I had purchased. It was lunchtime, and I boiled a few of the eggs and made simple egg-salad sandwiches spread with shallots and homemade mayonnaise. The eggs were difficult to peel because of their freshness, but the taste was like nothing I had ever had. The vivid-yellow yolks turned the mixture into a golden glow. We all happily chomped on our sandwiches, licking the egg salad that was dripping down our chins. And there was almost no sound as the three of us sat, mesmerized by the taste. When my younger son begged, "More, please," I knew I simply had to find a way to have my own eggs.

Six months after I started working from home, I began earnestly talking about raising chickens. "You're crazy," my husband said when he realized I might actually be getting serious. "We can't have a farm here; we live in the suburbs of St. Paul. It's the Twin Cities; we're urban." I assured him I didn't want a farm, just a couple of chickens. I pictured cute chicks, picturesque chicken coops, and indescribably delicious eggs. My husband imagined smelly farm animals, hard work, and mountains of chicken poop.

Friends often loved the idea at first, but quickly became squeamish. "You *cook* for a living!" they'd exclaim. "You're not a vegetarian, you cook *chickens*!" Then they would ask me accusingly, "How can you raise them in your backyard?"

I explained that I didn't intend to eat my chickens. "Besides," I said, "farmers do it all the time." "That's different," they muttered.

Was it?

Our yard is a fine place for chickens. It's bigger than a city lot, although quite cozy for a suburban yard—a mixture of grass, lots of bushes and trees for chickens to hide under, and wild growth in the back to romp in. There were no neighbors in the lot out back. It was owned by a cemetery but unoccupied. Whoever "moved in" probably wouldn't complain. Our neighbors on either side were close by, but we all got along well, probably aided by the high privacy fences between us. The remaining five houses on our cul-de-sac would be far removed from the chickens, so hopefully there would be no problem.

I didn't aspire to have chickens as pets; except for cats I wasn't that much of an animal lover. Dogs scare me, fish are a lot of work for no return, and although I'd let the kids keep their share of hamsters and rats, the eeeek! factor still got me. I wanted chickens for only one reason—really good eggs.

I couldn't understand why Marty didn't automatically share my passion. I thought it would be fun, the perfect project to do together. Maybe that's what worried him. Perhaps the idea of mucking out a chicken coop was more than he could bear. Mucking about with anything has never been his idea of fun. For instance, he can't remember, even as a boy, ever playing in the mud. I think it has to do with his Scandinavian-Germanic heritage, or maybe with being raised Lutheran. Garrison Keillor has elevated Scandinavian Lutherans to comedic heights. But really. Have you ever noticed how everything is so darn tidy and neat and organized in a Lutheran church? Far different from the jumbled, statue-filled, incense-fogged Slavic churches of my childhood.

I thought keeping a few chickens in the back was a reasonable idea. What Marty didn't know was that deep down I really wanted goats. Imagine making your own goat cheese.

In the end, Marty and I settled our differences by agreeing to disagree. He could sense my passion building, and he sighed with resignation, "Well, if you really want to do this, that's fine. Just remember that they'll be your chickens. Don't involve me in it!"

"No problem," I said defiantly. The fact that I knew nothing about chickens didn't bother me. How hard could it be? As the snow began to fall, I made plans. Spring should be the perfect time to get chickens.

I'm not an impulse shopper. I carefully research every important purchase I make, compare several stores, look online, and locate the best deal. Then I think about it. That's why what happened next was so out of character.

I planned to get the chicks in May. The weather would be warm, they'd be able to go outside, and I'd have eggs by summer. I wanted baby chicks. The reason? Deep down I was really quite afraid of chickens, especially large grown-up hens. I couldn't imagine holding a large chicken. My plan was to bond with the chicks when they were tiny, and hopefully we'd all learn to get along together.

Although I hadn't done all my usual research, I figured there was plenty of time. I did sign up for a one-night adult-education course in March at a Minneapolis inner-city school on keeping city chickens. I assumed I'd be one of a couple of students, but the class filled to capacity with a wide range of people. Who knew? By the end of the night my head was overloaded, but two things stood out: (1) Keeping chickens is less work than having a dog; (2) I knew that I had to get my chicks *immediately*.

When I got home, I burst through the door shouting, "Did you know chickens don't start laying until they're at least five months old?" Without waiting for Marty's response, I continued, "That means if I don't get chicks

until May they won't lay until October, when there's less light, the temperatures are cool, and they naturally start laying fewer eggs." Marty continued watching a basketball game on the television, not really responding, until I said, "That means I have to get the chicks this weekend!" Then he sat up. "You're kidding, right?" A few days later I was the proud owner of three baby chicks.

CHAPTER · TWO

EARLY

SPRING

"Hello, this is Clare from Omlet. What can I do to help you?" Her British accent sent tingles up my spine. I'm a sucker for anyone with a British accent. I think some Americans must buy the English-designed Eglu coop just to talk to Clare on the phone. Making no effort to hide the excitement in my voice, I ordered my Eglu.

I decided to go with the mod, designer-label coop because it was easy. No building required, no fencing to cut, and everything you needed for a backyard flock, including ready-to-lay chickens, if desired, was delivered directly to your house. Plus, even though I wanted chickens, I didn't want our yard looking like a farm. All of the other coops had that barnyard look and feel. I wanted urban chicks, and the wacky contemporary look of the brightly colored, plastic Eglu seemed to capture that.

It's so nice dealing with a small company. I had the feeling Clare was almost as excited as I was. "Now the fun part," she said. "What color do you want?" "Blue!" I answered immediately, as I had my heart set on a royal blue coop. "Blue?" she said with genuine surprise.

My heart began to sink. What if they were out of blue coops? I couldn't bear to have one of their other colors in my backyard, especially pink.

"Don't you have any blue Eglus?" I asked.

"Oh, don't worry, luv; we have blue. It's just that people don't normally order the blue." My astonishment was apparent as I all but shouted "Really?" at her. "Well, we sell some blue coops, but the favorite is green. I guess because it blends into the grass." Those silly sods! I thought to myself. Or maybe I said it out loud; I'm not sure. Brit-com slang had been filling my head while I was talking to her. That large plastic overgrown-outdated-iMac-computer-look-alike thing sitting in your garden is never going to blend in, no matter what color it is, I thought.

My belief, now restored, regarding the foolishness of other people increased my confidence as I confirmed that my choice was blue. I confided in Clare how I absolutely loved blue and how the coop would match the cushions on my deck furniture. I don't think she cared that much. She did ask where we were going to put the Eglu, and I said in our backyard. Actually, I might have said "in our garden" with my best British accent because I was really getting into it by that time. We finished the transaction, and she reminded me the coop and run would be delivered in two parts, along with the grub bowl, the glug bowl, chicken instructions, and a set of six mini egg cartons, each ready to hold four eggs. I had *actually* ordered my chicken coop. Now all I needed were chickens.

Three days after the chicken class, I drove to a local feed store to get my chicks. Tom, the owner, greeted me heartily and asked what I was looking for. I reminded him that we had spoken the day before about the chicks he was getting in, and I wanted two. "These round washtubs are the day-olds," he said. I watched the little peeps as they tottered, fell, pecked at each other, climbed on top of each other, ate and drank, and did it all again. Some slept in the midst of the chaos.

As I bent down to look more closely, Tom asked again, "Are you sure you want only two? Chickens are social creatures; they like a crowd." Never ask a woman if she wants more baby chicks while she's looking at a tub full of bobbing fluff balls. "Well . . . maybe I could take three." If my coop had been bigger, I might have walked out with the entire washtub of fuzzy orbs that morning.

I knew I wanted an Easter egg chick, the mixed breed of Araucana and Ameraucana that lays colorful green, blue, or pink eggs. Beyond that I was clueless. "The brown-and-black ones will lay colored eggs," Tom explained. "The gold ones are Buff Orpingtons, and they're a good hen," he added.

Now that I was getting three, I wanted three different breeds. "Well, I don't have any other day-olds but these over here are just a few weeks old." They looked huge next to the baby chicks. I decided to stay with the day-olds. As I peered into the fuzzy, swarming tubs, I recalled an old *Star Trek* episode about Tribbles. It was disconcerting.

Was there some trick to choosing baby chicks, like examining a mare's teeth and hooves when you buy a horse? If so, the feed store owner wasn't going to let me in on the secret. So I developed my own criteria: (1) Let sleeping chicks lie. Any chicks that could sleep in that cacophony must be comatose; (2) If you can grab it, take it. The fluff balls never stopped moving. By the time your hand shot out to grab the one you wanted, it had moved three times and you had no idea where it went; (3) Take the one at the top. Nature is always guided by survival of the fittest. Those chicks that reached the summit must be stronger than the ones squashed at the bottom.

My chosen three were unceremoniously put into a tiny box with air holes. "Now, they're all females, right?" I wanted reassurance from Tom that I didn't have a rooster hidden in the group. "Well, they should be," Tom fudged. "What do you mean they should be," I shot back with a small note of panic. "We can't guarantee it. But don't worry; we'll take back any roosters," he replied. Oh, great, now I have to worry about crowing, I thought as I paid $3.95 per chick and headed to the car. Marty will *really* love that.

I stopped worrying about whether I might have a rooster and drove home, excited that I finally had my own chickens. It wasn't until years later that I learned what happens to all the roosters no one wants. The dark side of the hatchery business is shocking. Half of the chicks born are males. Most of them are ground up live by the binful or smothered to death for dog food or fertilizer. Those of us who don't have a place for noisy roosters in our picturesque backyard flocks are but a tiny part of the problem. The simple fact is roosters don't lay eggs. They also take longer to raise for meat, requiring more feed, which costs extra money. So the meat industry has no use for them. Plus, the meat doesn't taste the same as the bland chicken we've all become accustomed to. Roosters are like the daughters in some cultures around the world—no one wants them.

I arrived home from the feed store frazzled and slightly deaf in one ear from the chicks' high-pitched peeping. I'd only been with them for forty minutes, and they were already driving me nuts. If the next two months are going to be like this, I thought as I walked into the house, God help us all. You see, these chicks had to bunk with us inside the house until they feathered out and the weather warmed up. Marty had no idea what he was in for. I'll admit I may have left out a few of the specifics before rushing off to the feed store, figuring he'd find out soon enough. I really thought the cute baby chicks would win him over. I was wrong.

My less-than-excited husband played his part by ignoring the whole situation. It was a major feat, since the large plastic storage tub I turned into a brooder sat in the family room within view of my office, the kitchen, and the living room. Any thought of moving the brooder to the basement or an out-of-the-way bedroom was no longer an option, as I decided the fragile chicks needed monitoring.

The chicks needed names. I considered the two Easter egg chicks. Their gold and black markings are striking when they're small, and the chickens look regal as they age. The smaller one had eye markings that rivaled Elizabeth Taylor's makeup in *Cleopatra*, so I named her Cleo, although Marty argued she was going for the goth look. I named the second Easter egg chick Lulu, which quickly changed to Crazy Lulu as her personality became evident. Larger, stronger, and more forceful than Cleo, she was determined to get her own way all of the time.

I decided to let Marty name the last chick, my Buff Orpington, an energetic girl covered in golden fluff. I should have known better. He named her after "Roxanne," the hit song by the Police, because of the red heat light that hovered over the brooder the chicks were in. Maybe that's why this chick struts around with so much attitude and stays up half the night!

Extra-Creamy Scrambled Eggs over Buttermilk-Chive Biscuits

I call these eggs my risotto-style scrambled eggs because the cooking method is similar to the one for risotto. You cook the eggs slowly over low heat, stirring constantly while you gradually add the cream. The eggs should form very tiny curds or no curds at all. The result is velvety, delicate eggs, tender and moist. Served over fresh-from-the-oven biscuits, it's a breakfast worth getting up for!

Preheat the oven to 450°F. Line a baking sheet with parchment paper.

TO MAKE THE BISCUITS: Whisk together the flour, baking powder, baking soda, and salt in a medium bowl. Blend the butter into the flour mixture with a pastry blender or your fingertips until the butter is the size of blueberries. Gently stir in the buttermilk and chives with a fork until the dry ingredients are moistened.

Put the biscuit dough on a lightly floured surface and pat into a 5-inch round, ³/₄ inch thick. Using a floured dough cutter or knife, cut into four wedges. Place them on the baking sheet ¹/₂ inch apart.

Bake for 10 to 12 minutes or until rich golden brown on the top and bottom. Cool slightly on a wire rack.

TO MAKE THE EGGS: While the biscuits are baking, vigorously whisk the eggs in a medium bowl for 1 minute or until light and very frothy. Melt the butter over medium heat in a small nonstick skillet. (A larger skillet will cook the eggs too quickly for this recipe.) Add the eggs and cook for 1 minute, stirring constantly with a heat-proof silicone spatula.

Reduce the heat to medium-low, or low if the eggs begin to cook too fast. Add 1 tablespoon of the cream and cook for 1 minute, stirring constantly and scraping the bottom and sides of the pan. Continue cooking and stirring, adding 1 tablespoon of cream per minute. Add the salt and pepper with the last tablespoon of cream. The total cooking time should be about 6 to 7 minutes, or until the eggs are creamy but not liquid.

Split the warm biscuits and smear with butter, if desired. Spoon the eggs over the split biscuits and garnish with the chives before serving.

SERVES 4

BISCUITS

1 cup all-purpose flour

1 teaspoon baking powder

¹/₄ teaspoon baking soda

¹/₈ teaspoon salt

4 tablespoons cold unsalted butter, cut up

¹/₂ cup buttermilk

1 tablespoon thinly sliced fresh chives

EGGS

4 eggs

1 tablespoon unsalted butter

5 tablespoons heavy (whipping) cream

¹/₈ teaspoon salt

¹/₈ teaspoon freshly ground pepper

Butter for serving (optional)

Sliced fresh chives for garnish

CHICKEN CRAZY

Wondering why so many people across the nation are going crazy for chickens? Here are some of the answers:

EGGS: Nothing beats the flavor of a freshly laid egg, still warm from the nest. Chickens that run through the backyard, feed on vegetable scraps, and dig in the soil produce ultrafresh, intensely flavored eggs and vibrantly colored egg yolks. There is also growing evidence that free-range pasture-fed chicken eggs are more nutritious.

MEAT: A small group of backyard chicken enthusiasts not only raise chickens for eggs, but also for their meat. Many cities ban the slaughter of backyard birds, but there are areas where it's legal. The meat from home-ranged chickens is more succulent and flavorful because of the exercise it's had. Studies have shown that it's also healthier, with less fat, fewer calories, and more vitamin A and omega-3 fatty acids. Although most urban chicken owners wouldn't dream of eating their own birds, some enthusiasts like controlling all aspects of their food production.

COMPANIONSHIP: One of the unexpected pleasures of raising chickens is the pleasure and entertainment they provide, just like more conventional pets. Chickens are highly intelligent creatures with distinct personalities. They're social animals and most of them love human companionship. Chickens will readily cuddle on your lap, beg to be petted, jump on your shoulder, and follow you around. They respond to your voice and get to know various members of the family. Chickens, like other pets, will cheer you up or offer a shoulder for you to cry on.

BETTER GARDENS: People who garden appreciate chickens for the compost they provide and the pests they eat. Composted chicken waste contributes highly valuable nutrients to plants and soil. Gardeners also find chickens useful for turning over the garden soil in the spring and fall. Just remember that chickens need boundaries to keep them out of growing gardens. These clever birds will help themselves to anything that looks tasty.

Fluffy Omelet with Early Spring Herbs

Rev up your morning by stirring and shaking your way to a fluffy, tender omelet. The best omelets are made with the French method. Their motto is keep the eggs moving. Stirring the eggs and shaking the pan keeps them from overcooking and creates a delicate omelet that's creamy on the inside.

SERVES 1

3 eggs

1/8 teaspoon kosher salt

2 or 3 grinds of pepper

2 teaspoons sliced fresh chives

2 teaspoons chopped fresh tarragon

2 teaspoons chopped fresh mint

2 tablespoons unsalted butter, cut up

Whisk the eggs, salt, and pepper in a medium bowl for 1 full minute or until foamy and very well blended. Don't skimp on the whisking time—you want the eggs to be light and runny like liquid when you lift the whisk up.

Combine the chives, tarragon, and mint together in a small cup. Stir 1 tablespoon of the mixed herbs into the eggs.

Heat a medium nonstick skillet over medium-high heat until hot. Add the butter. It will sizzle and begin to melt, foaming slightly. When the foaming stops, immediately pour in the eggs and begin stirring with a heat-proof silicone spatula. While you're stirring, shake the pan back and forth across the burner. When the eggs start to form moist curds and no longer flow like liquid (this happens fast, in about 30 seconds), spread out the eggs across the bottom of the pan and sprinkle the remaining 1 tablespoon of mixed herbs over the moist eggs.

To serve, remove the pan from the heat and tilt it slightly while folding the top edge of the omelet toward the center. Loosen the bottom of the omelet with the spatula and slide the bottom edge onto a plate. Tip the pan over so the omelet rolls off the pan and onto the plate. The omelet should be golden yellow in color, and the center should be moist, soft, and tender.

NOTES

This technique is very simple to master as long as you keep both hands moving at the same time. The whole process goes very quickly; from start to finish it should take less than 1 minute.

To make more than one omelet, beat the eggs ahead of time and set up an assembly line with the remaining ingredients. Use 3/4 cup of beaten eggs per omelet, and cover each omelet to keep it warm.

To make a 2-egg omelet, reduce the amount of herbs to 1 1/2 teaspoons.

Poached Eggs over Spring Watercress and Croutons

Although watercress is now available year-round, its bright-green color and peppery bite still evokes spring to me. The beauty of this dish is revealed when you pierce the egg with your fork: the yellow yolk oozes over the egg white and onto the watercress and crisp, golden toast. It's a study in contrasts—exactly what springtime is here in the northland.

SERVES 4

Crack each egg into its own small cup. Set aside. Combine the garlic and 1 tablespoon of the olive oil in a small bowl. Brush the garlic oil over one side of each of the bread slices.

Heat a large nonstick skillet over medium heat until hot. Pour 1 tablespoon of the olive oil into the pan and swirl around to coat the bottom of the pan. Heat the oil. Add the bread, garlic-oil-side up, and cook for 4 to 6 minutes, or until lightly browned on both sides, turning once. Increase the heat to medium-high if necessary. Place the toasted croutons on individual plates. Set aside the skillet.

While the bread is toasting, fill a medium nonstick skillet with water; cover and bring to a gentle boil over high heat. Remove from the heat and gently slide the eggs into the water. Cover and let sit for 3 minutes or until the whites are set but the yolks are still soft. Remove each egg with a slotted spoon and drain briefly on paper towels (while still in the spoon).

While the eggs are poaching, add the remaining $1/2$ tablespoon of olive oil to the large skillet and sauté the watercress over medium heat for 20 to 30 seconds, or until bright green and slightly wilted. Sprinkle with $1/8$ teaspoon each of the salt and pepper. Arrange the watercress over the croutons, and top with the poached eggs. Sprinkle with the remaining $1/8$ teaspoon salt and pepper before serving.

4 eggs

1 garlic clove, minced

$2^1/2$ tablespoons extra-virgin olive oil

4 slices artisan Italian bread (from an oval loaf, cut $1/2$ inch thick)

3 cups chopped watercress or spinach (about 8 ounces)

$1/4$ teaspoon coarse sea salt

$1/4$ teaspoon freshly ground pepper

Lemon-Tarragon Deviled Eggs

Soft, fresh goat cheese is the surprise ingredient in these ultracreamy deviled eggs. The first sprigs of tarragon that emerge in the spring have a light, delicate flavor that pairs perfectly with the bright-yellow yolks of spring eggs. Fresh grass and other greens in a hen's spring diet enhance the flavor of these eggs.

Cut the hard-cooked eggs in half lengthwise. Scoop out the egg yolks with a small spoon and put them in a medium bowl. Blend with a pastry blender or a fork until crumbly, about the consistency of coarse sand. Stir in the goat cheese until well blended, add the mayonnaise, and stir until smooth and creamy. Stir in the green onion, grated lemon zest, salt, and pepper.

Spoon the egg yolk filling into a pastry bag fitted with a ½-inch star tip and pipe the mixture into the egg whites. Or, spoon the filling into the egg whites. Garnish with tarragon sprigs and slivered lemon zest before serving.

NOTE To hard-cook eggs, put the eggs in a medium saucepan and add enough hot tap water to just cover the eggs. Bring to a boil over high heat. Reduce the heat immediately to medium-low or low and gently boil for 9 minutes. Keep the water at a very slow, steady boil (the eggs should never bounce or rattle because of quickly boiling water), adjusting the heat as necessary. Remove the eggs from the water immediately with a slotted spoon and put in a bowl of ice water until cool. Remove the shells under running water.

SERVES 6
MAKES 12 DEVILED EGGS

6 hard-cooked eggs
(see Note)

⅓ cup fresh goat cheese,
softened

⅓ cup mayonnaise

1 tablespoon finely chopped
fresh tarragon, plus sprigs
for garnish

1 tablespoon thinly sliced
green onion (green part only)

Scant ½ teaspoon grated
lemon zest, plus slivered zest
for garnish

⅛ teaspoon salt

⅛ teaspoon freshly ground
pepper

Tossed Greens with Strawberries, Avocado, and Farm-Fresh Eggs

This beautiful salad is a perfect way to use the first strawberries of the season. The spring greens, avocado, and bright sweet strawberries complement the five-minute eggs, with their creamy, tender whites and softly set yolks. Serve this salad for lunch on the patio, as part of a brunch, or as an elegant first course for dinner. If you have fresh chive blossoms, scatter the purple flowers over the salad before serving.

TO MAKE THE DRESSING: Whisk together the ingredients in a small bowl and set aside.

TO MAKE THE SALAD: Arrange the eggs in a single layer in a small saucepan and add enough hot tap water to just cover the tops of the eggs. Cook over high heat until the water just begins to boil. When you see the first bubbles appear, immediately lower the heat to medium-low or low and cook for 5 minutes at a gentle boil. Remove the eggs with a slotted spoon and place in a bowl of ice water until cool. Peel and cut each egg crosswise into six slices. The egg whites should be firm yet tender, and the yolks should be soft but not runny.

Toss the greens in a large bowl with enough dressing to lightly coat the leaves. Divide the greens among 4 plates and top with the sliced avocado. Place the egg slices in the center of the greens and arrange clusters of strawberries around the edges. Sprinkle the salads generously with freshly ground pepper and pass the remaining dressing when serving.

SERVES 4

BALSAMIC-MAPLE DRESSING

2 tablespoons extra-virgin olive oil

2 tablespoons pure maple syrup

1 tablespoon thinly sliced fresh chives

2 teaspoons balsamic vinegar

1/4 teaspoon honey mustard

SALAD

4 eggs

5 cups lightly packed mixed greens

1 avocado, peeled, pitted, and sliced

1 1/2 cups quartered fresh strawberries

Freshly ground pepper

Chicken and Egg Salad Sandwiches with Fresh Dill Mayonnaise

Two classics—chicken salad and egg salad—are blended with a fresh dill mayonnaise. The result is an updated sandwich that appeals to everyone. It's a perfect way to stretch a little leftover chicken into a great new meal.

SERVES 6

Gently toss the chicken and eggs together in a medium bowl with a fork, being careful not to mash the eggs. Sprinkle the shallots, ¼ teaspoon of the salt, and ¼ teaspoon of the pepper over the mixture and gently toss to mix.

Stir together the mayonnaise and mustard in a small bowl until smooth. Stir in the dill and the remaining ¼ teaspoon each of the salt and pepper. Add to the chicken and eggs and stir gently until mixed.

Place a lettuce leaf on each of 6 slices of the bread. Top with the chicken-and-egg-salad mixture and cover with the remaining 6 slices of bread. Serve immediately.

NOTE — To poach chicken, fill a medium skillet with water. Add a couple of onion slices, 1 bay leaf, ¼ teaspoon of dried thyme, and 5 dill stems, if available. Bring to a boil over medium-high heat, add 1 large boneless, skinless chicken breast half (about 10 ounces), reduce the heat, and simmer for 8 to 10 minutes or until no longer pink in the center. Remove from the liquid and cool completely. Shred into bite-sized pieces. If you're poaching chicken breast for another recipe, omit the dill.

1½ cups shredded poached chicken breast (see Note)

4 hard-cooked eggs (see Note, page 31), chopped (1½ cups)

½ cup chopped shallots (about 3 large)

½ teaspoon salt

½ teaspoon freshly ground pepper

1 cup mayonnaise

¾ teaspoon Dijon mustard

3 tablespoons coarsely chopped fresh dill

6 Boston "butter" lettuce leaves

12 slices crusty country French or sourdough bread (½ inch thick)

Fettuccine with Crisp Bacon, Spring Mushrooms, and Eggs

This pasta is a study in contrasts. The tender pasta and earthy mushrooms are accented with the taste of smoky bacon, while lightly fried eggs create a delicate sauce. An assortment of mushrooms gives this recipe the best flavor. Nutty morels are the perfect spring mushroom choice, but the more common shiitake and oyster mushrooms are also fine. Feel free to use half cremini (also known as baby bellas) or button mushrooms and half exotic mushrooms.

SERVES 4

6 ounces bacon (about 6 slices), coarsely chopped

2 tablespoons unsalted butter

8 ounces assorted mushrooms

$\frac{1}{4}$ teaspoon of kosher salt, plus a pinch

$\frac{1}{4}$ teaspoon freshly ground pepper, plus $\frac{1}{8}$ teaspoon

$\frac{1}{4}$ cup sliced shallots

2 garlic cloves, minced

One 8- to 9-ounce package fresh fettuccine

$\frac{1}{2}$ cup freshly shredded Parmigiano-Reggiano cheese

4 eggs

$\frac{1}{3}$ cup sliced fresh chives

Bring a large pot of salted water to a rapid boil.

Heat a large nonstick skillet over medium-high heat. Add the bacon and cook for 7 to 9 minutes or until the bacon is golden brown and crisp, stirring occasionally and reducing the heat to medium if necessary. Drain the bacon on paper towels, and put in a medium bowl. Pour 1 tablespoon of the drippings into a small heat-proof cup and set aside. Discard the remaining drippings.

Add the butter to the same skillet and melt over medium heat. Increase the heat to medium-high and add the mushrooms. Cook for 3 to 4 minutes or until the mushrooms are tender, stirring often. Sprinkle with the $\frac{1}{4}$ teaspoon each of salt and pepper. Stir in the shallots and cook 30 to 40 seconds or until they just begin to cook. Add the garlic and cook, stirring, for 30 seconds or until the garlic becomes fragrant. Combine the mushroom mixture with the bacon in the bowl. Set aside the skillet.

Cook the pasta in the boiling water for 2 to 3 minutes or until tender, reserving $\frac{1}{3}$ cup of the cooking water. Drain the pasta. Toss in a large warm pasta bowl with the reserved cooking water and the cheese.

While the pasta is cooking, add the reserved tablespoon of bacon drippings to the skillet. Heat until warm over medium heat. Add the eggs and sprinkle with the remaining pinch of salt and $\frac{1}{8}$ teaspoon pepper. Cover and cook $1\frac{1}{2}$ to 2 minutes, or just until the whites are set but the yolks are still soft.

Divide the pasta among 4 plates, top with the bacon and mushroom mixture, and place an egg on top of each serving. Shower with fresh chives before serving.

READY TO TAKE THE CHICKEN PLUNGE?

Chickens are trendy and, yes, you'd love a couple in your backyard. But is raising chickens right for you? Here are some questions for you to consider:

1. IS KEEPING CHICKENS LEGAL IN YOUR AREA? If yes, follow the recommendations set forth by your city or town. If not, talk to officials about the possibility of changing the regulations to allow a small number of hens. Many cities are realizing the benefits of allowing small flocks of chickens as their residents seek locally grown, sustainable food.

2. DO YOU HAVE THE SPACE? Chickens can exist in very small spaces (think industrial battery hens), but for the best quality of life, they need room to stretch and roam. The recommendations range from about 10 to 25 square feet per bird. This means even small city lots can support a couple of hens. If the chickens are allowed to roam the yard, they'll need less coop space than if they're kept confined to a coop and run.

3. WILL YOU HAVE THE TIME? Chickens are low-maintenance animals. In fact, they're easier to care for than dogs. They still require a commitment from you, however. At the minimum, you will need to get up early to let them out of the coop and into their run. You'll have to set out their food and clean water and check for eggs. At night, you'll have to make sure they're in the coop and secure from predators. Once a week you'll want to do a routine cleanup of the coop and the run, and once a month the area should get a thorough cleaning. So be realistic. Hundreds of people get baby chicks at Easter, only to later abandon them. If your lifestyle includes frequent traveling and staying out late, chickens may be a bad choice. Once you make the decision, you're responsible for their well-being, safety, and good health.

4. DO YOU HAVE THE RESOURCES? If you think you're going to save money on eggs, think again. The actual cost of home-raised eggs may be higher than those from the store. Although chickens are relatively inexpensive to keep compared to other pets, they do require an initial investment. The main expense will be the coop. Depending on where you live, the coop may be a simple shelter from the rain and sun or an insulated structure with heat and light. Keeping the roaming areas free from predators requires adequate fencing all around, including the top. (Many chicken owners do keep their expenses to a minimum, though, by creative planning and the use of recycled materials.)

Chicken Breasts with Bunches of Chives

The simplicity of this dish calls for the finest of ingredients. Use the best pasture-fed chicken available. The puréed fresh chives create an emerald-green vinaigrette that's used as both a marinade and a sauce, infusing the chicken with the delicate pungency of spring chives. There are two types of chives: round-stem chives, the most common, are called onion chives, while the flat-stem chives are known as garlic chives. Either can be used in this recipe. When available, garlic chives can also be quickly sautéed like greens and served as a tasty side dish.

TO MAKE THE VINAIGRETTE: Put all the ingredients in a blender container and blend until smooth and bright green in color.

TO MAKE THE CHICKEN: Drop the chicken breasts into a large resealable plastic bag and pour half the vinaigrette (about ¼ cup) over the chicken. Seal the bag, eliminating as much air as possible, and massage the vinaigrette into the chicken. Put in a shallow pan and marinate in the refrigerator for 8 to 12 hours. Cover and refrigerate the remaining vinaigrette.

Preheat the oven to 425°F. Bring the reserved vinaigrette to room temperature. Line a small, rimmed baking sheet with foil. Remove the chicken from the marinade, shaking off any excess and discarding the marinade. Heat a large skillet over medium-high heat. Add the 1 tablespoon olive oil. When the oil is hot, cook the chicken for 4 minutes or until golden brown on one side. (Be careful; the chicken may splatter slightly from the marinade.) Remove from the heat. Place the chicken, browned-side up, on the baking sheet and sprinkle with the salt and pepper.

Bake the chicken for 5 to 8 minutes or until no longer pink in the center (see Note). Remove from the oven and let rest for 5 minutes. Pour any accumulated pan juices into the reserved vinaigrette.

SERVES 4

CHIVE VINAIGRETTE

½ cup extra-virgin olive oil

¼ cup plus 2 tablespoons sliced fresh chives

2 teaspoons grated lemon zest

2 teaspoons fresh lemon juice

¼ teaspoon kosher salt

¼ teaspoon freshly ground pepper

CHICKEN

4 boneless skinless chicken breast halves (about 1½ pounds)

1 tablespoon extra-virgin olive oil

¼ teaspoon kosher salt

¼ teaspoon freshly ground pepper

TO MAKE THE SAUTÉED CHIVES, IF DESIRED: Heat a large skillet over medium-high heat and lightly film with the olive oil. Sauté the chives for 3 minutes or until slightly wilted. The greens should sizzle and lightly brown as you sauté them. Sprinkle with the salt.

To serve, slice the chicken breasts diagonally into thirds. Divide the sautéed chives (if using) among 4 plates. Drizzle with the vinaigrette. Garnish with fresh chive blossoms, if desired. Place the chicken slices over the chives.

NOTES For moist chicken, do not overcook. To test for doneness, press lightly on the chicken breasts with a pair of tongs. They should spring back slightly when gently pressed.

For even more flavor in the chives, cook them in the same pan as the chicken. The garlic chives will become infused with the flavor of the meat drippings.

SAUTÉED GARLIC CHIVES (OPTIONAL; SEE NOTE)

1 tablespoon extra-virgin olive oil

1 large bunch garlic chives or spring onion tops (about 4 ounces), cut into 2-inch lengths

1/4 teaspoon kosher salt

Chive blossoms for garnish (optional)

Roasted Chicken Thighs with Feta and Cherry Tomatoes

This is one of those dishes you'll find yourself making time and time again. A blender makes quick work of the marinade, which gives the chicken an intense flavor. It's perfect in spring, while you're waiting for local tomatoes to ripen, because the roasting intensifies the sweetness of the plump cherry tomatoes.

Combine the olive oil, lemon juice, garlic, dried oregano, salt, the 1/4 teaspoon black pepper, and the red pepper flakes in a blender or small food processor and blend until smooth. Drop the chicken thighs into a large resealable plastic bag and pour the marinade over them. Massage the marinade into the thighs. Put in a shallow pan and refrigerate overnight or up to 24 hours, turning occasionally.

Preheat the oven to 425°F. Line a large, rimmed baking sheet with foil. Remove the chicken thighs from the marinade and arrange on the baking sheet. Discard the remaining marinade.

Roast the chicken for 35 minutes. Remove from the oven and arrange the tomatoes around the chicken, coating the tomatoes with the chicken juices in the pan. Spoon some of the feta over the chicken thighs and the rest over the tomatoes. Arrange the fresh oregano sprigs (if using) over the tomatoes. Roast for another 10 minutes or until the chicken is no longer pink in the center, the tomatoes have softened and deflated a little, and the feta is lightly browned and soft.

Place the chicken thighs on a serving platter and arrange the tomatoes around them. Spoon any feta from the bottom of the pan over the chicken and tomatoes. Garnish with the roasted oregano sprigs, if desired. Grab your pepper mill and grind a good dose of pepper over the whole dish before serving.

3 tablespoons extra-virgin olive oil

3 tablespoons fresh lemon juice

3 garlic cloves, coarsely chopped

1 teaspoon dried oregano, preferably Greek

1/2 teaspoon salt

1/4 teaspoon freshly ground black pepper, plus more for garnish

1/4 teaspoon red pepper flakes

8 bone-in, skin-on chicken thighs (about 2 1/2 pounds)

2 cups cherry tomatoes

6 ounces feta cheese, crumbled (3/4 cup)

Fresh oregano sprigs (optional)

Fast and Crispy Roast Chicken

This chicken is juicy, crunchy, and addictive. The secret to success is flat roasting at a high temperature. Ask your butcher to remove the backbone and, if possible, the keel bone (center breastbone), leaving you to simply sprinkle the bird with olive oil and garlic before placing it in the oven. To make the most of the extra-crispy skin this recipe produces, carve the bird immediately after removing it from the oven.

SERVES 4

2 tablespoons extra-virgin olive oil

3 garlic cloves, minced

One 3½-pound chicken, backbone removed (see Note)

½ teaspoon kosher salt

¼ teaspoon freshly ground pepper

1½ cups hot water, or as needed

Preheat the oven to 475°F. Position a wire rack inside a large, rimmed baking sheet lined with foil. Coat the rack with nonstick cooking spray.

Stir together the olive oil and garlic in a small cup. Slather about 2 tablespoons of the mixture over the skin side of the chicken, and rub the remainder, about 1 tablespoon, over the back.

Open up the chicken like a book and spread out across the rack, skin-side up, so it's as flat as possible. Position the legs so they are knock-kneed (facing each other). Tuck the wing tips behind the chicken. Sprinkle the chicken with the salt and pepper. Pour enough hot water into the pan to cover the foil. This will keep the drippings from smoking and burning in the high heat, and the steam will help cook the chicken from the bottom up.

Roast for 30 minutes. Cover the breast loosely with foil if it browns too quickly. Continue roasting for 10 to 15 minutes, or until the meat is no longer pink and an instant-read thermometer inserted in the thickest part of the thigh (without touching a bone) registers 175°F.

To carve the chicken, make a diagonal cut below the breast and remove the legs. Cut between the drumsticks and thighs to separate them. Cut the breast in half down the center and cut each breast half in half again crosswise, leaving the wings attached, for a total of 8 pieces of chicken. Serve immediately.

NOTE To remove a chicken's backbone, place the chicken, breast-side down, on a cutting board. Start at the tail end and, with a sturdy pair of kitchen shears, cut along one side of the back-bone, cutting through the tiny back rib bones. Repeat on the other side. Remove and discard the backbone, or save to make stock. Turn the chicken over and press on the breastbone to flatten slightly.

Herb-Buttered Chicken with Spring Vegetables

Your local farmers' market is the best place to shop for this meal. Look for a locally raised chicken that's been free-ranged on pasture, and accompany it with garden-fresh carrots, new potatoes, and asparagus. The herbs used in this dish can be varied to suit your taste or the time of the year. In the spring, I prefer lighter, delicate herbs so they support but don't overpower the flavor of the chicken and the young vegetables.

Preheat the oven to 425°F. Place a roasting rack in the center of a large, rimmed baking sheet or shallow roasting pan. Stir together the butter and ¼ cup herbs in a small bowl until completely blended.

Loosen the skin of the chicken over the breast by slipping your hand between the skin and the meat to create a pocket, being careful not to tear the skin. Spoon 1 tablespoon of the herb butter into the pocket, pressing on the skin to spread the butter around. Tuck the wing tips behind the chicken so they lie flat.

Reserve 1 tablespoon of the herb butter and smear the rest all over the outside of the chicken. Sprinkle with ½ teaspoon of the salt and ¼ teaspoon of the pepper. Place the chicken, breast-side down, on the roasting rack and roast for 15 minutes.

Meanwhile, melt the reserved tablespoon of herb butter. Toss with the potatoes, carrots, and onion in a large bowl and sprinkle with the remaining ¼ teaspoon of salt and ¼ teaspoon of pepper.

Remove the chicken from the oven and, using tongs, carefully turn the chicken breast-side up. Scatter the potatoes, carrots, and onion in a single layer around and under the chicken. Roast for an additional 20 minutes. Baste the chicken and vegetables with the pan juices. Continue to roast for another 15 minutes. Add the asparagus and coat with the pan juices. Roast for 5 minutes more, or until an instant-read thermometer inserted in the thickest part of the thigh (without touching a bone) registers 175°F and the vegetables are tender.

Remove the chicken from the oven and let rest for 10 minutes. Carve and arrange on a large platter, surrounded by the vegetables. Garnish with the 3 tablespoons herbs before serving.

SERVES 4

4 tablespoons unsalted butter, softened

¼ cup chopped fresh spring herbs, such as tarragon, chives, chervil, and/or dill, plus 3 tablespoons

One 3½- to 4-pound chicken

¾ teaspoon kosher salt

½ teaspoon freshly ground pepper

8 ounces unpeeled tiny new potatoes (about sixteen 1-inch potatoes), halved (quartered if large)

8 medium-thick carrots with 1 inch of the green tops left on

1 large onion, cut into 1-inch wedges

16 pencil-thin asparagus spears, trimmed

HOW TO ENJOY CHICKENS WITHOUT THE HASSLE

Admit it. You love the idea of raising chickens but can't see yourself actually doing it. Happily, you're in luck. There are many ways to enjoy the benefits of backyard chickens without having to raise them yourself. Here are a few suggestions:

Offer to help chicken owners in your area. You can take care of their coops while they're away or lend a helping hand now and then. You'll find chicken owners are more than happy to pay you in delicious home-raised eggs.

While many communities bar the *sale* of backyard eggs, the bartering system is alive and well. Chicken keepers are often happy to exchange some of their eggs for something of equal value.

If you're a gardener, you can help chicken owners and yourself by offering to take some of the chicken waste for compost. Owners of large flocks are especially appreciative and will probably offer you some of their eggs as a thank-you.

Finally, frequent your local farmers' market. In some communities you'll find a few back-yard chicken owners setting up tables there. You'll also be able to meet the wonderful farmers in your area who've made the choice to offer humanely raised, organic, free-range eggs and meat.

Rhubarb-Ginger Custard Bars

This is one of my family's favorite recipes, and is requested each year by both of our boys for their birthday celebrations. The buttery, tender crust is enough reason to make these bars, but the hint of ginger in the tart rhubarb custard makes them irresistible. Although rhubarb desserts are common in the Midwest, I haven't been able to find the source of this recipe. I've adapted it through the years and added the ginger to jazz it up, but a huge thank-you to whoever first developed the tasty treat.

CRUST

1 cup all-purpose flour

$\frac{1}{2}$ cup powdered sugar

1 tablespoon minced crystallized ginger

$\frac{1}{8}$ teaspoon salt

$\frac{1}{2}$ cup (1 stick) cold unsalted butter, cut up

FILLING

$1\frac{1}{2}$ cups granulated sugar

$\frac{1}{3}$ cup all-purpose flour

$\frac{3}{4}$ teaspoon baking powder

Pinch of salt

2 eggs plus 1 egg yolk

$\frac{1}{2}$ teaspoon vanilla extract

3 cups thinly sliced rhubarb (about $1\frac{1}{4}$ pounds)

2 tablespoons minced crystallized ginger

TO MAKE THE CRUST: Preheat the oven to 350°F. Butter or coat an 11-by-7-inch glass baking dish with nonstick cooking spray. Stir together the flour, powdered sugar, crystallized ginger, and salt in a medium bowl until blended. Work the butter into the flour mixture with a pastry blender or your fingertips until the butter is evenly distributed and about the size of small blueberries. (The mixture will be dry and crumbly.) Spread the flour mixture over the baking dish and firmly press into the bottom of the dish to form the crust. Bake for 20 minutes or until the crust is golden brown on the edges and pale brown in the center. Leave the oven on.

TO MAKE THE FILLING: While the crust bakes, whisk the granulated sugar, flour, baking powder, and salt together in a medium bowl. (It's okay to use the same bowl you mixed the crust in.) Whisk together the eggs, egg yolk, and vanilla in a large bowl until smooth. Whisk in the sugar mixture until smooth. Toss in the rhubarb and crystallized ginger and stir until the rhubarb is evenly coated.

Pour the filling over the warm crust. Bake for 30 to 35 minutes or until the top is golden brown and crisp. Cool on a wire rack for 20 to 30 minutes. Cut into 12 bars and serve warm; or cool completely, cut into bars, and serve at room temperature. Store any leftovers in the refrigerator for up to 2 days.

 NOTE This dessert is best served the day it is made as the crispy top crust softens overnight.

Hong Kong Sweet Egg Tarts

I first tasted these incredible tarts from the famous Tai Cheung bakery when I was in Hong Kong. They were introduced to the Hong Kong area by Portuguese colonists, and have become a dim sum dessert specialty. The tarts are miniature one-bite wonders of flaky pastry filled with a golden egg custard. If made with home-grown or free-range summer eggs, they have that signature golden color that makes the tart look like a fresh egg yolk surrounded by pastry. If you make these in the winter with commercial eggs, you'll have to resort to a few drops of yellow food coloring to get the right hue.

TO MAKE THE TART SHELLS: Combine the flour and sugar in a medium bowl. Blend in the butter with a pastry blender or your fingertips until the butter is the size of small blueberries. Stir in the beaten egg and 2 teaspoons of the water with a fork. The dough will be crumbly but should hold together when pressed with your fingers. If necessary, add additional water. Shape into a flat round, cover with plastic wrap, and refrigerate for 1 hour or until chilled.

On a lightly floured surface, roll out the dough to a $\frac{1}{8}$-inch thickness. Using a $3\frac{1}{4}$-inch round cutter, cut the dough into twelve rounds. Gather up the dough scraps and roll them out if necessary. Gently press the rounds into twelve muffin cups (the dough will come about a third of the way up the cups). Press the blunt side of a small knife around the top $\frac{1}{4}$-inch edge of each tart to make decorative indentations. Place the muffin pan in the freezer for 15 minutes to firm the dough.

Preheat the oven to 400°F. Line each tart shell with foil (about 3 inches square), pressing the foil into the bottom and sides of the muffin cups. Bake for 15 minutes, or until set and the tops are light brown. Remove the foil liners and bake an additional 2 to 3 minutes, or until the tart shells are pale brown in the center. Remove the tart shells from the oven and reduce the oven temperature to 325°F. Cool on a wire rack.

SERVES 12
MAKES 12 TARTS

TART SHELLS

1 cup all-purpose flour

1 tablespoon sugar

6 tablespoons cold unsalted butter, cut up

1 egg, beaten with a pinch of salt

2 to 3 teaspoons ice water

FILLING

3 egg yolks

$\frac{1}{4}$ cup sugar

$1\frac{1}{4}$ teaspoons cornstarch

$\frac{3}{4}$ cup heavy (whipping) cream

TO MAKE THE FILLING: While the tart shells bake, whisk the egg yolks and sugar together in a small bowl until blended. Whisk in the cornstarch and heavy cream until combined.

Gently remove the tart shells from the muffin cups and place on a baking sheet. Spoon off and discard any foam that has formed on top of the egg mixture and pour 1 to 1$\frac{1}{2}$ tablespoons of filling into each tart shell. (There may be some filling left over, depending on the size of the tart shells.)

Bake for 15 to 20 minutes or until the custard is slightly puffed and set. Cool on a wire rack for 12 to 15 minutes. Serve warm or at room temperature. Store any leftovers in the refrigerator for up to 2 days.

NOTE The tarts can be made up to 1 day ahead and stored in the refrigerator. To warm, heat in a 325°F oven for 3 to 5 minutes or until warm.

Key Lime Cream Pie with Billowy Meringue

This is the ultimate Key lime pie. The extra-tart, creamy lime filling is piled high with a delicate meringue, making this pie lighter than the traditional whipped cream–topped version. The classic crumb crust has a slightly caramelized taste from the addition of brown sugar. Use the freshest organic free-range eggs available for the meringue. They'll whip up higher and hold the air longer than older eggs.

TO MAKE THE CRUST: Preheat the oven to 350°F. Stir together the graham cracker crumbs, brown sugar, and lime zest with a fork in a medium bowl until blended. Pour in the butter and stir until all of the crumbs are moistened. Press the crumb mixture over the bottom and up the sides of a 9-inch glass or metal pie plate with your fingers. Use a small measuring cup to press the crumb mixture evenly against the bottom and sides of the dish to firm the crust. Bake for 10 minutes or until set and slightly deeper brown in color. Cool on a wire rack. Leave the oven on.

TO MAKE THE FILLING: Beat the cream in a medium bowl with an electric mixer on medium-high speed until soft peaks form. In a large bowl, whisk the egg yolks until smooth. Whisk in the condensed milk and the lime zest until blended. Slowly whisk in the lime juice. Gently fold in the whipped cream. Pour the filling into the cooled pie crust.

Bake the pie for 15 minutes, or until the filling is set but still quivers when gently shaken. Leave the oven on.

TO MAKE THE MERINGUE: While the filling is baking, dissolve the cornstarch in the water in a small saucepan. Bring to a boil over medium heat and boil for 30 seconds or until very thick, stirring constantly. Remove from the heat and cover to keep warm. Beat the egg whites and cream of tartar in a large bowl with an electric mixer on medium-low speed until the whites are frothy. Increase the speed to medium and beat until soft peaks form. With the mixer running, slowly beat in the granulated sugar. Continue beating while slowly adding the warm cornstarch mixture, one spoonful at a time. Increase the speed to medium-high and beat until the egg whites are glossy and will hold a stiff peak. *(continued)*

CRUST

1½ cups graham cracker crumbs

¼ cup packed light brown sugar

2 teaspoons grated lime zest

6 tablespoons unsalted butter, melted

FILLING

½ cup heavy (whipping) cream

6 egg yolks

One 14-ounce can sweetened condensed milk

2 teaspoons grated lime zest

⅔ cup Key lime juice

MERINGUE

1 tablespoon cornstarch (see Note, page 48)

⅓ cup water

6 egg whites

¼ teaspoon cream of tartar

¾ cup granulated sugar

As soon as you remove the baked pie from the oven, immediately spoon half of the meringue over the hot filling, carefully and gently spreading the meringue so it touches the crust all around (this will keep it from shrinking). Pile the remaining meringue on top and swirl decoratively.

Bake for 15 to 18 minutes or until the meringue is dry to the touch and light brown. Cool on a wire rack to room temperature, about 2 hours. Refrigerate for 3 hours or until cold before serving. Store any leftovers in the refrigerator for up to 2 days.

 The addition of the cornstarch mixture to the meringue is a food styling technique that helps stabilize the egg whites. It produces a tender meringue that is less likely to shrink from the edges, bead up, or weep on a humid day.

Bittersweet Fudge Pound Cake

Pound cake recipes no longer require a pound each of flour, sugar, butter, and eggs. The classic recipe has been refined through the years to reflect our taste for lighter, sweeter cakes with a more delicate texture. This chocolate rendition is moist and light and always a favorite—probably because of the half-pound of chopped chocolate mixed into the batter. Buttermilk makes this cake extra-tender, and the additional egg yolk adds to the richness.

TO MAKE THE CAKE: Preheat the oven to 325°F. Grease a 12-cup Bundt pan with shortening or coat with nonstick cooking spray. Sprinkle with unsweetened cocoa, turning the pan upside down and tapping to remove any excess cocoa. Whisk together the flour, $^3/_4$ cup cocoa powder, baking powder, baking soda, and salt in a medium bowl until blended. Set aside.

Beat the butter in a large bowl with an electric mixer at medium speed for 1 minute until creamy. Reduce the speed to low and add the brown sugar, beating just until blended. Increase the speed to medium and, with the mixer running, slowly pour in the granulated sugar in a steady stream. Beat for 3 minutes or until light and fluffy. Reduce the speed to low and slowly beat in the canola oil and coffee until blended.

Add the eggs and the egg yolk, one at a time, beating each egg only until blended into the batter. Alternately add the flour mixture and buttermilk in thirds, beginning and ending with the flour mixture. Stir in the 8 ounces chopped chocolate. Gently ease the batter into the pan. Run a spatula or knife through the batter and tap the pan on the counter several times to eliminate air bubbles.

Bake for 50 to 60 minutes or until a wooden skewer inserted in the center of the cake comes out almost clean, with a few moist crumbs clinging to it. Cool in the pan on a wire rack for 10 minutes. Invert the cake onto the rack and remove the pan. Cool to room temperature.

TO MAKE THE GLAZE: While the cake is cooling, put the 6 ounces chocolate, the butter, and corn syrup in a medium heat-proof bowl. Place over a saucepan filled with 1 inch of simmering water. Melt the chocolate, stirring occasionally until smooth.

Pour the glaze over the top of the cooled cake, letting the glaze drip down the sides. Let the glaze set before serving.

SERVES 12

CAKE

$1^1/_2$ cups all-purpose flour

$^3/_4$ cup unsweetened cocoa powder

$1^1/_4$ teaspoons baking powder

$^1/_4$ teaspoon baking soda

$^1/_2$ teaspoon salt

$^3/_4$ cup ($1^1/_2$ sticks) unsalted butter, softened

$1^1/_2$ cups packed dark brown sugar

$^3/_4$ cup granulated sugar

$^1/_3$ cup canola oil

1 tablespoon strong coffee at room temperature

4 eggs plus 1 egg yolk at room temperature

$^3/_4$ cup buttermilk

8 ounces bittersweet chocolate (60% cacao), chopped

GLAZE

6 ounces bittersweet chocolate (60% cacao), chopped

3 tablespoons unsalted butter, cut up

1 tablespoon dark corn syrup

CHAPTER·THREE

MID-SPRING

The chicks invaded our space and took it over. We were like

the parents of newborns whose lives are abruptly turned upside down. It was a blur of constant feeding, cleaning, watering, pooping, more cleaning, checking bottoms for pasted bums, holding, cuddling, and feeding some more. I was enthralled. I was also exhausted.

Baby chicks are like the Energizer bunny on speed—in constant motion. Like toddlers, they're curious about the world around them. Had these chicks been hatched under a broody hen, their mother's voice would have been imprinted on them while they were still in the shell. Instead, I became their surrogate mom. They became excited at the sound of my voice. As they grew, they even learned to recognize my footsteps. If my husband or sons stepped out onto the deck, the girls didn't really respond. But as soon as I walked out, even when I hadn't said a word, they came running.

None of the neighbors knew about the chicks, so the constant red glow in the front window from the light over the brooder began eliciting comments. My friend who lived across the street pounded on our door and demanded, "What's with the red light—what's going on over here?" Others made jokes or rude comments. Marty started enjoying himself for the first time since the chicks had arrived. He was delighted that the name Roxanne was appropriate after all.

I checked the brooder constantly. When the three chicks hugged the walls of the brooder like shy seventh-grade boys at their first dance, they were too hot. But when they huddled together under the heat lamp, reenacting a football scrum, they were too cold. I began obsessively raising and lowering the makeshift heat lamp inch by inch.

At night I'd pull up a chair and watch the girls while Marty watched sports. I tried to get him to watch my Reality Chick Show, but he'd glance and then turn back to his own program. He was a hard case. Chickens are natural comedians, sort of like Steve Martin or Chevy Chase. They're funny just standing there doing nothing. Chickens force you to slow down, stop, and watch simply for the entertainment value. Our two cats were fascinated by them as well. They watched the chicks in their brooder as if the chicks were fish in an aquarium. I made sure the cover was secure.

The chicks quickly became the center of attention at our home. People came to see them, not us. The girls' personalities began to shine. Roxanne was the gangly one; everything on her body looked a little too big, as if she hadn't yet grown into the oversized clothes she was given. But unlike teenagers who grow too big too fast and are slow to develop the coordination to control it, Roxanne used her size to her advantage. Maybe it was from living in hockey country; body checking was her specialty. She hip-checked the other two—up against the boards if necessary—so she could get her share of the food, water, or whatever she wanted. But she was lovable and didn't mind a quick cuddle.

Lulu's psychotic personality developed early on. She began running and squawking frantically around the box whenever a hand approached. She always acted as if the hand carried a knife instead of the food, treats, or soft touch it offered. I've never been able to decide if she suffers from an overactive imagination or actually had a scare right after she was hatched. Unfortunately, those friends who were successful in picking her up were always left with a slimy gift.

Cleo was the runt of the litter. She looked cute with her black stripe running down the center of her golden back. The pecking order began early and Cleo was on the bottom, but she was unperturbed as the other two bullied her. I felt protective of this little one and she loved to sit in my arms, exploring the world beyond her box.

My three swingin' chicks entertained their guests by dancing in unison from one end of the large plastic tub to the other in the blink of an eye. They formed towers by climbing on top of each other, bouncing down like SuperBalls. They never tired of reenacting the "Walk This Way" scene from *Young Frankenstein* as they traversed the pine shavings.

These in-the-moment birds would stop suddenly in the middle of a walk and keel over, sound asleep. Two minutes later, one of them would be up running again. Nighttime was particularly entertaining. Their bedtime routine resembled the skillful moves of a con man's shell game or kids playing pickle-in-the-middle. The chicks nuzzled together side by side. After a few minutes, the outside two would pop up and force their way into the warm center. I could always tell where golden-feathered Roxanne ended up, but the other two had me conned.

I had finally settled into an evening routine with the girls, when Cleo suddenly disappeared one night. I was relaxing in front of the TV, holding and slowly petting her. Perhaps I nodded off and she grabbed an opportunity to escape, or she saw something of interest. Whatever the reason, she bolted out of my arms in a flash, landed on the couch, and then on the floor. I screamed; she ran. Marty yelled, and the other two cheeped frantically. It was a symphony of confusion.

We couldn't find her. Marty and I quickly got ourselves under control and listened for her peeps as we searched. But it was impossible to hear anything over the bawling of the two girls in the box, who were frightened by the sudden burst of noise. As Marty tried to find the cats to keep them away, I crawled around on my belly, peering under the couch and the bookcases looking for a fluff ball among the dust bunnies. I needed to find Cleo before one of the cats did.

Cats and dogs can coexist with chickens quite easily, depending on the personalities of the individual animals. I've seen chickens crawl into a dog's bed and cuddle up next to the sleeping pooch. I also know of dogs that have snatched up chickens in their jaws like McNuggets thrown up in the air. Chickens and cats get along remarkably well, but cats can easily kill a chick with one quick swipe. So introductions should be made slowly and carefully under close supervision. This wasn't the time to give the cats a nose-to-nose personal presentation.

I continued to slide along the wood floor, looking for Cleo. Petunia, our sixteen-year-old cat, wasn't my biggest concern as she was the gentlest cat we'd ever had. When Petunia was eight, she had once helped save our son's hamster when the exercise ball it was rolling around the room in accidentally fell down the stairs, breaking open and flinging the poor critter onto the carpet. Miss Petunia kept guard, keeping the hamster on the stairway and away from the jaws of our other cat, Mugsy, until we arrived. Mugsy was a hunter and wouldn't have hesitated had he seen the rodent. This time I hoped neither cat would find Cleo before I did. It seemed wise not to tempt fate twice.

I finally found Cleo quivering in a corner, where she gratefully let me close my hand around her to carry her away. The cats watched with interest as I brushed her off and gently placed her in the safety of the plastic tub.

The chicks ate ravenously and grew quickly, seeming to double in size week by week. Obviously, what goes in needs to come out, and the pine shavings used for bedding needed constant changing. At first I took to my new barnyard chores with the enthusiasm of the newly converted. But the chores quickly grew tiresome—a never-ending cycle. The baby chicks rapidly grew feathers and wings and practiced flying in the limited space of their hangar. The brooder was definitely becoming too small. They were ready to be outdoors, but the weather refused to warm up.

I had read about someone who rigged up a teeter-totter in their brooder to keep their chicks entertained, but their brooder was the size of a kiddy swimming pool. Mine was the size of a double kitchen sink. I tried adding a few small toys, such as balls, but they weren't amused. What did amuse them was water.

The simple watering device in the brooder was designed for small chicks; it was a plastic bottle that sat upside down on a wider base. The base was small, so tiny chicks couldn't crawl in, get wet, or even drown. Now that they were bigger, however, my chicks found they could move the tube and knock it over. It became a game they played every night.

I stoically did my chores daily, cleaning, mucking, and feeding endlessly, but I also started referring to them under my breath as "those damn dirty chicks." I'm not a stoic person by nature, so putting on a stiff upper lip was getting me down.

To top it off, I began suspecting that Marty was beginning to enjoy the girls. He went out of his way to act uninterested, but while I was in another room, I'd hear him talking baby talk to the chicks. I should have been glad, but maybe I didn't really want to share the girls, now that I'd had them to myself. Or maybe it was because he also started checking up on me, as in, "Did you feed the girls today?" or "Do you think their heat is too high?" And the worst, "Isn't it about time to change their bedding?" Paranoia started in as I thought, "He truly wanted these chickens and only pretended not to because he just didn't want the extra work." I felt like the Little Red Hen, my favorite story when I was growing up. No one wanted to help her grow the wheat and bake the bread, but everyone wanted to eat it. "Guess who will be first up when the eggs start rolling out?" I muttered to myself.

It soon became evident why chickens do not make good house pets. They were ready to start running outside, but unfortunately, the weather wouldn't cooperate. As a born-and-bred Northerner who loves the changing seasons, I began to envy those in warmer climates. Once-a-day cleanings were no longer enough, and our house was starting to smell like a barnyard. They weren't going to produce eggs for another three to four months. Maybe I should have gone for the ready-to-lay hens.

Raising chicks is a little like raising kids; if can you get them into adulthood unscathed, you've done a good job. But, as with raising children, most of the time you don't know what you're doing, so you do what you can and hope for the best. To everyone's relief, the girls finally moved outside in May. They were no longer baby chicks; they'd grown into gangling teenagers called pullets and were settling nicely into their coop and the surrounding yard. My reluctant partner began more openly enjoying them from a distance as we sat on the deck in the evenings with a couple of glasses of wine, watching them play.

A surprising thing about keeping chickens is how quickly you start acting and sounding like a new parent. Conversation topics dwindle and focus solely on your little darlings and their latest antics. For a while, friends may feign interest and amusement, but soon you've become a new-parent bore.

I was certainly delighted to talk chickens for quite awhile, but, finally the topic started to bore even me. Just when I was happy to leave the subject alone, my keep-me-out-of-the-chicken-business spouse discovered the conversational value of chickens. He would eagerly ask new acquaintances, "Did you know my wife raises chickens in our backyard?" Everyone but the new captive would drift away as quickly as possible. We'd never been social butterflies, but now we were in danger of not being invited anywhere.

Poached Eggs over Walnut-Crusted Cheese and Whole-Grain Toast

Looking for an energy boost to start the day? Try these tender eggs over melting cheese, crunchy walnuts, and hearty artisan bread. Grab the freshest eggs for poaching; you'll notice they keep their shape better and the whites stay tight, with fewer flyaway strands.

TO MAKE THE WALNUT-CRUSTED CHEESE: Preheat the oven to 375°F. Line a small baking sheet with foil. Beat the egg white until frothy and transfer to a wide, shallow bowl. Put the walnuts in another shallow bowl. Cut the cheese crosswise into four pieces. Press each piece into a thin round about 3 inches in diameter and ¼ inch thick. Dip the cheese rounds into the egg white, then coat with the walnuts, pressing lightly to adhere. Place on the baking sheet. Refrigerate for at least 15 minutes or until ready to bake. Bake the cheese rounds for 4 to 5 minutes or until soft and melty.

Crack each egg into its own small cup. Fill a medium nonstick skillet with water, cover, and bring to a gentle boil over high heat. Remove from the heat and gently slide the eggs into the water. Cover and let sit for 3 minutes or until the whites are set and the yolks are still soft. Remove with a slotted spoon and drain briefly on paper towels (while still in the spoon).

Place a warm cheese round on each slice of toast, top with a poached egg, and sprinkle with salt, pepper, and chives before serving.

SERVES 4

WALNUT-CRUSTED CHEESE

1 egg white

½ cup finely chopped walnuts

One 4-ounce log cold fresh goat cheese

4 eggs

4 slices artisan whole-grain bread, toasted and buttered

Kosher salt

Freshly ground pepper

2 tablespoons thinly sliced fresh chives

HOW CAN YOU HAVE EGGS WITHOUT A ROOSTER?

The answer involves a sex education review. When a woman ovulates, she passes an egg each month, whether a man is present or not. Chickens do the same thing, except a hen passes an egg every twenty-five hours instead of once a month. (Can you imagine?) If you just want eggs, you don't need a rooster. If, however, you want baby chicks, then a rooster is necessary.

Does a hen *need* a rooster? Does a woman need a man? The answer is no.

Strawberry Soufflé Omelet with Maple-Caramelized Almonds

This delicate, airy, open-faced omelet topped with fresh strawberries and caramelized nuts makes a spectacular springtime presentation. It's a cross between a soufflé and an omelet. The egg whites and yolks are beaten separately, making the omelet rise like a soufflé in the oven. It will rise even higher if you use the freshest eggs available.

TO MAKE THE ALMONDS: Line a small baking sheet with parchment paper. Melt the butter in a medium nonstick skillet over medium heat. Add the almonds and cook, stirring occasionally, for 3 minutes or until the almonds are just starting to lightly brown. Add the maple syrup and cook, stirring constantly, for 30 seconds to 1 minute, or until the mixture is thickened and the almonds are glazed. Spread out over the parchment and cool. Break into bite-size pieces.

TO MAKE THE OMELET: Preheat the oven to 400°F. Beat the egg whites in a large bowl with an electric mixer at medium speed until frothy. Add the sugar, increase the speed to medium-high, and beat until soft peaks form, being careful to not overbeat the egg whites. Pour the egg whites into another large bowl.

Add the egg yolks to the same mixing bowl the whites were beaten in (there's no need to clean the bowl or the beaters), sprinkle with the salt and pepper, and beat on medium speed for 3 minutes or until pale yellow and very thick. Stir half of the egg whites into the egg yolks to lighten the mixture. Pour the egg yolk mixture over the remaining egg whites and gently fold in until completely blended.

Melt the butter in a large nonstick ovenproof skillet over medium heat. Swirl to coat the bottom of the pan completely. Pour in the egg mixture and gently smooth the top. Cook for 1 minute (do not stir). Place the pan in the oven.

MAPLE-CARAMELIZED ALMONDS

$\frac{1}{2}$ tablespoon unsalted butter

$\frac{1}{2}$ cup sliced almonds

2 tablespoons pure maple syrup

OMELET

6 eggs, separated

2 tablespoons sugar

$\frac{1}{4}$ teaspoon salt

$\frac{1}{8}$ teaspoon freshly ground pepper

2 tablespoons unsalted butter

Powdered sugar for sprinkling

1 pound fresh strawberries, sliced (about 3 cups)

Bake for 10 minutes or until golden brown, puffed, and set. Run a spatula around the sides of the pan to release the omelet and slide onto a large platter. Sprinkle with the powdered sugar, top with the sliced strawberries, and scatter the caramelized almonds over the top. Cut into wedges and serve.

 The Maple-Caramelized Almonds can be made up to 2 days ahead of time. Store at room temperature in an airtight container. You can also sprinkle them on top of salads and desserts.

WHICH COMES FIRST—THE CHICKEN OR THE EGG?

You've decided to raise chickens, but where should you start? You can: (1) Play mother hen and hatch your own eggs; (2) Get baby chicks from your local feed store or through the mail; (3) Skip the baby steps and start with pullets, which are young chicks that are about to start laying; or (4) Start at the end and adopt adult hens with a proven track record.

The cute factor was a big draw for me, so I started with baby chicks. For instant eggs, go with pullets or adults. If you want a challenge, hatch your own eggs, a perfect thing to do if you're obsessive-compulsive. It requires constant monitoring of temperature and humidity, along with turning the eggs a minimum of three times daily. Any variation will kill the embryos. Just remember, there's no way to sex eggs before they hatch. The ratio of hens to roosters in a batch of eggs can be 50-50. The big question is, what do you plan to do with all the roosters?

Golden Egg Pancakes with Berries and Honey Yogurt

What makes these pancakes special, beyond using freshly laid eggs from your backyard, is the addition of cornmeal. It not only adds a subtle crunch and sweetness to the batter, but also complements the golden color of these egg-rich cakes. For those who like even more texture, use medium- or coarsely ground cornmeal.

12 PANCAKES

TO MAKE THE TOPPINGS: Combine the berries and sugar in a medium bowl and stir, crushing the berries slightly so the juices will run. Stir together the yogurt and honey in a small bowl until blended. Set aside while you make the pancakes.

TO MAKE THE PANCAKES: Whisk together the flour, cornmeal, sugar, baking powder, nutmeg, and salt in a large bowl and set aside. Whisk the eggs and egg yolk together in a medium bowl until blended and smooth. Whisk in the yogurt and slowly add the buttermilk and melted butter. Pour the egg mixture into the dry ingredients and whisk just until moistened.

Preheat the oven to 200°F. Heat a griddle to 375°F or a large non-stick skillet on medium to medium-high heat. Brush with melted butter using a silicone heat-proof brush and heat the butter until sizzling. Pour about 1/4 cup of batter per pancake onto the griddle and cook for 3 minutes or until bubbles form on the surface, the edges are set, and the pancakes are golden brown on the bottom. Turn and cook for 1 to 1 1/2 minutes or until lightly browned.

Keep the pancakes warm in the oven until all are done. Serve topped with the berries and a dollop of honey yogurt.

TOPPINGS

3 cups assorted fresh berries, such as sliced strawberries, raspberries, blueberries, and/or blackberries

3 tablespoons sugar

3/4 cup plain nonfat yogurt, preferably Greek

1 1/2 tablespoons honey

PANCAKES

1 1/4 cups all-purpose flour

1/3 cup finely ground yellow cornmeal, preferably stone-ground

1/3 cup sugar

2 teaspoons baking powder

1/2 teaspoon ground nutmeg

1/4 teaspoon salt

3 eggs plus 1 egg yolk

3/4 cup plain nonfat yogurt, preferably Greek yogurt

1/2 cup buttermilk

5 tablespoons unsalted butter, melted and cooled

Melted unsalted butter or canola oil for frying

Florentine Fried Eggs over Roasted Asparagus with Crispy Prosciutto

Asparagus and eggs are a classic pairing. This version has an Italian twist, with olive oil–fried eggs and crispy prosciutto. Look for young, thin asparagus for this dish because they will cook in the same amount of time it takes to crisp the prosciutto. A shower of shredded Parmigiano-Reggiano cheese is always a welcome addition.

SERVES 4

24 pencil-thin asparagus spears (about 12 ounces), trimmed

1 teaspoon extra-virgin olive oil, plus 2 tablespoons

$\frac{1}{8}$ to $\frac{1}{4}$ teaspoon freshly ground pepper

3 ounces thinly sliced prosciutto, cut into $\frac{1}{4}$-inch strips

4 eggs

Pinch of kosher salt

Preheat the broiler on high. Line a large, rimmed baking sheet with foil. Arrange the asparagus on half of the baking sheet, brush with the 1 teaspoon oil, and sprinkle with $\frac{1}{8}$ teaspoon of the pepper. Toss the prosciutto, fluffing it slightly to separate the strands into strips, and place on the other half of the baking sheet.

Broil for 2 to 4 minutes or until the asparagus is crisp-tender and the prosciutto is crispy. Remove from the broiler and cover lightly with foil to keep warm.

Crack the eggs into individual small cups. Warm the remaining 2 tablespoons of oil in a medium nonstick skillet over medium heat. Gently ease the eggs into the oil, cover, and cook slowly for 2 minutes, reducing the heat to medium-low or low if the eggs begin to cook too quickly or bubble. Tilt the skillet and spoon any olive oil in the pan over the egg yolks to baste them. Cover and continue cooking 1 to 2 minutes, or until the whites are set and the yolks are still soft. Sprinkle lightly with salt.

To serve, arrange the eggs over the asparagus and scatter the crisp prosciutto over both. Sprinkle with additional freshly ground pepper, if desired.

Warm Slab Bacon Salad with Sunny-Side Eggs

A warm, tangy dressing provides the perfect note for the hearty cubes of bacon and blue cheese without overpowering the eggs. Be aware that the red wine vinegar smells strong when the dressing is warmed, but it mellows before it's tossed with the salad.

TO MAKE THE DRESSING: Whisk together all of the ingredients except the oil in a small saucepan until blended. Slowly whisk in the oil and set aside.

TO MAKE THE SALAD: Put the greens in a large bowl and sprinkle with the cheese. Heat a medium nonstick skillet over medium-high heat. Add the bacon and cook for 10 minutes or until golden brown and crisp, stirring frequently. Remove the bacon and drain on paper towels. Leave a tablespoon of bacon drippings in the pan, and reserve another tablespoon in a small cup. (If you don't have a full tablespoon, add some olive oil.) Discard any remaining drippings.

Add the onion to the skillet. Cook over medium-high heat for 3 minutes or until lightly browned and softened, stirring occasionally. Remove the onion with tongs or a slotted spoon and toss with the greens.

Crack the eggs into individual cups. Add the reserved tablespoon of bacon drippings to the same skillet and heat until warm. Add the eggs and season with the salt and pepper. Cover and cook over medium to medium-low heat for 3 minutes, or until the whites are set and the yolks are still soft. Remove from the heat. (Do not overcook the eggs, as they will continue to cook as they sit.)

Bring the dressing to a simmer over medium-high heat. Pour the warm dressing over the greens, onion, and cheese and toss. Mound the salad on individual plates and top each serving with a fried egg. Scatter the bacon over the egg and greens. Serve immediately.

NOTE: The onion and eggs can be fried in extra-virgin olive oil instead of the bacon drippings, if you prefer.

SERVES 4

DRESSING

2 tablespoons red wine vinegar

$\frac{1}{4}$ teaspoon Worcestershire sauce

$\frac{1}{4}$ teaspoon Dijon mustard

$\frac{1}{8}$ teaspoon kosher salt

$\frac{1}{8}$ teaspoon freshly ground pepper

2 tablespoons extra-virgin olive oil

SALAD

6 cups torn escarole, spinach, or mixed greens (bite-size pieces)

$\frac{1}{4}$ cup crumbled blue cheese, preferably Maytag blue

6 ounces slab bacon or thickly sliced bacon, cut into $\frac{1}{2}$-inch pieces

1 medium onion, halved and sliced (1 cup)

4 eggs

$\frac{1}{8}$ teaspoon kosher salt

$\frac{1}{8}$ teaspoon freshly ground pepper

Chicken Risotto with Asparagus and Saffron

Chicken risotto is pure comfort food, basically a tony version of the Midwestern favorite, chicken and rice. You don't need to chain yourself to the stove for this recipe. Although purists insist on constant stirring, your risotto will be creamy even if you're not quite so diligent. Accompany the risotto with mixed greens tossed with fresh herbs, grape tomatoes, and a light lemon vinaigrette.

SERVES 4

Two 14-ounce cans reduced-sodium chicken broth

2 boneless, skinless chicken breast halves (about 12 ounces total)

$1/4$ teaspoon saffron threads (see Note)

3 tablespoons unsalted butter

$1/2$ cup finely chopped shallots (3 large)

2 garlic cloves, minced

1 cup Arborio rice

8 ounces asparagus spears, trimmed and cut diagonally into 1-inch pieces ($1^1/2$ cups)

$1/2$ teaspoon kosher salt

$1/4$ teaspoon freshly ground pepper

$1/2$ cup grated Parmigiano-Reggiano cheese

Pour the chicken broth into a medium saucepan and add the chicken breasts. Bring to a boil over medium-high heat. Reduce the heat and simmer, partially covered, for 8 to 10 minutes or until the chicken is no longer pink in the center. Remove the chicken to a plate and let cool for 10 minutes. Add enough water to the broth so you have $3^1/2$ cups; set aside. Shred the chicken.

Toast the saffron in a large saucepan over low heat for 2 minutes or until slightly darker in color, stirring constantly and being careful not to let the saffron burn. Transfer to a plate to cool.

Bring the broth to a simmer over low heat and cover. Melt 2 tablespoons of the butter in the same large saucepan over medium heat. Cook the shallots and garlic for 1 minute or until fragrant. Stir in the rice, coating the grains with the butter, and cook for 1 minute, stirring constantly. Crush the saffron and add it to the rice along with $1/2$ cup of the hot broth. Cook until the liquid has been almost completely absorbed, stirring.

Continue to add the broth, $1/2$ cup at a time, cooking and stirring until 2 cups have been added, adjusting the heat as necessary to keep the rice mixture simmering. Stir in the asparagus. Continue adding broth until 3 cups have been added. Stir in the chicken, salt, and pepper and keep adding broth until the mixture is creamy and the rice is tender but slightly firm in the center. Stir in the remaining tablespoon of butter and $1/4$ cup of the Parmesan. Serve sprinkled with the remaining $1/4$ cup Parmesan.

NOTE — Although saffron is known as the world's most expensive spice, tiny amounts will yield enormous flavor. For the best results, buy saffron threads and crush them between your fingers.

Grilled Japanese Chicken Skewers (Yakitori)

Yakitori is Japanese street food. In Tokyo, tiny stalls tucked under railway tracks and on back-streets, some with no more than a few stools, are packed with businessmen stopping for a quick bite and a beer. You can smell the charcoal braziers as you walk the city. The word *yakitori* literally means "grilled chicken," including all its parts. Morsels of chicken livers, hearts, gizzards, and skin are regularly part of the yakitori experience, along with ground chicken and chicken wings. Meat from the thigh, however, is considered the best. The skewers are brushed with a sweet soy grilling sauce, which glazes the meat as it cooks. Serve them as appetizers or the main course.

SERVES 4
AS A MAIN COURSE OR 12 AS AN APPETIZER

1 cup mirin

$1/2$ cup soy sauce

$1/2$ cup sake or dry sherry

1 tablespoon canola oil

$1^1/_4$ pounds boneless, skinless chicken thighs, cut into thirty-six 1-inch pieces

12 green onions (white and light green parts), each cut into two $2^1/_2$-inch lengths (24 pieces)

12 shiitake mushroom caps (about 3 ounces)

1 orange bell pepper, seeded, deveined, and cut into 12 pieces

Stir together the mirin, soy sauce and sake in a glass measuring cup. Pour 1 cup of the mixture into a small saucepan for the grilling sauce and set aside. Add the canola oil to the remaining mixture for the marinade. Put the chicken pieces in a large resealable plastic bag. Pour the marinade over the chicken, seal the bag, and put in a shallow pan. Marinate in the refrigerator for 6 to 8 hours.

Meanwhile, bring the grilling sauce in the saucepan to a boil. Boil for 4 to 5 minutes over medium-high heat until slightly syrupy and reduced to a generous $1/2$ cup. Soak twelve 8-inch bamboo skewers in water for 20 minutes so they are less likely to burn.

Preheat the grill to medium-low. Remove the chicken from the marinade, saving the marinade. To assemble each skewer, alternate three pieces of chicken with two pieces of green onion, placing one mushroom cap in the middle of the skewer and one piece of bell pepper on the end. Brush the skewers with the marinade.

Oil the grill grate. To reduce the charring on the skewers, put a piece of triple-folded heavy-duty foil at one end of the grill and place the bare ends of the skewers on the foil. Cover the grill and cook the skewers for 10 minutes or until the chicken is no longer pink in the center, turning every 2 minutes and brushing with the reserved grilling sauce during the last 6 minutes.

Serve immediately.

NOTE The skewers can be assembled and refrigerated for up to 2 hours before cooking.

Crispy Orange Chicken with Spring Vegetables

For this dish, the chicken breasts are dipped in orange juice and then coarse bread crumbs, resulting in crunchy-crisp oven-fried chicken, permeated with the bright, fresh flavors of oranges. The orange flavor is echoed in the colorful Asian-style carrots, asparagus, and leeks served alongside.

SERVES 4

Preheat the oven to 400°F. Line a small, rimmed baking sheet with foil. Stir together 1/4 cup of the orange juice, 1 teaspoon of the orange zest, 1 teaspoon of the ginger, and half the garlic in a shallow bowl. Put the panko in another shallow bowl and toss with the melted butter until the crumbs are moistened. Sprinkle the chicken with 1/4 teaspoon each of the salt and pepper.

Dip the chicken into the orange juice mixture, pressing some of the ginger, garlic, and orange zest onto the meat. Coat with the panko mixture, pressing and patting the crumbs on to adhere. Place on the baking sheet. Bake for 20 minutes or until lightly browned and no longer pink in the center.

Meanwhile, stir together the remaining 1/2 cup of orange juice, 1/4 teaspoon of orange zest, 1/2 teaspoon of salt, 1/4 teaspoon of pepper, and the sesame oil in a small bowl. Heat a large nonstick skillet over medium-high heat. Heat the canola oil. Add the carrots and asparagus and cook for 1 minute, stirring constantly. Add the leeks and cook for 1 minute. Add the remaining teaspoon of ginger and the remaining garlic and cook for 30 seconds, or until fragrant. Pour in the orange juice mixture, bring to a simmer, cover, and cook for 2 minutes, or until the vegetables are almost crisp-tender. Uncover, increase the heat to high, and boil for 1 minute, or until the sauce is slightly thickened. Serve the vegetables with the chicken.

3/4 cup orange juice

1 1/4 teaspoons grated orange zest

2 teaspoons minced fresh ginger

2 garlic cloves, minced

1 cup panko (coarse bread crumbs)

3 tablespoons unsalted butter, melted

4 boneless, skinless chicken breast halves (about 1 1/2 pounds)

3/4 teaspoon kosher salt

1/2 teaspoon freshly ground pepper

1 teaspoon dark sesame oil

1 tablespoon canola oil

1 cup julienned carrots

8 ounces asparagus spears, trimmed and cut diagonally into 2-inch pieces (1 1/2 cups)

1 1/2 cups sliced leeks trimmed and cut 1/2 inch thick, white and light green parts

Creamy Deviled Egg–Stuffed Chicken Breasts

Deviled eggs take on a new role when stuffed into chicken breasts for a creamy filling with a rich egg taste. This play on the chicken and egg question will delight your guests as they cut into the chicken breast and find it stuffed with eggs.

Preheat the oven to 400°F. Line a small, rimmed baking sheet with foil and coat with nonstick cooking spray. Halve the eggs, remove the yolks, and reserve the egg whites for another use. Mash the egg yolks in a small bowl with a pastry blender or a fork until they resemble fine crumbs. Stir in the mayonnaise, blending until smooth. Stir in the shallot, mustard, salt, and pepper. Gently stir in 2 tablespoons of the parsley.

Place the chicken breasts on a cutting board and make a ½- to 1-inch horizontal slit into the plump side of the breast with a thin knife. Very carefully, slide the knife into the slit, keeping the knife parallel to the cutting board, cutting to create a larger pocket inside and being careful not to cut through to the other side. (Making only a small cut on the outside of the breast and creating a larger pocket on the inside helps prevent the filling from oozing out during cooking.) Put the deviled egg filling into a disposable pastry bag. Or put it into a small resealable plastic bag and cut off the corner. Pipe about 3 tablespoons of filling into the pocket of each chicken breast half. Secure the opening with toothpicks.

Heat a large nonstick skillet over medium-high heat and heat the oil. Add the chicken breasts and cook for 4 minutes or until deep golden brown, lowering the heat to medium if the chicken is cooking too fast. Turn and cook for 30 seconds. Transfer to the baking sheet, brown-side up.

Bake the chicken for 10 minutes or until no longer pink in the center. Sprinkle with the remaining 2 tablespoons of parsley before serving.

NOTE The chicken breasts can be assembled, covered, and refrigerated for up to 8 hours before baking.

6 hard-cooked eggs (see Note, page 31)

½ cup mayonnaise

2 teaspoons minced shallot

¾ teaspoon Dijon mustard

¼ teaspoon kosher salt

⅛ teaspoon freshly ground pepper

4 tablespoons chopped fresh flat-leaf parsley

4 boneless, skinless chicken breast halves (about 1½ pounds)

1 tablespoon extra-virgin olive oil

Pan-Roasted Chicken Breasts over Roasted Potato Salad

Pan-roasting, the technique of browning food on top of the stove and finishing it in a hot oven, is a perfect way to ensure moist chicken breasts. The whole process takes only 8 to 10 minutes. Roasted potato salad—made with crisp, golden potatoes—is a fantastic accompaniment to the chicken.

TO MAKE THE POTATO SALAD: Preheat the oven to 400°F. Toss the potatoes in a large bowl with the olive oil. Lightly rub a rimmed baking sheet with olive oil and spread out the potatoes in one layer, if possible. Bake for 30 to 35 minutes, or until the tops of the potatoes are light brown and the bottoms are golden brown. Leave the oven on for the chicken.

Meanwhile, stir together the mayonnaise, salt, pepper, and mustard in the same large bowl. Gently toss the hot roasted potatoes with the mayonnaise and stir in the green onion, radishes, and egg.

TO MAKE THE CHICKEN: Combine 2 teaspoons of the olive oil with the garlic and spread over the chicken; sprinkle with the salt and pepper.

Heat a large ovenproof skillet over medium-high heat. Add the remaining 2 teaspoons of olive oil and swirl to coat the bottom of the pan. Add the chicken, reduce the heat to medium, and cook for 4 minutes or until brown. Turn the chicken and immediately place in the oven. Bake 4 to 6 minutes or until the chicken is no longer pink in the center. Remove from the oven and let rest for 5 minutes.

To serve, slice the chicken and fan over the potato salad.

SERVES 4

ROASTED POTATO SALAD

1 pound unpeeled red new potatoes, sliced $1/4$ inch thick

2 teaspoons extra-virgin olive oil

6 tablespoons mayonnaise

$1/2$ teaspoon coarse sea salt

$1/4$ teaspoon freshly ground pepper

$1/4$ teaspoon Dijon mustard

$1/4$ cup sliced green onion (green part only)

4 radishes, halved and thinly sliced

1 hard-cooked egg (see Note, page 31), chopped

CHICKEN

4 teaspoons extra-virgin olive oil

2 garlic cloves, minced

4 boneless, skinless chicken breast halves (about $1^{1}/_{2}$ pounds)

$1/4$ teaspoon coarse sea salt

$1/4$ teaspoon freshly ground pepper

Lemon-Spiked Chicken with Sage

Sage lends a delicate green color and pungent flavor to the lemony marinade, which mellows during grilling. The grilled fresh sage sprigs add a nice touch to this dish, similar to deep-fried sage leaves but more delicate and less oily. I like to use different varieties of sage, such as tricolor or golden sage. They're easy to grow and offer unique foliage, so I always tuck a few plants into my container gardens at the start of the growing season.

Drop the chicken pieces in a large resealable plastic bag. Combine all the remaining ingredients, except the sprigs of fresh sage, in a blender container and blend until smooth. Pour the marinade mixture over the chicken, seal the bag, and massage the chicken to coat all of the pieces. Put in a shallow pan and marinate for 6 to 8 hours in the refrigerator, turning occasionally.

Preheat the grill to medium and then arrange for indirect heat: For a charcoal grill, arrange the coals on one side or around the edges, leaving the center clear. For a two-burner gas grill, turn one side off, and for a three-burner gas grill, turn the center burner off.

Place the chicken directly over the heat, cover, and cook for 8 minutes, turning once. Turn the chicken again and place over the indirect heat. Cover and grill for an additional 40 to 50 minutes or until the chicken is no longer pink in the center, turning every 10 minutes.

Place 1 sage leaf on each piece of chicken and place the remaining sage sprigs over the direct heat during the last 2 to 4 minutes of grilling time. Grill the sage sprigs until lightly dried and crumbly. Crumble the grilled sage over the chicken before serving, or place the grilled sprigs on the platter with the chicken, letting diners crumble the sage themselves.

SERVES 4

One 3-pound chicken, cut into 8 pieces

1 medium onion, coarsely chopped (3/4 cup)

4 garlic cloves

1/2 cup fresh lemon juice

1/4 cup extra-virgin olive oil

1 tablespoon grated lemon zest

1 tablespoon coarsely chopped fresh sage, plus 6 sprigs fresh sage

1 tablespoon poultry seasoning

1 teaspoon kosher salt

1/2 teaspoon freshly ground pepper

1/4 teaspoon ground allspice

Tender Shortcakes with Raspberry Cream

These cardamom-scented shortcakes are as easy to make as drop biscuits, with no rolling or cutting required. The raspberry cream filling is similar to a fruit fool, the classic British dessert of whipped cream folded with fresh fruit.

TO MAKE THE SHORTCAKES: Preheat the oven to 425°F. Line a baking sheet with parchment paper. Whisk together the flour, granulated sugar, baking powder, cardamom, and salt in a medium bowl. Blend in the butter with a pastry blender or your fingertips until the butter is about the size of large blueberries. Whisk together the egg yolks and half-and-half in a small bowl until blended. Make a well in the center of the flour mixture, pour in the cream mixture, and stir with a fork just until moistened. The dough will be lumpy and very moist. Drop by large spoonfuls onto the baking sheet to make eight 2$\frac{1}{2}$-inch mounds. Pat the tops to flatten the mounds so they're about 1$\frac{1}{2}$ inches high.

Bake the shortcakes for 10 to 15 minutes or until light golden brown on top and deeper golden brown on the bottom. Cool on a wire rack.

TO MAKE THE RASPBERRY CREAM: Pile the raspberries in a medium bowl and sprinkle with the $\frac{1}{4}$ cup sugar. Lightly mash some of the berries to start the juices running. Let sit for 30 minutes or until the sugar has dissolved, stirring occasionally. Whip the heavy cream in a large bowl with an electric mixer at medium speed until slightly thickened, sprinkle in the remaining 2 tablespoons of sugar, and beat until firm, but not stiff, peaks form. Gently fold the cream into the raspberry mixture.

To serve, split the shortcakes horizontally in half. Fill each short-cake with a generous $\frac{1}{2}$ cup of raspberry cream. Sprinkle with powdered sugar.

NOTE: As with any quick bread, avoid overmixing the dough for tender and light results.

SERVES 8
MAKES 8 SHORTCAKES

SHORTCAKES

2 cups all-purpose flour, preferably bleached

$\frac{1}{2}$ cup granulated sugar

2$\frac{1}{2}$ teaspoons baking powder

1 teaspoon ground cardamom

$\frac{1}{4}$ teaspoon salt

$\frac{1}{2}$ cup (1 stick) cold unsalted butter, cut up

2 egg yolks

$\frac{1}{2}$ cup half-and-half

RASPBERRY CREAM

3 cups fresh raspberries

$\frac{1}{4}$ cup granulated sugar, plus 2 tablespoons

1$\frac{1}{4}$ cups heavy (whipping) cream

Powdered sugar for sprinkling

Almond Poppy Seed Cake

I'd like to claim this poppy seed cake as my own personal dessert, since my mother has made it for my birthday ever since I can remember. But other members of my family might dispute that claim, since they all ask for this cake when their birthdays roll around, too. Although it's baked in an angel food cake pan, this is a chiffon cake, which contains egg yolks and oil in addition to the beaten egg whites. The eggs create the delicate rise and tender structure of this moist, long-lasting cake, which is perfect for any celebration.

TO MAKE THE CAKE: Preheat the oven to 325°F. Bring the milk to a boil in a small saucepan. Put the poppy seeds in a small bowl, pour the hot milk over the poppy seeds, and let sit 1 hour or until the milk has cooled to room temperature. Whisk together the flour, $1\frac{1}{2}$ cups of the sugar, the baking powder, salt, and baking soda in a medium bowl.

Beat the egg yolks and oil in a large bowl with an electric mixer on low speed until well blended. Slowly beat in the poppy seeds with the milk, and then the flour mixture and almond extract.

In another large bowl, beat the egg whites with an electric mixer at medium speed until foamy. Add the cream of tartar and beat on medium-high speed until soft peaks form. With the mixer running, slowly pour in the remaining $\frac{1}{4}$ cup of sugar, beating until stiff but not dry peaks form. Stir one-fourth of the egg whites into the batter to lighten. Then gently fold in the remaining whites. Pour into an ungreased 10-inch angel food tube pan with a removable bottom.

Bake for 55 to 60 minutes or until the top is golden brown and springs back when gently pressed, and a wooden skewer inserted into the center of the cake comes out clean. Turn upside down and set the cake pan on its feet, or if it has none, put the center tube upside down over the neck of a bottle. Cool the cake completely. Carefully slide a thin metal cake spatula or knife around the sides of the pan and tube to loosen the cake, pressing against the pan to avoid cutting the cake. Invert the cake onto a serving platter and remove the pan.

SERVES 12

CAKE

1 cup whole milk

$\frac{1}{2}$ cup poppy seeds

2 cups all-purpose flour, preferably bleached

$1\frac{3}{4}$ cups sugar

1 tablespoon baking powder

$\frac{1}{2}$ teaspoon salt

$\frac{1}{4}$ teaspoon baking soda

8 eggs, separated, at room temperature

$\frac{1}{2}$ cup canola oil

$1\frac{1}{2}$ teaspoons almond extract

$\frac{1}{2}$ teaspoon cream of tartar

FROSTING

$\frac{1}{2}$ cup (1 stick) unsalted butter, softened

$4\frac{1}{2}$ to 5 cups powdered sugar

$\frac{1}{4}$ cup whole milk

1 teaspoon almond extract

Poppy seeds for garnish

TO MAKE THE FROSTING: Beat the butter in a large bowl with an electric mixer at medium speed until creamy. Reduce the speed to low and slowly add 1 cup of the powdered sugar. With the mixer running, slowly pour in the milk and almond extract. Continue adding powdered sugar until the desired consistency is reached.

Spread the frosting over the sides and top of the cake. Garnish with additional poppy seeds around the top edge, if desired before serving.

NOTE Chiffon cake recipes have a distinctive method; follow it precisely for the best results.

THE BROODER: REPLACING MOTHER HEN

Chicks are in your future and mother hen has left the nest. It's up to you to provide the babes with a sheltered space of their own: in other words, a brooder. A brooder keeps the chicks warm and dry and protected from any drafts, just like a fussy mom does. It's set up with heat, so all you have to do is provide the food, water, and love.

A brooder can be as simple as a cardboard box, but hey, splurge a little and upgrade to a large plastic tub. It's still cheap, is much easier to clean, and is reusable. Buy the biggest one you can find, and don't forget the cover. My 32-by-16-by-18-inch tub was perfect for three chicks, even as they grew.

You'll need to snip away part of the cover and replace it with wire screening for good airflow, but otherwise the plastic tub is self-contained. Use paper towels on the bottom for the first couple of days (so the chicks don't mistakenly eat the bedding), and then switch to pine shavings. Anchor a thermometer inside and hang a red heat lamp overhead. Set up chick-size food and water feeders, and you're ready to go.

Strawberry-Coconut Meringue

This recipe was given to me by a friend in New Zealand, where the fruit-filled meringue known as Pavlova, or Pav, is the national sweet. It's become my new favorite dessert. Less sweet than some versions, its lovely crunchy exterior holds a marshmallow-tender center. Piled high with fruit and cream, it's the ultimate springtime treat.

TO MAKE THE MERINGUE: Preheat the oven to 300°F. Line a baking sheet with parchment paper. With a pencil, draw a 6-inch circle in the center of the parchment paper, using a bowl as a guide. Turn the parchment paper over so the outline of the circle shows through but won't touch the meringue.

Beat the egg whites with the salt in a large bowl with an electric mixer at medium-high speed until soft peaks form. Beat in the cornstarch, lemon juice, and vanilla and continue beating until firm peaks form. With the mixer running, very slowly beat in the sugar (this should take about 1 to 1½ minutes). Continue beating until the egg whites are stiff and glossy and the sugar has dissolved. Gently fold in ¼ cup of the coconut.

Pile the meringue in the center of the parchment circle and spread to the edges of the circle (it will puff and expand as it bakes to about 8 inches in diameter). Gently smooth the top and sides of the meringue. Sprinkle the top and sides with the remaining ½ cup of coconut.

Bake for 45 to 50 minutes or until the coconut is golden brown and the meringue is firm on the outside. Slide the meringue and parchment paper onto a wire rack and cool completely. Gently peel off the parchment paper.

TO MAKE THE FILLING: Beat the heavy cream in a medium bowl with an electric mixer at medium speed until soft peaks form. Add the yogurt and sugar. Continue beating until firm, but not stiff, peaks form.

Pile the cream in the meringue. Top with the strawberries before serving.

NOTE The meringue can be baked up to 2 days ahead of time and stored in an airtight container. To keep the meringue as crisp as possible, assemble the dessert right before serving.

SERVES 8

MERINGUE

4 egg whites

Pinch of salt

2 tablespoons cornstarch

1 tablespoon fresh lemon juice

1 teaspoon vanilla extract

1 cup sugar

¾ cup sweetened shredded coconut

FILLING

1 cup heavy (whipping) cream

¼ cup plain nonfat yogurt

1½ tablespoons sugar

2½ cups halved fresh strawberries, or quartered if large

CHAPTER · FOUR

GLORIOUS SUMMER

I was awakened one morning by an elbow jabbing

me in the ribs. It was my husband, who mumbled, "Your chickens are squawking; they'll wake the neighbors." I blearily opened my eyes and saw it was barely 6:30 on a Saturday. Chickens have no sense of timing. Or rather, they have a different sense of timing. They live by the sun, and the bright summer sunshine told them it was time to be up.

I slipped on a light jacket over my pajamas and donned my grass-green Wellies with white clovers all over them and went outside to get the girls. As I opened the door to the coop, out charged Roxanne, the largest of my three hens. As she ran, her fat little body bounced like a buxom Victorian lady with a bustle on her rear end. She had a bossy, matronly attitude about her and was serious about her duties, insisting on always being first.

Cleo came next. She'd grown into a gentle, sweet little girl who still loved to be cuddled. Her coloring had changed as she grew, and she had lost the sophisticated Egyptian look, but she was still quite regal, with golden feathers accented with black. She was usually the odd girl out of the tight clique formed by Roxanne and Lulu, but she didn't seem to mind as she dutifully took her place two steps behind the other two.

Crazy Lulu was still the difficult chick—kind of like having a teenager, except worse. She thought her job was to annoy me. When treats were given out, Lulu let me know that she would rather starve than come close and risk being petted or caught. I had thoughts about giving her away because she was such a nuisance. As I watched the girls gobble their layer feed and breakfast treat of yogurt, it was hard to believe these grown chickens were once the day-old peeps that fit into the palm of my hand when I brought them home that Saturday in March.

Petunia, our older cat, took to the chicks with a youthful enthusiasm. She was enthralled with the new creatures that had invaded her turf and watched them intently. When the chickens finally moved outside, Petunia joined in their fun. She'd run to the corner of the yard, where they stood scratching and pecking, and she'd stand in the group munching blades of grass. She kept to the edge of the flock, presumably knowing she was last in the pecking order. When they moved, she moved. When something distracted the group and off they ran in unison toward the opposite side of the yard, there went Petunia, holding up the rear.

Even when she grew tired and stopped running with the chicks, she still came to sit next to me when Cleo was in my lap. I felt quite honored as I petted Petunia the cat with one hand and Cleo the chick with the other.

....

That first summer was the year of the great chicken migration. The chickens were vagabonds, never staying in the same place for more than a week. They didn't travel far, just from one end of the yard to the other, along with their coop, but that summer they experienced life from many vantage points.

The chicks' journey started when the coop became a chicken tractor. The image of chickens driving a tractor—mowing, tilling, and planting—of course is over the top. But there is some basis in truth when you see the effect a chicken coop can have on a yard. A chicken tractor, also known as an ark, is much more low-tech than its name implies; it's merely a mobile coop or grazing pen without a floor. The chickens peck and scratch, thereby tilling the ground; eat the bugs and weeds; and recycle it all back in the form of fertilizer. When the chickens finish with one area, you simply move them to another, and quite soon everything has been weeded, debugged, and fertilized. The hens are protected and happy and the yard is enriched. Or so the theory goes.

At the time I thought I was simply moving the coop. It wasn't until much later that I found out I was in the forefront of the chicken movement and what I had was a chicken tractor. And the chickens were driving.

My chickens migrated like wildebeests all summer long. The nifty little plastic Eglu has an attached run that's open to the ground, and the entire unit can be easily moved—or at least Omlet, the coop company, so claims. Each weekend, after the weekly coop cleaning, I'd drag the whole thing to the other end of the yard looking for a stable and level area on which to set it down. Everything looks different when you lie on your stomach to get a chick's perspective. Except for the cleaning, the backbreaking hauling, and the twisted run that had to be stomped back in place each time, the system worked great—for the first couple of weeks.

I frankly admit my decision to turn the chickens into migratory birds had nothing to do with the well-being of the chicks. It had everything to do with the lawn. I worried that if the coop stayed in one spot, I'd end up with a large area of dead grass in the middle of the yard. Mind you, the arrival of chickens seemed like an odd time to start worrying about the state of our lawn. We've never had a gorgeous lawn—the sod was laid in November for heaven's sake. It never had a chance. It snows in November up here. So our lawn has never been much of a priority. Nevertheless, I suddenly became possessive about the grass the way some people become possessive about the junk they put in their garbage. It's fine for the landfill, but heaven help anyone who swings by early in the morning and loads up a perfectly usable chair that's sitting out with the trash. I didn't mind ruining the grass myself, but I certainly didn't want the chickens doing it.

The trouble with the chicken tractor system began as the chickies started to grow. As their feet became bigger, their scratches went deeper. Each week they became more excited by the fresh grass, bugs, and other treats in their new patch of lawn, attacking the ground with gusto. They also started taking dust baths. Granted, dust bathing is a good thing, as it keeps the creepy crawlies off the birds. The problem is, when chickens don't have an area of dirt to bathe in, they create one.

The more the chickens traveled, the worse our yard looked. Friends who came out back to visit the chicks heard "Oh, just ignore the lawn. We're moving the coop around to help the yard." And they'd glance around at the worn yellow areas with puzzlement.

Thinking back to the day I ordered my Eglu, I'm now certain that Clare snickered when I told her we were going to move the coop around the yard weekly. We ended the summer with, to put it generously, a unique lawn: large yellow rectangles of sod, stunted from being pecked to death; dirt-filled, bathtub-size depressions scattered randomly around the backyard, shallow enough to miss but deep enough to twist an ankle; and trampled areas that looked like elephants had slept there, not baby chicks. Our yard was a mess, but I learned not to care. I was raising chickens and growing eggs, not sod. Eventually I abandoned the tractor idea, put up a temporary fence on the sides of the yard that were open, and let the chickens free-range most of the time. As I learned later, most chicken tractors are too small and don't provide enough room for the chickens. Chickens should have at least six square feet per bird in their run. Depending on the number of birds you have, that gets too big to move without a crew.

....

I was upstairs one day when a sound I'd never heard from the chickens echoed from the backyard. An intense high-pitched shriek, a staccato warning that continued in repeated measures like some deafening tornado siren. The shrill babble that followed sounded like my flock of three had increased tenfold. As I lunged toward the window, everything suddenly went silent. Nothing moved, not even the leaves on the trees. It was like the eerie stillness before the storm hits.

Chickens make over thirty different sounds, more than most of the bird population. When they're happy and satisfied, they putter about scratching and pecking, mumbling softly to themselves. When everything is right in their world, for instance when they're sunbathing after a tasty lunch and leisurely dust bath, they emit a throaty, guttural vibration that sounds eerily similar to a cat's purr.

They occasionally let out a deep, panicked bonk-bonk-bonk when they suddenly find themselves alone with no one in sight. These social birds travel in cliques with a pack mentality and are struck with terror when separated from their group. But the sound I had just heard was different.

It was a bright, sunny Saturday morning and a lawnmower buzzed in the distance as Marty and I thundered down the stairs. I didn't hear another sound and wondered why we were racing like greyhounds to beat each other out the door. Then I heard someone shout "No!" Someone else added, "Get her!"

Had the chickens escaped? If so, we were going to have a devil of a time catching them. Chickens are extremely sensitive to vibrations. They can pick up movement by feeling the vibrations in the air or on the ground through their skin, especially their legs. Meaning, it's impossible to sneak up on a chicken. I know. I've tried.

As we rounded the corner, I both saw and heard it in the same instant. Marty reached for me as if to hold me back. The light outside was dappled, but the sun seemed to be at a weird angle, causing everything to look slightly out of focus. My eyes started rapidly blinking. We slowly and reluctantly walked over to look, like gawkers at an ambulance scene. The leash was back in our neighbor's hand, taut and barely holding back the dog, which was still straining against it. Her bark had subsided. Apparently there was a gap in the fence. Luckily, the chickens had made it to the coop. I found them cowering in the deep recesses, away from the door.

It's hard to build a fence when your hands are shaking. I couldn't let go of the guilt as I worked that weekend. Chickens are prey animals. With few natural defenses, they are easy targets for all manner of predators. The list is long: eagles, hawks, owls, raccoons, possums, mink, skunks, foxes, snakes, coyotes, weasels, and yes, sometimes even dogs and cats. Birds of prey attack from above, while raccoons are smart enough to manipulate the door of a coop. A small possum can

slip through chicken wire, and a fox will dig to get under a fence. I felt overwhelmed. I had thought my birds were safe. As I worked on the fence, I kept worrying: What about next time? The neighbors might not be there to catch their runaway dog. Next time the chicks might not be so lucky. My hands continued to shake as I strengthened the fence.

COOP TOUR

You're hooked. Chickens are what you want, but first you need a coop. Where do you start? If you're all thumbs, or prefer to keep your hands clean, look for a premade house. They come in all styles, from barnyard to chic, delivered right to your door. At least one company, Omlet, will also deliver your chickens to complete the deal.

You can also build a coop yourself. Just remember, if you're in an urban area, you have neighbors. Keep them in mind when you're building your coop, and make it aesthetically pleasing. A nice-looking coop doesn't have to cost anything more than a ramshackle one. Many urban areas now host coop tours. Plan to attend one and talk to those in your area who have built coops. You'll find they're glad to give you lots of ideas and tips.

Coops come in all shapes and sizes, so how do you know how much room to provide? Recommendations will vary, but the accepted rule is four square feet per bird. There should be a total of at least ten square feet per bird for the outdoor and indoor space combined. If the birds are simply sleeping in the coop and not spending any daytime there, other than laying time, you can get by with a smaller coop. Also, smaller birds make do with less space than larger birds.

Keep in mind the coop is a home for birds, not people. Chickens are ground-dwelling birds that enjoy roaming during the day, looking for new food sources. They are creatures of habit and always return to the same area every evening to roost. Chickens in the wild will roost in trees, so every coop should have a sheltered, elevated roosting area for the chickens to comfortably sleep at night. Hens also need a secluded area to lay their eggs. They prefer an area that gives them privacy, so try to be accommodating and they'll reward you with eggs.

Birds need the normal amenities of light and air, but the most important consideration is keeping your chickens safe from predators. That means all openings must be protected with closures that predators are unable to open.

Baked Eggs with Basil-Mint Pesto

I've been making basil-mint pesto for years, since the time I didn't have enough basil for my usual pesto and added mint to make up the difference. The combination is very refreshing—perfect for early summer. This recipe is like a deconstructed pesto: the herbs are combined with a hint of garlic and just enough olive oil to make a paste. The cheese is a tangy soft goat cheese, which is spread over toast, and the nuts are pecans, which toast lightly as they bake on top.

Preheat the oven to 350°F. Butter four 5-by-1-inch gratin or crème brûlée dishes or coat them with nonstick cooking spray and place on a rimmed baking sheet. Pulse the basil and mint in a food processor until finely chopped. Add the garlic, ⅛ teaspoon of the salt, and half of the pepper and pulse to combine. With the processor running, slowly add the olive oil.

Toast the baguette slices and spread each with ½ tablespoon of the goat cheese. Arrange two slices in each baking dish. Top each slice with about ¾ teaspoon of the basil-mint mixture and gently spread to cover.

Break the eggs, one at a time, into a small cup and gently pour one egg over each slice of toast. (The eggs may slip off the toast and the toast may float, but don't worry, they will bake just fine.) Sprinkle the eggs with the remaining salt and pepper. Top each dish with 1 teaspoon of pecans.

Bake the eggs for 12 to 16 minutes or until the egg whites are set and the yolks are to your preferred doneness.

Serve immediately.

Ingredients

- ½ cup lightly packed fresh basil leaves
- ¼ cup lightly packed fresh mint leaves
- ¼ teaspoon minced garlic
- ¼ teaspoon salt
- ⅛ teaspoon freshly ground pepper
- 1½ tablespoons extra-virgin olive oil
- 8 slices baguette (½ inch thick), cut into rounds or on a slight diagonal, depending on the shape of the baking dishes
- ¼ cup fresh goat cheese, at room temperature
- 8 eggs
- 4 teaspoons chopped pecans

NOTES The basil-mint mixture can be made 1 day ahead and refrigerated, or make a batch when the herbs are in season and freeze it for up to 6 months.

This is an easy dish to make for guests because the herb mixture can be made in advance and the bread can be toasted and spread with the cheese and pesto up to 2 hours ahead.

Smoky Cheddar and Bacon Puffed Eggs

This easy brunch dish is a cross between an omelet and a soufflé. It's baked in a shallow dish, rising like a soufflé when the eggs hit the oven. The center is filled like an omelet, with fried onions, smoky cheddar cheese, and bacon. Choose an extra-smoky bacon, to make this dish extra-special.

Preheat the oven to 400°F. Coat a 6-cup shallow baking or gratin dish with nonstick cooking spray. Fry the bacon in a medium skillet over medium-high heat for 4 to 6 minutes or until brown and crisp, stirring frequently. Scoop the bacon from the pan using a slotted spoon and drain on a paper towel-lined plate. Keep the drippings in the pan.

Add the onion to the pan and cook over medium heat for 8 to 10 minutes, stirring frequently, until softened and golden brown, increasing the heat to medium-high toward the end of cooking if necessary to facilitate the browning. Add to the bacon.

Meanwhile, whisk the egg yolks, milk, salt, and pepper together in a medium bowl for 1 to 2 minutes or until light and fluffy. Whisk in half of the green onion. In a large bowl, beat the egg whites with an electric mixer at medium speed until firm but not stiff peaks form (do not overbeat). Gently stir half of the whites into the egg yolk mixture to lighten. Pour the egg yolk mixture into the egg whites and gently fold until blended.

Gently spoon half of the egg mixture into the baking dish. Sprinkle with the bacon, fried onion, the remaining green onion, and half of the cheese. Gently pour the remaining egg mixture over the filling. Sprinkle with the remaining cheese. (The puffed eggs can be made to this point up to 2 hours before baking. Cover and refrigerate, adding an additional 5 minutes for the baking time, if needed.)

Bake the eggs for 10 to 15 minutes or until puffed, golden brown, and set in the center (tap to make sure they don't wobble like liquid). Serve immediately.

SERVES 4

4 slices applewood-smoked bacon, chopped (3/4 cup)

1 onion, halved and sliced (1 cup)

6 eggs, separated

1/4 cup milk

1/4 teaspoon kosher salt

1/4 teaspoon freshly ground pepper

1/3 cup sliced green onion (green part only)

3/4 cup shredded smoked cheddar cheese (3 ounces)

Sweet Chili Shrimp and Egg Bruschetta

This truly is a global recipe. It originated in Iceland and came to me via my nephew, who studied there for a year. Based on Italian bruschetta, the dish is made with Thai sweet chili sauce instead of tomato, giving the dish an Asian spin.

TO MAKE THE SAUCE: Stir together all of the ingredients and set aside.

TO MAKE THE BRUSCHETTA: Preheat the oven to 375°F. Arrange the baguette slices on a baking sheet. Brush both sides with about 1½ tablespoons of the olive oil. Bake for 5 to 8 minutes or until slightly crisp and the edges are just beginning to turn brown. Cool on a wire rack to room temperature.

Heat a large skillet over medium heat and heat the remaining 1 tablespoon of olive oil. Add the shrimp and garlic and cook for 3 to 4 minutes, stirring frequently, until the shrimp turn pink and are slightly firm. Remove to a plate and cool to room temperature.

Spoon about ½ teaspoon of the sauce over each baguette. Top with a slice of egg, spoon another ½ teaspoon of sauce over the egg, and top with a shrimp. Garnish with the cilantro sprigs. Serve with lemon wedges.

NOTE: A red-colored chili powder will lend the best color to the sauce.

SERVES 6 TO 8
MAKES 18 BRUSCHETTA

SAUCE

½ cup sweet chili sauce

2 tablespoons chopped fresh cilantro

1 teaspoon fresh lemon juice

½ teaspoon chili powder (see Note)

BRUSCHETTA

18 slices baguette (⅜ inch thick)

2½ tablespoons extra-virgin olive oil

18 large raw shrimp (21 to 30 count), peeled and deveined, tails removed

2 garlic cloves, minced

4 hard-cooked eggs (see Note, page 31), peeled and sliced

Cilantro sprigs for garnish

Lemon wedges for serving

Cucumber-Basil Egg Salad

The glories of summer are captured in this pale green egg salad redolent of fresh basil, green onions, and crunchy cucumbers. Serve it surrounded by greens or tucked into pita pockets or slices of crusty bread for a satisfying lunch.

Gently combine the eggs, cucumber, shallots, green onions, and basil in a medium bowl. Stir in the mayonnaise, salt, and pepper.

Store in the refrigerator for up to three days.

SERVES 6

6 hard-cooked eggs (see Note, page 31), diced (2 cups)

$^3/_4$ cup seeded, diced cucumber (about $^1/_2$ cucumber)

$^1/_4$ cup minced shallots

$^1/_2$ cup sliced green onions (green part only)

3 tablespoons lightly packed chopped fresh basil

$^1/_2$ cup mayonnaise

$^1/_4$ teaspoon kosher salt

$^1/_4$ teaspoon freshly ground pepper

IT'S JUST CHICKEN FEED

Chickens are like teenaged boys—always hungry. What you should feed them will depend on how old they are. Provide a complete chicken feed to make sure they're getting all of the nutrients they need. Commercial feed comes in starter formula for chicks, grower for growing pullets, and layer for hens that have started to lay eggs. The formulas are adjusted to meet the chickens' nutritional needs at each stage of life.

Try to get organic chicken feed if possible. You can also make your own chicken feed utilizing a combination of twelve to seventeen different grains. Chickens are omnivores, meaning they eat meat as well as grains and vegetables. They eat worms, bugs, moths, and other goodies in your backyard. When they are molting, or the weather is cold, or they are sick or otherwise stressed, extra protein will provide the nutrients to pull them through.

Layered Antipasto Chicken Salad with Fresh Basil Dressing

This is the perfect potluck salad—it's colorful and travels well. In fact, it's best made ahead of time. The layers of antipasto ingredients, including salami, cheese, artichokes, and olives, make a nice change of pace from the usual pasta salad, which shows up at so many potlucks. Use leftover chicken, or look for a rotisserie chicken (that's certified as humanely raised) at your grocery store.

TO MAKE THE DRESSING: Combine all of the dressing ingredients in a blender container and blend until smooth. Set aside.

TO MAKE THE SALAD: Arrange the romaine over the bottom of a 10-cup glass bowl and sprinkle with the red bell pepper. Spread the chicken over the bell pepper and layer with the tomatoes, artichoke hearts, soppressata, mozzarella and olives. Cover and refrigerate for up to 1 hour before serving.

When ready to serve, pour in enough dressing to lightly coat the salad ingredients.

SERVES 4

DRESSING

¼ cup plus 2 tablespoons extra-virgin olive oil

⅓ cup chopped fresh basil

2 tablespoons red wine vinegar

1 tablespoon grated Parmigiano-Reggiano cheese

1 garlic clove, chopped

¼ teaspoon kosher salt

¼ teaspoon freshly ground pepper

SALAD

2 cups sliced romaine lettuce (½ inch thick)

1 red bell pepper, seeded, deveined, and chopped

2 cups cubed (¾-inch cubes) cooked chicken (see pages 13 to 14)

1 cup grape tomatoes, halved

¾ cup quartered artichoke hearts, drained

1½ ounces thinly sliced soppressata or dry salami, cut into thin strips (½ cup)

1 cup halved fresh mozzarella balls

1 cup pitted Kalamata and/or green olives, halved

Spanish Tuna Salad with Smoked Paprika Dressing

This salad is brimming with the lusty flavors of tuna, smoky paprika, sherry vinegar, salty olives, roasted peppers, and hard-cooked eggs. It's a little like a Spanish alternative to the French salad niçoise, a light meal that leaves you satisfied.

TO MAKE THE DRESSING: Combine all of the ingredients in a small food processor or blender and pulse until smooth. Set aside.

TO MAKE THE SALAD: Blanch the green beans in a large pot of boiling salted water for 2 to 3 minutes, or until bright green in color. Plunge the beans into ice water to cool; drain and pat dry with paper towels.

Toss the green beans, mixed greens, green bell pepper, roasted red peppers, red onion, and ⅓ cup of the cheese in a large bowl until mixed. Toss with enough dressing to lightly coat. Arrange on a large platter. Top with the tuna, quartered eggs, olives, and the remaining ⅓ cup of cheese. Drizzle with about 3 tablespoons of the remaining dressing before serving.

SERVES 4

DRESSING

¼ cup plus 2 tablespoons extra-virgin olive oil

2 tablespoons sherry vinegar

2 tablespoons slivered almonds

2 garlic cloves, coarsely chopped

1 teaspoon smoked paprika (*pimentón*)

¼ teaspoon kosher salt

¼ teaspoon freshly ground pepper

SALAD

6 ounces green beans

6 cups mixed greens

1 green bell pepper, seeded, deveined, and sliced

2 roasted red bell peppers, drained, patted dry, and chopped (about ½ cup)

½ cup thinly sliced red onion

⅔ cup diced Manchego cheese

One 4½- to 5-ounce can tuna packed in olive oil, drained and flaked

4 hard-cooked eggs (see Note, page 31), quartered

⅓ cup pitted Kalamata olives, halved

Egg-Stuffed Baguette with Fresh Lemon Mayo

Hold this sandwich tightly, because it's packed full of eggs, tomatoes, and arugula slathered in a homemade lemon mayonnaise. (Some of the filling may slip out if you're not careful.) It's best assembled ahead of time, so all of the flavors mingle together and all you have to do at the last minute is slice and serve.

SERVES 4

FRESH LEMON MAYO

1 egg yolk (see Note)

1½ teaspoons fresh lemon juice

½ teaspoon Dijon mustard

⅛ teaspoon salt

⅛ teaspoon freshly ground pepper

¼ cup canola oil

½ teaspoon grated lemon zest

SANDWICH

1 small baguette or half a standard-size baguette (about 5 ounces)

1 cup lightly packed arugula or spinach

1 tomato, sliced

4 hard-cooked eggs (see Note, page 31), halved lengthwise

TO MAKE THE MAYONNAISE: Beat the egg yolk, lemon juice, mustard, salt, and pepper with an electric mixer at medium speed for 1 to 1½ minutes or until thick and foamy. Continue beating and slowly begin adding the oil drop by drop in a very thin stream. When about half of the oil has been added, the mayonnaise will begin to thicken. At that point, the oil can be added at a slightly faster rate. Once all of the oil has been added, stir in the lemon zest. (If making ahead, cover and refrigerate the mayonnaise for up to 1 week.)

TO ASSEMBLE THE SANDWICH: Slice the top third of the baguette horizontally, but do not cut all the way through. Open the top of the bread like a book and remove all but ½ inch of the bread inside, leaving a shell. (Reserve the bread for another use, such as bread crumbs or croutons.)

Spread the mayonnaise over the inside of the bread shell. Layer the arugula over the bottom, and top with the tomato slices. Arrange the eggs down the length of the bread. Cover with the top of the bread shell and tightly wrap the baguette in plastic wrap. Refrigerate for at least 1 hour, and up to 8 hours. Cut crosswise into 4 servings.

NOTES — The mayonnaise is made with a raw egg yolk. If you prefer, you may substitute 1 pasteurized egg yolk. To ensure success in making this homemade mayonnaise, start with a warm, dry bowl. If you prefer a thicker mayonnaise, continue adding oil until it reaches the desired consistency.

You may also substitute a simpler lemon mayonnaise: Stir together ⅓ cup of mayonnaise with 1 teaspoon of fresh lemon juice and ½ teaspoon of grated lemon zest.

Smoked Wings with Cilantro Dip

These wings are addictive. The smoked paprika, cumin, and chipotle chile powder are key to their smoky, bold flavor. Don't be put off by the length of the ingredient list; it's a very quick and easy recipe. Simply measure and dump, then marinate the wings for up to a day before grilling.

TO MARINATE THE CHICKEN WINGS: Put the wings in a large resealable plastic bag. Stir together the remaining wing ingredients, except the oil, in a small bowl. Add the olive oil and stir until smooth. Add the seasoning mixture to the chicken wings, seal the bag, and squish the bag to coat the wings with the seasoning. Put in a shallow pan and refrigerate overnight, or up to 24 hours.

TO MAKE THE DIP: Blend all of the ingredients together in a blender until smooth. Cover and refrigerate. Bring to room temperature before serving.

Preheat the grill to medium. Remove the wings from the rub and discard any remaining seasoning mixture. Grill, covered, for 10 to 12 minutes or until no longer pink in center, turning every 3 to 4 minutes to brown on all sides. Serve the chicken wings with the dip.

NOTES

To separate the wings, cut between the wing joints with a large chef's knife or kitchen shears. Discard the wing tips or save for chicken stock.

When grilling wings, dump all of the wings onto the grill, and then use tongs to quickly arrange the wings on the grill. I find that trying to place the wings individually on the grill grate takes too long, and the first ones begin to cook before the rest even get near the heat.

SERVES 4
MAKES ABOUT
32 CHICKEN WINGS

CHICKEN WINGS

2½ pounds chicken wings (about 16 wings), separated at the joint (see Note), or 32 chicken drumettes

3 tablespoons smoked paprika (*pimentón*)

2 tablespoons red wine vinegar

1 tablespoon dried oregano, preferably Greek

1 tablespoon ground cumin

¾ teaspoon chipotle chile powder

¾ teaspoon garlic powder

¾ teaspoon kosher salt

½ teaspoon freshly ground pepper

¼ cup extra-virgin olive oil

CILANTRO DIP

¾ cup lightly packed coarsely chopped fresh cilantro

¼ cup plus 2 tablespoons extra-virgin olive oil

⅓ cup water

¼ cup chopped pecans

3 tablespoons fresh lemon juice

2 tablespoons chopped fresh mint

2 garlic cloves

½ teaspoon ground cumin

¼ teaspoon kosher salt

¼ teaspoon freshly ground pepper

Rosemary Chicken Burgers with Fried Onions

When I go to a classic old-time diner, I order a burger with fried onions. At home, however, I like to jazz up the classics a bit. This moist chicken burger is flavored with fresh rosemary, sun-dried tomatoes, and green onions, and topped with a pile of golden fried onions.

TO MAKE THE BURGERS: Gently mix together all of the ingredients, except the egg, in a large bowl, being careful not to overmix the chicken, or it will become compacted and dry. Gently stir in the egg. Form into four 4-inch patties, ¾ inch thick, and place on a baking sheet. Cover and refrigerate for 30 minutes or until chilled.

Meanwhile, heat a medium skillet over medium-high heat. Heat the 2 tablespoons of oil. Fry the onions for 10 to 12 minutes or until golden brown and tender. Reduce the heat to medium if the onions begin to brown too quickly.

Preheat the grill to medium. Oil the grill grate. Grill the burgers, covered, for 10 minutes or until no longer pink in the center, turning once. Place the hamburger buns on the grill during the last minute and cook until lightly toasted.

Right before serving, reheat the onions over medium heat until warm. Spread the mayonnaise over the buns. Place a tomato slice on each bottom bun and follow with a burger and onions. Finish each with the top bun and serve.

SERVES 4

BURGERS

1½ pounds ground chicken

½ cup panko (coarse bread crumbs)

½ cup thinly sliced green onions (green part only)

⅓ cup chopped oil-packed sun-dried tomatoes, drained patted dry

2 tablespoons extra-virgin olive oil

1 tablespoon chopped fresh rosemary

1 garlic clove, minced

½ teaspoon kosher salt

¼ teaspoon freshly ground pepper

1 egg, beaten

2 tablespoons extra-virgin olive oil

2 large onions, halved and sliced

4 hamburger buns, split

¼ cup mayonnaise, preferably Fresh Lemon Mayo (page 90) or Garlic Mayonnaise (page 148)

4 slices tomato

Summer Solstice Chicken

Fresh dill and cilantro are unlikely partners that blend beautifully in the vivid green marinade for the chicken. Perfect for celebrating the start of the summer and the longest day of the year, the grilled chicken maintains the emerald color of the marinade, evoking the lushness of green grass and the fragrance of an herb garden in its true summer glory.

Combine all of the ingredients, except the chicken, in a blender container and blend until smooth and bright green in color. Put the chicken breasts in a resealable plastic bag and pour the marinade over them. Put in a shallow pan and marinate in the refrigerator for 8 hours or overnight.

Preheat the grill to medium. Remove the chicken from the marinade and discard the marinade. Oil the grill grate and grill the chicken, covered, for 8 to 10 minutes or until no longer pink in the center.

Serve immediately.

VARIATION: Slice the grilled chicken and serve in warm pita bread (flatbread) pockets with sliced tomatoes, cucumbers, and onion. Spoon in some sour cream flavored with chopped fresh dill.

SERVES 4

4 green onions (green part only), coarsely chopped (scant 1 cup)

$3/4$ cup coarsely chopped fresh cilantro

$1/3$ cup coarsely chopped onion

$1/3$ cup extra-virgin olive oil

$1/4$ cup coarsely chopped fresh dill

4 garlic cloves, coarsely chopped

1 tablespoon fresh lemon juice

$1/2$ teaspoon kosher salt

$1/4$ teaspoon freshly ground pepper

4 boneless, skinless chicken breast halves (about $1 1/2$ pounds)

Pan-Seared Chicken Breasts with Green Olive Tapenade

Stuffing the tapenade under the skin of the chicken breast not only adds flavor but also keeps the breast moist during baking. While there's no denying the convenience of boneless, skinless chicken breasts, there are times when they just won't do. This recipe is one of those times. The pungent olive spread tastes best with the extra flavor and moisture you get with bone-in breasts.

SERVES 4

1 garlic clove, smashed with the side of a chef's knife

$\frac{1}{2}$ cup coarsely chopped fresh flat-leaf parsley, plus 1 tablespoon

2 tablespoons slivered almonds

One $3\frac{1}{2}$-ounce jar pitted green olives (scant 1 cup), drained and patted dry with paper towels

$\frac{1}{4}$ teaspoon freshly ground pepper

2 tablespoons extra-virgin olive oil

4 bone-in, skin-on chicken breast halves (3 pounds)

Preheat the oven to 425°F. Lightly oil a small, rimmed baking sheet. With the food processor running, drop the garlic into the processor and process until finely chopped. Add the $\frac{1}{2}$ cup parsley and pulse until finely chopped. Add the almonds and pulse until finely chopped. Add the olives and $\frac{1}{8}$ teaspoon of the pepper and pulse until the olives are finely chopped. With the processor running, pour in 1 tablespoon of the oil to form a coarse paste.

Trim away the back rib bones on the chicken breasts with kitchen shears. Using your fingers, make a pocket in the center of each breast between the skin and the meat, keeping the skin attached around the edges. Spoon a generous $2\frac{1}{2}$ tablespoons of the tapenade into the pocket of each breast. Press and smooth the skin over the filling to distribute evenly.

Heat a large skillet over medium-high heat, and heat the remaining tablespoon of oil. Add the chicken, skin-side down, in batches if necessary, and cook for 3 to 4 minutes or until golden brown. Place skin-side up on the baking sheet. Sprinkle with the remaining $\frac{1}{8}$ teaspoon pepper.

Bake for 25 minutes or until golden brown and the chicken is no longer pink in the center. Sprinkle with the 1 tablespoon chopped parsley before serving.

NOTES   The tapenade can be made up to 3 days ahead of time. Cover and store in the refrigerator.

The chicken breasts can be assembled up to 8 hours before cooking. Cover and refrigerate until ready to cook.

Charred Tandoori Chicken with Mint

This flavorful marinade gets deep into the chicken, thanks to the slits you cut in the meat before marinating. For the best flavor, let the chicken marinate overnight before grilling. I like to serve this dish with basmati rice cooked with coconut milk and tossed with fresh cilantro.

SERVES 4

Measure all of the ingredients, except the mint and the chicken, into a blender container and blend until smooth. Stir in the $1/4$ cup mint.

Cut three $1/2$- to 1-inch-deep slits in each piece of chicken to allow the marinade to penetrate. Drop the chicken into a large resealable plastic bag and pour the yogurt mixture over the chicken, seal the bag, and turn and massage the bag to coat each piece of chicken. Put in a shallow pan and refrigerate for 6 hours or overnight to marinate.

Preheat the grill to medium. Remove the chicken from the marinade and discard the marinade. Oil the grill grate. Cover the grill and cook the chicken for 25 to 30 minutes or until the chicken is slightly charred and no longer pink in the center, turning every 5 minutes and moving the chicken to a cooler area of the grill if browning too quickly.

Cut the chicken breasts in half if large and sprinkle the chicken with the 1 tablespoon mint before serving.

One 8-ounce container plain yogurt

4 garlic cloves, coarsely chopped

One 1-inch piece fresh ginger, coarsely chopped

3 tablespoons canola oil

2 tablespoons fresh lemon juice

1 tablespoon ground cumin

1 tablespoon ground coriander

1 tablespoon paprika

1 teaspoon kosher salt

$1/2$ teaspoon freshly ground black pepper

$1/4$ teaspoon cayenne pepper

$1/4$ cup chopped fresh mint, plus 1 tablespoon

One 3- to $3\frac{1}{4}$-pound chicken, cut into 8 pieces

Chocolate-Cherry Fudge Brownies

These brownies are extreme—rich, fudgy, and chocolaty. The cherries not only add a sweet tartness, they also add moisture so the brownies will keep for several days. According to food scientist Shirley Corriher, eggs are the reason for the shiny top crust that forms on a brownie; that's because the egg whites and sugar create a meringue when beaten. The longer you beat the eggs, the crisper and shinier the crust becomes. If you beat the eggs too much, the crust will actually rise and separate from the rest of the brownie.

TO MAKE THE BROWNIES: Preheat the oven to 350°F. Coat a 13-by-9-inch baking pan with nonstick cooking spray. Melt the butter and the chopped bittersweet chocolate together in small saucepan over low heat, stirring occasionally until smooth. Remove from the heat and add the cocoa, whisking until smooth. Cool to room temperature.

Whisk together the flour, baking powder, and salt in a medium bowl. Beat the eggs in a large bowl using an electric mixer at medium speed for 1 minute. Add the granulated sugar, brown sugar, and vanilla and beat for 1 minute or until smooth. Beat in the chocolate mixture. Reduce the speed to low and beat in the flour mixture. Stir in the chocolate chips and cherries and pour the batter into the baking pan.

Bake for 25 to 30 minutes or until the brownies are set, the center is slightly puffed, and a toothpick inserted 2 inches from the edge comes out slightly moist, with a few crumbs attached. (This last test is a little difficult because of all of the chocolate chips; it may take several tries before you can actually test the brownie without piercing a melted chocolate chip.) Cool completely in the pan on a wire rack.

TO MAKE THE FROSTING: Combine the ingredients in a small saucepan. Heat over low heat until melted and smooth, stirring occasionally. Spread over the brownies.

Let the brownies sit until the frosting has firmed up before serving.

NOTE I love using tart dried cherries because they balance the sweetness of the chocolate. For a less expensive alternative, use cherry-flavored dried cranberries or other dried fruit.

MAKES 24 BROWNIES

BROWNIES

1 cup (2 sticks) unsalted butter, cut up

4 ounces bittersweet chocolate (60% cacao), chopped

3/4 cup unsweetened cocoa powder

1 3/4 cups all-purpose flour

1 1/4 teaspoons baking powder

1/2 teaspoon salt

4 eggs, at room temperature

1 cup granulated sugar

3/4 cup packed light brown sugar

2 teaspoons vanilla extract

One 12-ounce package semisweet chocolate chips

1 cup dried tart cherries (see Note)

FROSTING

One 12-ounce package semisweet chocolate chips

4 tablespoons unsalted butter

1/4 cup heavy (whipping) cream

Blueberry Sour Cream Tart

Fresh blueberries crown a sour cream custard that's reminiscent of light, tangy cheesecake, with a sugar cookie crust that melts in your mouth.

TO MAKE THE CRUST: Whisk together the flour, nutmeg, and salt in a small bowl. Beat the butter and sugar in a large bowl with an electric mixer at medium speed for 1 minute or until smooth. Add the egg yolk and beat until blended. Reduce the speed to low and add the flour mixture, beating just until a dough forms. On a lightly floured work surface, press the dough into a flat disk. Press into the bottom and up the sides of a 14-by-4½-inch rectangular or a 9-inch round tart pan with a removable bottom.

Refrigerate for 30 minutes, or freeze for 15 minutes or until firm. Preheat the oven to 375°F. Whisk the egg white until frothy. Lightly brush the inside of the crust with the egg white. Bake for 15 minutes or until pale brown and set. Cool for 10 minutes on a wire rack.

TO MAKE THE FILLING: Beat the butter and sugar in a large bowl with an electric mixer at medium speed for 2 minutes or until light and fluffy. Beat in the flour. Add the eggs, one at a time, beating well after each one. Beat in the sour cream, vanilla, and orange zest. Pour into the baked crust.

Bake the tart for 20 minutes or until slightly puffed around the edge. Cool completely on a wire rack.

Pile the blueberries on top of the tart. Brush the red currant jelly over the blueberries. Serve immediately or store in the refrigerator for up to 2 days.

CRUST

1¼ cups all-purpose flour

½ teaspoon ground nutmeg

⅛ teaspoon salt

½ cup (1 stick) unsalted butter, softened

¼ cup sugar

1 egg, separated

FILLING

6 tablespoons unsalted butter, softened

½ cup sugar

1 tablespoon all-purpose flour

2 eggs

¾ cup sour cream

1½ teaspoons vanilla extract

½ teaspoon grated orange zest

2 cups fresh blueberries

¼ cup red currant jelly, warmed

Triple-Cheese Cheesecake with Strawberries

As a family of cheesecake connoisseurs, we've done our part to never let any cheesecake go untouched. When everyone tasted this tangy-sweet combination of mascarpone, goat cheese, and cream cheese it became an instant favorite. Even the crust is special; it's like eating a shortbread cookie with a hit of lemon.

TO MAKE THE CRUST: Preheat the oven to 350°F. Line the outside of a 9-inch springform pan with heavy-duty foil. Whisk together the flour, sugar, and salt in a medium bowl. Blend in the butter with a pastry blender or your fingertips until the butter is the size of small blueberries. Combine the egg yolk and lemon zest and stir into the flour mixture with a fork. The dough will be crumbly but should cling together when pressed with your fingers. If necessary, add additional water. Press into the bottom of the springform pan.

Bake the crust for 20 minutes or until light brown. Partially cool on a wire rack.

TO MAKE THE FILLING: Combine the cream cheese, mascarpone, goat cheese, and butter in a large bowl. Beat with an electric mixer on low speed until smooth, using the paddle attachment if possible. Beat in the sugar and flour until mixed. Add the sour cream, lemon juice, and vanilla and beat until combined. Add the eggs, one at a time, beating only until incorporated. Pour the cheesecake batter over the crust.

Place the springform pan in a large, shallow pan or broiler pan. Add hot tap water to come 1 inch up the sides of the springform pan. Bake for 50 to 60 minutes or until the top is golden brown and the edges are slightly puffed. The center will wobble slightly when tapped, but it should not be liquidy.

Remove the springform pan from the water and remove the foil. Cool on a wire rack to room temperature and refrigerate, uncovered, overnight.

SERVES 12

CRUST

1 cup all-purpose flour

$1/3$ cup sugar

Pinch of salt

4 tablespoons cold unsalted butter, cut up

1 egg yolk, beaten with 2 teaspoons water

1 teaspoon grated lemon zest

FILLING

One 8-ounce package cream cheese, softened

One 8-ounce container mascarpone cheese, softened

8 ounces fresh goat cheese, softened

$1/2$ cup (1 stick) unsalted butter, softened

$1^{1}/3$ cup sugar

$1^{1}/2$ tablespoons all-purpose flour

$1/3$ cup sour cream

1 tablespoon fresh lemon juice

2 teaspoons vanilla extract

3 eggs

TO PREPARE THE STRAWBERRIES: Stir together the berries, sugar, vanilla, and lemon zest in a medium bowl. Let sit for 30 minutes or until the sugar has dissolved and a sauce has formed, stirring occasionally.

Serve the cheesecake topped with the strawberries.

NOTES The key to a good cheesecake is to avoid overbeating, especially once the eggs are added. The more air that is beaten into the mixture, the greater the chance that cracking will occur. Start with softened cheeses and beat only until the ingredients are blended, no more.

For an extra-smooth cheesecake with no lumps, pour the finished batter through a medium strainer, pressing with a large rubber spatula.

To avoid overbaking the cheesecake, another common cause of cracking, follow the baking doneness tests as described. The cheesecake will firm up as it cools.

STRAWBERRIES

1 pound fresh strawberries, sliced (3 cups)

3 to 4 tablespoons sugar, depending on the sweetness of the berries

1 teaspoon vanilla extract

1 teaspoon grated lemon zest

HOT CHICKS

The temperature is ninety-five degrees Fahrenheit. You've got a group of hot chicks on your hands. Sound exciting? It won't be the swinging time you're expecting because chickens don't tolerate heat well. They're built to survive the cold better than the heat. Chickens are covered in a coat of downy feathers and have no sweat glands. It's difficult for them to cool themselves off. If they become too hot, they start panting like a dog. Make sure your birds have shade so they can escape the sun in hot weather; lots of fresh, cool water; and a well-ventilated coop with good airflow.

Raspberry-Peach Upside-Down Cake

This moist, tender cake rises high above the brown-sugar-and-butter-glazed peaches and raspberries. Allspice adds a hint of exotic spiciness to the fruit. For the best results, bring the eggs to room temperature before using; they'll beat up higher with more air, adding extra lightness to the cake.

Preheat the oven to 350°F.

TO MAKE THE TOPPING: Coat a 9-by-2-inch round cake pan with nonstick cooking spray. Melt the butter in a small saucepan over medium heat. Add the brown sugar, lemon juice, and allspice and cook for about 2 minutes, or until the sugar has dissolved and the mixture is thick and bubbly. Pour into the bottom of the cake pan. Arrange the peach slices over the sugar mixture and scatter the raspberries over and around the peaches.

TO MAKE THE CAKE: Whisk the flour, baking powder, baking soda, and salt together in a medium bowl. Beat the butter in a large bowl with an electric mixer at medium speed for 1 minute or until smooth. Add the granulated sugar and almond extract and beat for 3 minutes or until light and fluffy; the mixture will be almost white in color. Add the eggs, one at a time, beating well after each one. Reduce the speed to low and beat in the flour mixture in three parts, alternating with the buttermilk, beginning and ending with the flour mixture. Spoon the batter over the fruit and gently spread to cover.

Bake the cake for 45 minutes or until a toothpick inserted in the center of the cake comes out clean and the top is deep golden brown and springs back when gently pressed. Cool in the pan on a wire rack for 15 minutes. Run a thin knife or spatula around the sides of the cake and invert onto a large serving plate. Cool for 20 minutes, and serve warm or at room temperature.

NOTES: To peel peaches, plunge them into a large pot of boiling water for 30 to 60 seconds, or just until the skins are loose. Cool in a bowl of ice water. Using a small knife, gently peel.

To bring the eggs to room temperature quickly, put them in a bowl of very hot tap water and let sit for about 10 minutes.

SERVES 8

TOPPING

Nonstick cooking spray

4 tablespoons unsalted butter, cut up

$1/2$ cup packed light brown sugar

1 tablespoon fresh lemon juice

$1/2$ teaspoon ground allspice

2 large peaches (about 1 pound), peeled (see Note) and sliced $3/4$ inch thick

1 cup fresh raspberries

CAKE

$1 1/2$ cups all-purpose flour, preferably bleached

$3/4$ teaspoon baking powder

$1/2$ teaspoon baking soda

$1/4$ teaspoon salt

$1/2$ cup (1 stick) unsalted butter, softened

1 cup granulated sugar

$1/2$ teaspoon almond extract

2 eggs, at room temperature (see Note)

$1/2$ cup buttermilk

LOOK—I'M FLYING!

My chickens get this surprised look every time their wings synchronize and they gain loft. It's like they can't believe they're in the air. Yes, chickens can fly. The smaller and lighter they are, the farther they can travel, which is why small bantams are the best fliers of all. Granted, most chickens don't fly well and they don't fly far, but they can glide over a low fence if the grass looks greener on the other side. And it always does. For the best protection, build your fences high enough to keep the chickens in.

To ground your high fliers, one wing tip can be clipped to keep the bird off balance. This procedure, if done correctly, is like clipping fingernails. The wing tip will grow back after molting. But talk to an expert or get hold of detailed photos before attempting it yourself. If you cut too far, you will sever part of the wing, not only hurting the bird but permanently damaging the wing.

RUN, CHICKEN, RUN

As much as they love their coop, chickens can't wait to go outside in the morning. For their safety, provide them with a run, which is a secure outdoor area. It's at least as important as the coop itself. The bigger the run, the happier everyone will be. If you have a fenced area with lots of cover by way of bushes, trees, and plants, you may be able to let them run free in your backyard. If your yard is open, or if you are a gardener and need to keep the chickens away from most areas in the yard, you will need a separate place for the chickens to roam.

The run needs to be fenced on the sides and from above to protect your birds from aerial predators. The side fencing should go below the ground by at least 6 inches, and then out at a 90-degree angle to deter digging predators. Chicken wire is not recommended, as the holes are actually too big. Weasels or small rodents can slip through the chicken wire. Use hardware cloth instead; it's a tight screening material that's stiff and resistant to almost all wild intruders.

If possible, provide different levels for your birds to use in the run, and roosting branches of varying diameters to exercise their feet. If you live in a wet or snowy climate, the run should have a portion that is covered to offer your flock protection from the elements. In the summer, the birds should have ample shade.

CHAPTER
· FIVE

LATE SUMMER

Thwack!

The drumstick cleanly disconnected from the meaty thigh. I quickly arranged the chicken parts, skin-side up, on the baking sheet and grabbed another bird. It was 7:00 A.M., another busy Saturday morning, and I still had forty-nine chickens left to dismember. The glamorous job of a chef. Did you know that if you turn the thigh and leg portion of the chicken skin-side down there is a thin line of fat running between the two parts? If you cut right down that line of fat, you can sever the two parts without ever touching a bone.

I shook my head with a start. Why had I been daydreaming about working in a restaurant after all these years? And cutting apart chickens, of all things! In the past, I had been proud of my knowledge of chicken anatomy. It was the result of years of cutting apart chickens quickly and efficiently. I even taught classes in it. But on that morning I wished I was ignorant. The chicks were growing up and beginning to look like real chickens. My eyes still saw cute, adorable chicks, but my brain often instinctively registered drumsticks, thighs, breastbone, and wings. I knew right where to cut their legs apart, and the worst of it was, I actually thought about it.

I'd always said flippantly that I could easily become a vegetarian for moral reasons, but then I'd have to give up my day job. Now that I had chickens, I wondered just what kind of morals I had as I continued to throw family packs of chicken in my grocery cart and casually pounded chicken breasts and sautéed them until golden brown.

Maybe I moved so easily between chickens and chicken meat because the meat had been a part of my life a whole lot longer than the live chickens. Or because those featherless, anemic supermarket chickens didn't seem to have anything in common with my cute, fluffy chicks, except for their parts. And that was beginning to bother me.

The brain has an incredible capacity to compartmentalize. We all do it all the time; it's part of how we get through a bad day or the uncomfortable parts of our lives. Give a mind something else to focus on, and it will tuck away the inappropriate thought it was having. And it will forget those embarrassing moments, like the time you walked into a conference with toilet paper dragging behind, or asked an acquaintance when her baby was due and was told she wasn't pregnant. Or the painful time you suffered with friends over the death of their child. For a split second, your brain will reach for the immediate and let your dreaded thoughts and hurtful memories slip under the table.

This was one of the reasons I'd come to love having chickens. They provided the immediate, the goofy, and the take-your-mind-away-from-serious-moral-dilemmas type of fun. All I needed to do was walk outside. It was my therapy.

As I headed toward the backyard, all three chicks came galloping eagerly toward me, as if on horses, and pulled up the reins about a yard from me. They were hoping for treats, but they also seemed genuinely pleased to see me. I couldn't help but smile. When they saw my empty hands, it looked like they were going to gallop past me, but they stopped, swung off their saddles, and began grazing.

They scratched and pecked beneath the grass, occasionally stopping, standing on one foot, and looking around like short, dumpy flamingos. It always sent me into giggles. They were surprisingly good at balancing on their pencil-thin legs—better than most people I knew, with no wavering or quivering at all. Sometimes they'd stretch their foot out to the side as if to stretch out a kink, slowly flexing their toes.

As I stood there chuckling, Roxanne came closer and eagerly squatted down in front of me in an invitation to climb aboard. Not being a rooster, the offer didn't interest me, but I picked her up and she seemed pleased enough with that. She snuggled her large body into my arms as I petted her and we walked around the yard. As we settled onto the garden bench, Petunia came strolling over, wanting in on the action. She jumped up next to me and the three of us sat side by side, watching the shadows of treetops dance in the late-morning sunshine.

The stack of papers on my desk eventually beckoned, so I put Roxanne down and went back to work editing recipes. Was it just my imagination, or did all of the recipes I was reading call for chicken? Americans eat a lot of chicken. In fact, since 1970, we've doubled the amount of chicken we consume. I knew chicken recipes were always one of the most popular features in the magazine I was working for, but right then I just didn't want to read another chicken recipe. That morning, after being with my chicks, I just couldn't bear to think about eating chicken. Our magazine readers loved desserts. So where were the dessert recipes? I could do with reading about—or better yet, eating—an intensely rich chocolate caramel tart recipe right about then. Anything but another chicken recipe.

....

One sunny morning in early August, it finally happened. The precious first egg arrived. It had taken five months and over six hundred dollars, but there it was. It was worth it. The egg was beautiful—light blue in color with a green tint, and it was perfectly shaped. It lay in the nesting box while the three chicks scurried around looking terribly nonchalant, as if this were an everyday occurrence.

I had no idea which of the girls laid it, but I placed it in the handmade Amish egg basket I had purchased for the occasion and praised the chicks. Then I called family and friends around the country and snapped a bazillion photos, as though a birth had just occurred. What a shame I was the only one home; such an exciting event seemed to call for a group celebration, such as dancing around the coop and maybe a Champagne toast.

I wanted to know which girl had laid the first egg, but I was clueless. Easter egg chicks can lay blue, green, or pink eggs, so I knew it had to be either Cleo or Lulu. Roxanne, the Buff Orpington, was going to lay brown eggs, so I could rule her out. But it wasn't until later that I was able to determine for sure that Lulu's blue egg was the first.

How do you prepare an egg of such significance? I thought about it during the day and settled on one of the foundations of good cooking: use the best ingredients, keep it simple, and let the ingredients shine. After Marty got home, I cracked the egg into a custard cup and was surprised to find the tinted eggshell had a glorious light blue interior, like a sky blue silk lining in a wool jacket. Naturally, I snapped more photos, so the preparation of this egg took quite some time.

I gently fried the egg in unsalted butter, lightly seasoning it with a little sea salt and freshly ground pepper. That was it. I wanted to taste the egg on its own, without any competing flavors. The yolk was round and bright like a harvest moon. It was almost orange. The egg white was brilliant and tender, and it formed a perfect circle tight around the yolk. This egg was truly an amazing creation. I shared it with my love and helpmate, and we ate it with awe, knowing the work the chick had put into producing it. We knew

firsthand that a chicken never stops its constant scratching, pecking, and working in order to produce their gifts of eggs.

Two days later the other two laid their first eggs, and I had a total of three eggs in the nesting box that day. This was what I'd been waiting for. The next couple of weeks brought more eggs, many with double yolks. One week I had four double-yolk eggs. I never knew what I'd find when I cracked open an egg.

The first eggs chickens lay can be a mixed assortment. They're new at this, and it takes their bodies awhile to sort things out. The eggs are usually small to begin with and eventually they grow to size, often with double yolks, but sometimes the yolks are misshapen.

Once the chicks began laying consistently, I could see a change in their attitude. I wouldn't have been surprised if I'd opened the coop one morning and found them singing a rousing chorus of "I Am Woman." Each of them would give a loud cluck after she laid and run out of the coop, ready for congratulations. I never failed to thank them personally as I gathered up their gifts.

I soon found out that chickens are not automatic laying machines. All sorts of things interrupted their laying schedule. Thunderstorms, for instance. A good shaking of the heavens and pounding rain on the coop upset them enough so that they didn't lay for a couple of days. Stress also upset the girls. Change in temperature, change in light, change in feed all contributed to changes in egg laying. My little flock seemed to be affected by all of it.

"Dammit!" I muttered, as I grabbed the carrot that had rolled away and nearly caused me to slice my finger. I was busy chopping a pile of vegetables I'd picked up that morning at the farmers' market to use for minestrone. Making a large pot of soup is therapy for me. Smelling herbs, dicing onions, and sautéing garlic is calming. Extra-virgin olive oil and garlic are my meds of choice. The problem was, on that day it wasn't working. I wasn't calm. I wasn't soothed. In fact, I was hardly paying attention to what I was doing. All I could think of was what I had to do next, and I was dreading it.

I finished the soup, and left it simmering slowly on the stove. I had already used every delaying tactic I could think of. So I decided to just get it over with and slowly headed out the back door.

Roxanne came running over and squatted in front of me. I scooped her up with my disposable-glove-clad hands, feeling guilty. This wasn't going to be just our normal cuddle and it wasn't going to be easy. I'd enlisted the help of the unwilling participant in this entire adventure, the man who had wanted no part of any of this. I required an extra pair of hands in case anything went wrong and, as much as he hated it, his were available.

"Are you sure you want to do this?" he questioned. "No!" I shouted grumpily. "I don't want to do this at all." What I wanted to do was sit on the deck with a glass of wine. But Roxanne hadn't laid an egg in over a week, and there might be something wrong with her. According to the books, I had to check it out to be sure.

So there I was holding the wings of a cuddly, trusting hen, about to stick my finger up her rear end. I'd read that sometimes extra-large eggs can get stuck and endanger a chicken's health. If so, all I had to do was gently push my lubricated finger into her vent while pushing on her stomach and carefully ease the egg out. Yeah, right! If the egg were to break while inside her, she could die.

As I poked around at Roxanne's innards, she remained strangely calm for a chicken stuck on the end of my trigger finger like some bizarre lollipop. I guess if you're used to plopping out a Grade A large egg every day, a small finger is not a big deal.

I, on the other hand, felt like I was participating in some sort of primitive initiation rite to prove I was worthy of owning chickens. I slowly moved my finger around her smooth inner track, but encountered no egg-shaped objects or sharp, pointy bits. For the time being, Roxanne appeared to be fine, and I gently let her go.

....

As time went on, the girls settled into an egg-laying routine. Except for Lulu, they were not super layers. Certain breeds are known for their egg-laying ability, but I had chosen two of my girls for the color of their eggs. I should have done more research. They seemed to be sensitive birds that upset easily, like high-strung purebred racehorses or operatic prima donnas. If I were a real farmer, I'd have culled them from the flock a long time ago. But I wasn't a farmer. When you only have three birds it's hard to get rid of two-thirds of your flock during their first year.

My visions of piling eggs on my neighbors' doorsteps faded when I realized that I barely had enough to keep us in eggs. Each one became more special and more precious. It wasn't until their second year that I started to keep track of the eggs each of the girls laid. When they were all laying, we'd get around fourteen eggs a week. When a couple of them stopped laying, we went down to four or five eggs a week.

The main reason most chickens stop laying is because they're molting, which they do every year. After the first year, the chickens shed their coat of feathers and grow a fluffy, thick new covering of fresh feathers. Molting most often occurs in the fall, but it can happen at any time. Lulu molted in the winter one year. The poor dear looked so cold and forlorn with her few feathers that I started looking into chicken sweaters, which are normally made for rescued battery hens to keep them warm in the cold. The only thing that stopped me from making one was the thought that Lulu would never allow me to put it on her. On the other end of the spectrum, Roxanne has molted starting in July.

Some chickens molt quickly, which is scary the first time it happens. You open up the hen house one morning to find it covered in feathers, as if a huge pillow fight had happened during the night. Molting can also happen slowly, over a couple of months. Hens that lose their feathers quickly usually grow them back quickly. Those that take their time also take their time getting the new growth back, which means they don't start laying eggs again for a long time. Mine molt

lazily, dropping feathers around the yard for months, and seem to enjoy their lengthy break from egg laying.

It takes about twenty-five hours for an egg to be formed. The process starts with the yolk, which is either fertilized or not, depending on whether a rooster was present at the critical moment. The white forms around the yolk. The thin membrane around the white is formed next, followed by the shell and color. Finally, the protective layer, or bloom, is added just before the egg is released. The process usually starts up again immediately. It's truly amazing more things don't go wrong in this intricate process that plays out daily.

One of the problems I've encountered is soft-shelled eggs. One fall, Lulu consistently laid either soft-shelled eggs or eggs with no shell at all. No one knew why.

We routinely gave crushed oyster shells to the chicks to supplement the calcium in their diet so their shells would be hard. Lulu had plenty of calcium, and the other two laid perfect eggs, so it wasn't their diet. Lulu's eggs were strange. They looked like completely developed eggs minus the shell. Or they had a shell that could be poked and prodded with a finger into any shape, as if they had been soaked in vinegar for days in a school science experiment. A vet was stumped since Lulu continued to act perfectly normal in every other way. Eventually we decided it was the stress of her having her first molt. Instead of stopping her egg laying completely, Lulu continued to lay eggs for quite some time during her molt. It's just that some of them weren't quite perfect.

There were many times when the nest box was empty. I should have been disappointed, but it's not always about the eggs. Sometimes it's about the chickens themselves. I once sat on the deck and heard a sound like chanting. It was the girls. Picture monks in feather robes kneeling in reverence as a guttural sound rises from their throats in unison. It seemed to come from their hearts and grew in intensity, becoming higher in pitch but keeping the same tonal quality as a chant. It was similar to the chants the Orthodox priests sang in my grandmother's Ukrainian church. A strange, beautiful sound in a language I couldn't understand, and incredibly peaceful.

Greenmarket Scrambled Eggs in Ciabatta

Looking for a way to use up the small bits of vegetables that gather in the refrigerator by the end of the week? This egg-and-vegetable-stuffed loaf is the key. It's great for breakfast, lunch, or a light supper. Vary the vegetables and herbs according to what's in season and, if you like, substitute your favorite cheese.

Preheat the oven to 350°F. Remove the bread from the inside of each half of the ciabatta, making a shell for the eggs. (Reserve the bread for another use, such as bread crumbs or croutons.) Place the halves side by side on a baking sheet. Brush the inside of the loaf lightly with 2 tablespoons of the olive oil.

Heat 1 tablespoon of the oil in large nonstick skillet over medium heat. Cook the onion for 2 to 3 minutes or until it begins to soften. Stir in the zucchini and the red bell pepper and cook for 2 to 3 minutes or until crisp-tender. Sprinkle with the ⅛ teaspoon each of salt and pepper. Remove the vegetables to a plate.

Beat the eggs with the ¼ teaspoon each of salt and pepper in a large bowl for 1 minute or until frothy. Add the remaining 1 tablespoon of oil to the same skillet and cook the eggs over medium heat, stirring constantly until curds have formed but the eggs are still moist. Remove from the heat and stir in the vegetables, cheese, and basil.

Spoon the egg mixture into the bread shells and bake for 5 to 8 minutes or until the bread and vegetables are hot. To serve, cut each bread shell crosswise into thirds, for a total of six pieces.

SERVES 6

One 14-ounce loaf ciabatta bread, halved horizontally

4 tablespoons extra-virgin olive oil

1 medium onion, chopped

1 small zucchini, chopped

½ red bell pepper, seeded, deveined, and chopped

⅛ teaspoon kosher salt, plus ¼ teaspoon

⅛ freshly ground pepper, plus ¼ teaspoon

8 eggs

½ cup fresh goat cheese, crumbled

¼ cup chopped fresh basil or chives

Orange-Glazed Country Ham and Eggs

Breakfast orange juice takes on a new role when it's cooked into a sweet, tangy sauce and drizzled over eggs perched atop fried ham and cinnamon toast. The ham and cinnamon are a natural pairing, like baked cinnamon-glazed ham. It all works together for an easy, satisfying breakfast.

1 cup orange juice

1 tablespoon sugar

1 tablespoon unsalted butter

4 slices Black Forest or another deli ham

4 slices cinnamon bread, toasted and buttered

4 eggs

Bring the orange juice and sugar to a boil in a medium skillet over high heat, stirring to dissolve the sugar. Boil for 7 to 8 minutes or until the orange juice is reduced to $\frac{1}{4}$ cup, swirling the pan or stirring occasionally to blend the mixture.

Meanwhile, melt the butter in a large skillet over medium heat. Cook the ham for 6 to 8 minutes or until lightly browned and hot, turning occasionally. Arrange the toast on plates and place the ham slices over the toast.

Crack the eggs into individual cups. Fill a medium skillet with water and bring to a gentle boil over high heat. Remove from the heat and gently slide the eggs into the water. Cover and let sit for 3 minutes or until the whites are set but the yolks are still soft. Remove, one at a time, with a slotted spoon and drain briefly on paper towels (while still in the spoon).

To serve, place the eggs over the ham and drizzle with the orange sauce.

NOTE The orange sauce can be made up to 1 day ahead of time. Cover and store in the refrigerator. Reheat before serving.

THE LATEST SCOOP

You want chickens. But what's the scoop on poop? For some reason, they have an unde-served reputation for creating tons of waste. It's always one of the arguments cited against keeping chickens. Every animal produces waste and chickens are no exception. What goes in must come out. But in my experience, chickens do not produce more waste than other animals their size.

To compare how much actual waste they produced, I conducted an unofficial experiment. I measured the amount of chicken poop produced by my three chickens against the amount of waste produced by our family's three cats. After three days, the cats had so exceeded the chickens in the sewage department that I abandoned the experiment; it was not worth pursuing any further. Can you imagine how much waste one 50-pound dog produces when compared to one 5-pound chicken?

The ease of disposing of chicken manure is one of the benefits of keeping chickens. Nutrient-rich chicken droppings, unlike those of dogs or cats, can be added directly to the compost bin and eventually to your garden soil. Even if you're not a gardener, there are probably gardeners in your area who will gladly haul away your chickens' waste for their own compost piles.

EXIT THIS WAY

Just so we're all clear, chickens have only one exit point, and it's called the vent. Drop-pings and eggs are formed in separate areas, but they exit out of the same place. Is that a problem? Just deal with it. Chickens are very skilled and their anatomy ensures the two functions stay totally separate. Believe me; your eggs will emerge clean and droppings-free.

Six-Minute Eggs with Bright Beet Relish

This traditional Ukrainian combination of eggs and spicy beet relish is usually served at the Easter meal, but it can be enjoyed any time of the year as an appetizer or as a side dish, which goes particularly well with ham. The bright beet condiment will perk up your senses with its vibrant fuchsia color and spicy flavor. The eggs are gently cooked midway between a soft-cook and hard-cook stage, resulting in tender egg whites with creamy yolks, which provide the perfect counterpoint to the tangy relish.

SERVES 6

8 ounces unpeeled beets, with 1 inch of the tops left on

1 to 1½ tablespoons prepared horseradish (see Note)

1 tablespoon white wine vinegar

1 teaspoon sugar

½ teaspoon salt

6 eggs

Put the beets in a medium saucepan and add cold water to cover. Bring to a boil over medium-high heat. Reduce the heat to medium-low and simmer for 30 to 45 minutes (depending on how large the beets are), or until the beets are tender when pierced with a small knife. Drain and cool to room temperature.

Slip the skins off the beets under cold running water, scraping with a small paring knife if necessary. Pat dry with paper towels and finely grate the beets on the small holes of a box grater or with a food processor (there should be about ½ cup), and put in a small bowl. Stir in the horseradish, vinegar, sugar, and salt.

Arrange the eggs in a single layer in a large saucepan. Add just enough hot tap water to cover. Bring to a simmer over high heat. Reduce the heat immediately to medium-low or low and barely simmer for 6 minutes. Transfer the eggs quickly to a bowl of ice water to cool. Peel them carefully.

Serve the eggs with the beet relish on the side.

NOTE The amount of horseradish used in this recipe varies according to the cook. If you like a spicy relish, use lots of horseradish; if not, start with a small amount and add it slowly.

Italian Bread Salad with Tomatoes, Fresh Mozzarella, and Fried Eggs

Use the plumpest, ripest, and juiciest tomatoes you have for this salad. The tomato juices will soak into the bread, adding flavor and softening the texture of the ciabatta. Assemble the salad before quickly frying the eggs in olive oil. The warm eggs, with crispy bottoms and creamy yolks, complete this dish for a satisfying meal.

TO MAKE THE BREAD SALAD: Pile the ciabatta cubes in the bottom of a large bowl. Top with the tomatoes and layer the onion, cucumber, mozzarella, olives, and basil on top. Cover and let sit for 30 minutes to allow the tomatoes juices to soak into the bread.

Meanwhile, make a dressing by whisking together the vinegar, garlic, mustard, 1/4 teaspoon of the salt, and 1/4 teaspoon of the pepper in a small bowl. Slowly whisk in the oil until blended.

TO MAKE THE EGGS: Heat the 1 tablespoon oil in a large nonstick skillet over medium-high heat. Add the eggs and sprinkle lightly with salt and pepper. Cover and cook the eggs for 1 minute, or until the bottoms are lightly browned and crisp and the whites are set but the yolks are still soft.

Sprinkle the salad with the remaining 1/4 teaspoon each of salt and pepper. Toss the salad with enough of the dressing to lightly coat. Top with the eggs and serve.

NOTE: If the ciabatta is fresh, bake the bread cubes in a 350°F oven for 5 to 10 minutes or until slightly dry and crisp.

SERVES 4

BREAD SALAD

4 cups cubed (3/4-inch cubes) stale ciabatta bread (see Note)

3 cups chopped tomatoes (3 tomatoes)

3/4 cup halved and thinly sliced red onion

1 cup chopped unpeeled cucumber

One 8-ounce ball fresh mozzarella, cubed (about 1 1/2 cups)

1/2 cup pitted Kalamata olives, halved

1/2 cup coarsely chopped fresh basil

2 tablespoons red wine vinegar

1 garlic clove, minced

1/4 teaspoon Dijon mustard

1/2 teaspoon coarse sea salt

1/2 teaspoon freshly ground pepper

1/4 cup extra-virgin olive oil

EGGS

1 tablespoon extra-virgin olive oil

4 eggs

Pinch of coarse sea salt

1 to 2 grinds of pepper

Pasta Salad with Chicken and Roasted Tomatoes

Roasting intensifies the sweetness of garden-fresh tomatoes, adding extra flavor to this pasta salad. The tomato seeds and juice are removed before roasting, and then added later to the salad dressing because much of the fresh flavor of the tomato lies within the seeds and juice.

Preheat the broiler. Line a large, rimmed baking sheet with foil. Fill a large pot with water and bring to a boil.

Seed the tomatoes by squeezing the tomato halves over a bowl, reserving the seeds and juice. Coarsely chop the tomatoes and arrange in a single layer on the baking sheet. Broil the tomatoes for 6 to 10 minutes or until the tomatoes are lightly charred on top. Transfer to a large bowl and let cool.

Meanwhile, cook the pasta according to the package directions. Drain and rinse under cold running water to cool. Toss the pasta with the cooled tomatoes and add the chicken, chickpeas, green onions, olives, red onion, capers, salt, and pepper.

TO MAKE THE DRESSING: Whisk together all of the ingredients except the oil in a small bowl. Slowly whisk in the oil. Pour the reserved tomato juice and seeds into the dressing.

Toss the salad with enough of the dressing to lightly coat. Toss in the spinach and cheese right before serving.

3 large tomatoes, halved crosswise

6 ounces farfalle (bow-tie) pasta

3 cups shredded poached chicken (see Note, page 33)

One 15-ounce can chickpeas (garbanzo beans), rinsed and drained

$^3/_4$ cup sliced green onions (green part only)

$^3/_4$ cup pitted Kalamata olives, halved

$^1/_2$ cup chopped red onion

$^1/_4$ cup small capers, drained

$^1/_2$ teaspoon kosher salt

$^1/_4$ teaspoon freshly ground pepper

DRESSING

$^1/_4$ cup minced shallots

3 tablespoons red wine vinegar

$^1/_2$ teaspoon Dijon mustard

$^1/_4$ teaspoon kosher salt

$^1/_4$ teaspoon freshly ground pepper

$^1/_4$ cup extra-virgin olive oil

2 cups lightly packed baby spinach

$^3/_4$ cup finely diced Parmigiano-Reggiano cheese (4 ounces)

Salsa Verde Chicken Salad

Turn your leftover cooked chicken into a colorful salad topped with a spicy-tart green salsa dressing and homemade tortilla crisps. The salsa is easy to make in the blender and turns a beautiful pale green color. Look for tomatillos that are firm and bright green in color, with dry, tight-fitting husks.

TO MAKE THE DRESSING: Combine the ingredients in a blender container and blend until smooth. Set aside.

TO MAKE THE SALAD: Pour canola oil into a large, heavy skillet to a depth of ¼ to ½ inch. Heat over medium-high heat until bubbles form around a wooden spoon dipped into the oil in the middle of the pan (about 350°F). Fry the tortilla strips in the oil in batches for 1 to 2 minutes or until lightly browned, stirring with tongs. Drain on paper towels.

Arrange the lettuce on a large platter. Top with the chicken and layer with the beans, corn, red bell pepper, red onion, and avocado. Sprinkle with the tortilla strips and add the garnishes, if desired. Pass the dressing separately when serving.

 Tomatillos resemble small green tomatoes covered in a papery husk. Remove this outer layer and rinse off any sticky coating before chopping.

For best results, let the tortilla strips dry out at room temperature for 15 to 30 minutes before frying. The tortilla strips can be made up to 1 day ahead of time and stored in an airtight container at room temperature. You can also substitute tortilla chips for the fried strips.

DRESSING

9 ounces fresh tomatillos, husked, rinsed, and chopped (see Note; 1½ cups)

1 to 2 serrano chiles, chopped (seeded and deveined for less heat, if desired)

⅓ cup chopped fresh cilantro

⅓ cup chopped onion

3 tablespoons cold water

¼ teaspoon kosher salt

SALAD

Canola oil for frying

Four 5- to 6-inch corn tortillas, halved and cut into thin strips (see Note)

6 cups thinly sliced romaine lettuce

3 cups shredded poached chicken (see Note, page 33)

One 15-ounce can black beans, rinsed and drained

1 cup cooked fresh or frozen corn kernels

1 red bell pepper, seeded, deveined, and cut into strips

½ medium red onion, sliced

1 avocado, sliced

GARNISHES (OPTIONAL)

Mexican crema or sour cream

Crumbled queso fresco or shredded Monterey Jack cheese

Grilled Chicken Gazpacho

In late summer, when the tomatoes are ripe and the weather is hot, this cooling soup makes its traditional appearance at our house. The addition of grilled chicken turns it into a hearty main-course meal. Gazpacho is easily made in the food processor or blender, but remember that a good gazpacho retains the texture of its ingredients, so use a light touch when pureeing the vegetables.

TO GRILL THE CHICKEN: Preheat the grill to medium. Stir the olive oil and garlic together in a small dish and brush the chicken with the mixture. Sprinkle with the cumin, salt, and pepper. Grill, covered, turning once, for 4 to 5 minutes per side or until no longer pink in the center. Cool and shred into bite-size pieces. Set aside.

TO MAKE THE GAZPACHO: Drop the garlic cloves into the food processor through the feed tube with the motor running. Process until minced. Add the green bell pepper and onion and pulse a few times until mixed and chopped into smaller pieces. Add the cucumber and pulse a couple of times. Add the tomatoes and pulse until chopped into smaller pieces and mixed with the other vegetables, making sure the vegetables retain their texture. Pour the vegetable mixture into a large bowl. Stir in all of the remaining gazpacho ingredients, and then the chicken.

Serve at room temperature or refrigerate for 1 to 2 hours and serve cold.

SERVES 6

CHICKEN

2 teaspoons extra-virgin olive oil

1 garlic clove, minced

3 boneless, skinless chicken breast halves (about 1 pound)

2 teaspoons ground cumin

$\frac{1}{4}$ teaspoon kosher salt

$\frac{1}{4}$ teaspoon freshly ground pepper

GAZPACHO

2 garlic cloves

1 green bell pepper, seeded, deveined, and coarsely chopped

1 medium onion, coarsely chopped

1 cup coarsely chopped peeled cucumber

3 cups coarsely chopped tomatoes (3 medium tomatoes)

One $11\frac{1}{2}$-ounce can tomato juice (about $1\frac{1}{2}$ cups)

1 cup reduced-sodium chicken broth or water

2 tablespoons sherry vinegar or fresh lime juice

$\frac{1}{4}$ teaspoon crushed saffron threads

1 tablespoon extra-virgin olive oil

$\frac{1}{2}$ teaspoon coarse sea salt

$\frac{1}{4}$ teaspoon freshly ground pepper

$\frac{1}{4}$ cup chopped fresh basil

Ratatouille Gratin with Gruyère and Eggs

I have no self-control at farmers' markets and enthusiastically buy much more than we can possibly eat in a week. I'm the one with several cloth bags hanging from my shoulders, a bushel basket of tomatoes in my arms, and a loaf of French bread to clear the way in front of me. This recipe, with its abundance of vegetables, is perfect for those days.

Preheat the oven to 375°F. Brush a 6-cup gratin or baking dish with extra-virgin olive oil or coat with nonstick cooking spray.

TO MAKE THE RATATOUILLE: Pat the cut-up eggplant and zucchini dry with paper towels. Heat a large skillet over medium-high heat. Add 1 tablespoon of the oil and heat until the oil is shimmering. Add the eggplant and cook, stirring occasionally, for 3 to 4 minutes or until lightly browned; remove the eggplant. Add the remaining tablespoon of oil to the pan and reduce the heat to medium. Cook the zucchini, stirring occasionally, for 2 to 3 minutes or until lightly browned; remove the zucchini.

Add the onion and green bell pepper and cook for 3 minutes or until the onion begins to wilt. Add the garlic and cook for 30 seconds or until fragrant. Stir in the tomatoes and cook for 3 minutes. Return all of the vegetables to the pan and stir in the basil, salt, and pepper. Cover and cook for 5 minutes or until the juices are thickened. Stir, reduce the heat to medium-low and cook for an additional 5 minutes. Spoon the vegetables into the baking dish.

Make four indentations in the vegetable mixture with a large spoon. Crack each egg into a small bowl and gently slide one egg into each indentation. Lightly sprinkle with the salt and pepper. Sprinkle the cheese over the top.

Bake for 20 to 25 minutes or until the cheese is melted, the vegetables are hot, and the egg whites are set but the yolks are still soft. Sprinkle with the 2 tablespoons of basil right before serving.

NOTE The ratatouille can be made up to 1 day ahead. Cover and refrigerate until ready to use.

SERVES 4

RATATOUILLE

8 ounces unpeeled eggplant, chopped into 3/4-inch pieces (3 cups)

8 ounces zucchini, halved lengthwise and sliced cross-wise 1/2 inch thick (1 1/2 cups)

2 tablespoons extra-virgin olive oil

1 medium onion, chopped

1 small green bell pepper, seeded, deveined, and coarsely chopped

3 garlic cloves, minced

3 large tomatoes, seeded and chopped (2 1/2 cups)

1/4 cup chopped fresh basil

1/2 teaspoon kosher salt

1/4 teaspoon freshly ground pepper

4 eggs

Pinch of kosher salt

2 or 3 grinds of pepper

1 cup lightly packed shredded Gruyère cheese (about 5 ounces)

2 tablespoons chopped fresh basil

Bangkok-Style Chicken Saté

Vendors with roadside braziers line the streets of Bangkok, each selling his or her own specialty. The charcoal smoke coming from the saté stands is especially appealing as the vendors quickly turn their browned and glazed skewers to catch the searing heat. Adjust the amount of red curry paste to your taste. It's spicy and the Thais use a lot of it, but the recipe below is a toned-down version. Satés are versatile, perfect for a main course or as an appetizer.

TO MAKE THE CHICKEN: Put the chicken strips in a large resealable plastic bag. Whisk together all of the remaining ingredients in a small bowl and pour over the chicken. Seal the bag, put in a shallow pan, and refrigerate for 8 hours or overnight to marinate, turning the bag occasionally.

TO MAKE THE SAUCE: Stir together the peanut butter and the curry paste and slowly whisk in the coconut milk. Whisk in the fish sauce and the sesame oil. Stir in the cilantro.

Preheat the grill to medium. Have eight 10- to 12-inch metal or wooden skewers ready (see Note). If using wooden ones, soak them in water for at least 20 minutes to avoid charring. Remove the chicken from the marinade and discard the remaining marinade. Thread the chicken lengthwise onto the skewers.

Oil the grill grate. Grill the skewers, covered, over medium heat or coals for 7 to 9 minutes or until no longer pink in the center, turning once. Garnish with the peanuts and cilantro sprigs. Serve with the lime wedges (to squeeze over the chicken) and peanut sauce.

NOTES: Stir the coconut milk before using to incorporate the thick cream that rises to the top with the milk below.

To serve as an appetizer, thread 1 piece of chicken on each of 16 wooden skewers.

SERVES 4
AS A MAIN COURSE OR 16 AS AN APPETIZER

CHICKEN

4 boneless, skinless chicken breast halves (about 1½ pounds), cut lengthwise into ½-inch strips

½ cup coconut milk (see Note)

1 tablespoon canola oil

3 garlic cloves, minced

2 teaspoons fish sauce

1 to 2 teaspoons red curry paste

PEANUT SAUCE

½ cup crunchy peanut butter

1 to 2 teaspoons red curry paste

¾ cup coconut milk

1 tablespoon fish sauce

1 teaspoon dark sesame oil

⅓ cup chopped fresh cilantro

¼ cup salted roasted peanuts for garnish

Cilantro sprigs for garnish

Lime wedges for garnish

Chicken, Basil, and Corn Cakes

Like crab cakes, these chicken and corn cakes embody the taste of summer. Made with shredded cooked chicken, fresh-from-the-cob corn, and fresh basil, they're a tribute to summer's bounty. The cakes can be mixed and shaped ahead of time but should be served immediately after cooking.

Whisk together the mayonnaise, egg, lemon juice, hot sauce, salt, and pepper in a large bowl until smooth. Stir in the chicken, corn, red bell pepper, onion, and basil. Gently stir in the crackers.

Place eight ⅓-cup mounds of the chicken mixture onto a baking sheet. With the back of a fork, gently form the mounds into patties 3 inches in diameter and ½ inch thick. Cover and refrigerate for 1½ to 2 hours or until firm.

Heat 2 tablespoons of the oil in a large nonstick skillet over medium heat. Cook the chicken cakes in batches for 7 to 9 minutes or until browned, carefully turning once and adding the remaining tablespoon of oil when needed. Keep the cakes warm in a 250°F oven, if desired, until ready to serve.

 NOTES It's important to thoroughly chill the chicken and corn cakes before cooking to allow the moisture to distribute evenly, making them easier to cook.

These cakes are very delicate; for easier handling, make sure to cook the first side until golden brown before carefully turning to cook the second side.

SERVES 4
MAKES 8 CAKES

½ cup mayonnaise

1 egg

2 tablespoons fresh lemon juice

¼ teaspoon Asian hot chili sauce, such as Sriracha

¼ teaspoon salt

⅛ teaspoon freshly ground pepper

1¾ cups finely shredded poached chicken (see Note, page 33)

¾ cup cooked fresh or frozen corn kernels

⅓ cup finely diced red bell pepper

¼ cup finely diced red onion

¼ cup chopped fresh basil

10 saltine crackers, coarsely crushed

3 tablespoons canola oil

CHICKEN SENSES

If you own chickens, you've spent a lot of time watching them peck at the ground. So you know they have good vision. They can select and pick up minute pieces of grain, seeds, and bugs in rapid motion while distinguishing sudden movements in the distance out of the corners of their eyes. Scientific evidence has shown that chickens have well-developed color vision that surpasses that of humans. They see more hues and intensity of color than people, allowing them to recognize at least 100 members of their flock. It's been recently discovered, however, that all birds, including chickens, lose their color vision at twilight, which is much earlier in the evening than for other animals or humans. This may explain why free-range chickens return home to roost as dusk approaches each day.

In addition to good vision and hearing, chickens have a highly developed sense of smell. Until recently it was assumed that birds in general did not possess much of a sense of smell. However, scientists in New Zealand have found that olfactory receptor genes function and are well established in chickens and other birds. On the other hand, their sense of taste may be less sensitive than that of many animals. Chickens have a small number of genes in the taste receptor region of their genome. Anyone who has watched them eat a confusing mixture of foods can probably attest to this.

Garlicky Butterflied Chicken

When you butterfly a chicken by removing its backbone, you can lay the chicken flat while grilling, so it's all the same thickness. It's the best method for quick, even cooking. The chicken is basted with garlic oil on both sides while it's cooking, producing a heavenly aroma and crackling-crisp skin.

4 garlic cloves

1 teaspoon kosher salt

¼ cup chopped fresh flat-leaf parsley

1 tablespoon extra-virgin olive oil

½ teaspoon freshly ground pepper

One 4-pound chicken, back-bone removed (see Note, page 39)

Mash the garlic cloves and ½ teaspoon of the salt with the side of a chef's knife, or process in a small food processor, until the garlic and salt form a paste. Transfer to a small bowl and add the remaining ½ teaspoon of salt, the parsley, olive oil, and pepper. Stir together until blended.

Preheat the grill to medium. Spread the chicken out on a cutting board, breast-side up. Loosen the skin of the chicken over the breast meat and thighs by gently slipping your hand between the skin and the meat to create a pocket, being careful not to tear the skin. Spread a quarter of the garlic mixture under the skin and spread the remainder over both sides of the chicken.

Grill the chicken, covered, over medium heat or coals for 45 to 50 minutes, turning every 15 minutes, or until no longer pink in the center and the internal temperature of the chicken at the thickest point of the thigh (without touching a bone) registers 175°F. Remove from the grill, cover loosely with foil, and let sit for 10 minutes before carving and serving.

NOTE To carve the chicken, make a diagonal cut below the breast and remove the legs. Cut between the drumsticks and thighs to separate them. Cut the breast in half down the center and cut each breast half in half again crosswise (leaving on the wings), for a total of eight pieces of chicken.

Blue Cheese–Grilled Chicken over Balsamic Tomatoes

I love the simplicity of this dish. It contains only a few ingredients, but it's bursting with flavor. Choose your ingredients carefully, starting with great-tasting free-range chicken and mellow blue cheese, such as Maytag. The tomatoes should be sweet, tangy, and juicy because the tomato juice mingles with the balsamic vinegar, creating a light sauce for the chicken.

SERVES 4

4 boneless, skinless chicken breast halves (about 1½ pounds)

1 tablespoon extra-virgin olive oil

2 garlic cloves, minced

½ teaspoon kosher salt

½ teaspoon freshly ground pepper

2 tablespoons balsamic vinegar

½ cup crumbled blue cheese

12 tomato slices (about 2 tomatoes)

Preheat the grill to medium. Brush the chicken with the olive oil. Scatter the garlic over the chicken breasts and sprinkle with ¼ teaspoon each of the salt and pepper. Brush 1 tablespoon of the balsamic vinegar over the chicken.

Oil the grill grate. Grill the chicken, covered, for 8 to 10 minutes or until the chicken is no longer pink in the center, sprinkling the blue cheese over the chicken during the last 2 minutes of cooking.

Meanwhile, arrange the tomatoes on a platter and sprinkle with the remaining ¼ teaspoon each of the salt and pepper. Drizzle with the remaining 1 tablespoon balsamic vinegar. Serve the chicken over the tomatoes.

Double-Yolk Sour Lemon Bars

These lemon bars are tart, sweet, and delicate, all in the same bite. They're a perfect combination for those who like a little pucker with their dessert. These lemon bars honor a pullet's first-laid eggs, which often have double yolks. The first week my girls began laying, I had four eggs with double yolks. Don't worry, double yolks are not necessary to make these bars. But if you'd like some double yolks because of their novelty, you're more likely to find them in purchased extra-large or jumbo eggs than in standard large ones.

TO MAKE THE CRUST: Preheat the oven to 350°F. Butter a 13-by-9-inch baking pan or coat with nonstick cooking spray. Beat together the flour, powdered sugar, cornstarch, and salt in a large bowl with an electric mixer at low speed. Add the butter and beat until it's distributed throughout and the mixture is moist and crumbly. Sprinkle over the baking pan. With lightly floured hands, press the dough into the bottom of the pan to form a crust. Bake for 25 to 30 minutes or until golden brown. Remove from the oven and immediately reduce the oven temperature to 300°F.

TO MAKE THE FILLING: While the crust is baking, whisk together the eggs and egg yolks in a medium bowl until blended. Add the granulated sugar and flour and whisk until smooth. Whisk in the lemon juice and then the lemon zest. Pour the filling over the hot crust.

Bake the lemon bars at 300°F for 15 to 20 minutes or until set. Cool completely on a wire rack. Cut into 24 bars, and sprinkle with powdered sugar before serving.

CRUST

1½ cups all-purpose flour

½ cup powdered sugar

⅓ cup cornstarch

¼ teaspoon salt

1 cup (2 sticks) unsalted butter, softened and cut up

FILLING

4 eggs plus 2 egg yolks

1 cup granulated sugar

3 tablespoons all-purpose flour

¾ cup fresh lemon juice (about 3 large lemons)

1 tablespoon grated lemon zest

Powdered sugar for sprinkling

Frozen Chocolate–Almond Meringue Cake

This decadent cake is a marvel of textures, from the crisp meringues and crunchy almonds to the soft swirls of chocolate. The filling is so rich and creamy it's like eating your favorite chocolate ice cream. (Save the yolks when you separate the eggs for the meringue; you'll use them for the custard in the frozen chocolate filling.)

TO MAKE THE MERINGUE LAYERS: Preheat the oven to 275°F. Line two medium baking sheets or one very large baking sheet with parchment paper. Trace two circles using a 9-inch round springform pan as a guide. Turn the paper over so the circles show through but they won't transfer to the meringues.

Beat the egg whites with the salt in a large mixing bowl with an electric mixer at medium speed for 1 to 2 minutes, or until soft peaks form. Beat in the cornstarch and cream of tartar and continue beating for 30 to 60 seconds, or until firm peaks form. With the mixer running, slowly beat in the sugar. Continue beating for 1 to 1½ minutes, or until the mixture is glossy and firm but not dry. Beat in the vanilla and almond extract. Pile half the meringue inside each circle and spread out evenly, all the way to the edges. Sprinkle with the toasted almonds.

Bake for 2 hours or until dry and crisp and pale tan in color. Turn off the oven and let the meringues stand in the oven until cooled to room temperature.

TO MAKE THE FILLING: Combine 1 cup of the cream, the milk, egg yolks, and the ¼ cup sugar in a medium saucepan and cook over medium heat, whisking constantly, until the mixture thickens slightly and the temperature reaches 160°F. Remove from the heat and stir in the chocolate. Let sit until the chocolate is melted, stirring occasionally until smooth. Stir in almond extract. Pour the filling into a large bowl, cover with plastic wrap, and refrigerate until cold but not set, about 2 hours, stirring occasionally. (To speed up the cooling, place in a bowl of ice water and stir constantly until cooled.)

SERVES 12

MERINGUE LAYERS

4 egg whites

⅛ teaspoon salt

1 tablespoon cornstarch

1 teaspoon cream of tartar

¾ cup sugar

1 teaspoon vanilla extract

¼ teaspoon almond extract

½ cup sliced almonds, toasted (see Note)

FILLING

2 cups heavy (whipping) cream

½ cup milk

4 egg yolks

¼ cup sugar, plus 1 tablespoon

8 ounces semisweet chocolate, chopped

¾ teaspoon almond extract

Beat the remaining 1 cup of cream at medium speed with the 1 tablespoon sugar until soft peaks form. Fold into the chocolate filling.

To assemble the cake, place one meringue round, almond-side up, in the bottom of a 9-inch springform pan, trimming the edges if necessary to fit in the pan. Spread with the filling. Place the remaining meringue round on top, almond-side up. Cover with plastic wrap and freeze for at least 12 hours. Place in the refrigerator for 30 minutes before serving, to soften slightly for a creamier texture.

NOTE To toast the almonds, place them on a baking sheet and bake at 350°F for 4 to 7 minutes or until lightly toasted, watching carefully.

Raspberry-Swirl Angel Cake with Crème Fraîche

Forget everything you've heard about angel food cakes being difficult. My college-age son can whip this cake up in 15 minutes. This gem has a pale pink swirl of raspberries running through the cake and is decorated with a layer of sweetened whipped crème fraîche. It's truly the ultimate angel food cake, worlds away from the overly sweet and sticky supermarket version. If you are making your own crème fraîche, remember to start it 1 to 2 days ahead of time.

TO MAKE THE RASPBERRY PUREE: Puree the raspberries and granulated sugar in a blender or a food processor until smooth. Strain the puree through a fine-mesh strainer, pressing on the fruit with a rubber spatula. Discard the seeds and reserve the raspberry puree (about 1/2 cup).

TO MAKE THE CAKE: Preheat the oven to 350°F. Whisk the flour and powdered sugar together in medium bowl and set aside.

Beat the egg whites and salt in a large bowl with an electric mixer at medium speed for 30 to 60 seconds or until the whites become slightly foamy. Add the cream of tartar and beat for 30 to 60 seconds or until soft peaks form. With the mixer running, slowly add the granulated sugar in a steady stream. Add the vanilla and continue beating for 1 minute or until the egg whites are glossy and hold a firm peak.

Sift the flour mixture over the egg whites and gently fold in with a rubber spatula, being careful to keep the air in the egg whites as you fold in the flour. Pour in the raspberry puree and fold a couple of times just to swirl. Spoon the batter into an ungreased 10-inch angel food tube pan with a removable bottom. Run a thin knife through the batter to remove any large air pockets.

Bake for 30 to 35 minutes or until the top springs back when gently touched and a wooden skewer inserted into the center of the cake comes out dry. Cool the cake completely upside down on the legs attached to the pan, or if it has none, suspend it over the neck of a bottle. Carefully slide a thin metal cake spatula or knife around the sides of the pan and tube to loosen the cake, pressing against the pan to avoid cutting the cake. Invert the cake onto a serving platter and remove the pan.
(continued)

RASPBERRY PUREE

1 1/4 cups fresh raspberries (one 6-ounce package)

2 tablespoons granulated sugar

CAKE

1 1/4 cups all-purpose flour, preferably bleached

1/2 cup powdered sugar

12 egg whites

1/4 teaspoon salt

1 1/2 teaspoons cream of tartar

1 cup granulated sugar

1 1/2 teaspoons vanilla extract

TOPPING

1 cup crème fraîche, homemade (see Note) or purchased

2 to 3 tablespoons granulated sugar

1 1/4 cups fresh raspberries (one 6-ounce package)

TO MAKE THE TOPPING: Beat the crème fraîche and granulated sugar together until soft peaks form, adding additional sugar if necessary, depending on the tartness of the crème fraîche. Beat until firm peaks form.

Swirl the topping over the top of the cake, and sprinkle the raspberries over the top, or spoon a dollop of the topping over each slice as it is served.

 To make crème fraîche, combine 1 cup of heavy (whipping) cream and 1 teaspoon of buttermilk in a small saucepan. Heat over medium heat until warm (100° to 110°F). Remove from the heat and pour into a nonreactive bowl. Cover with plastic wrap and let sit at room temperature for 24 hours or until slightly thickened. (Crème fraîche can be kept refrigerated for up to 2 weeks; it will continue to thicken and become slightly more sour as it sits.)

Fresh Peach Custard Pie

Buttermilk adds a slight tang to the egg-rich custard that surrounds the fresh peaches in this pie. Wide strips of pastry create a simple lattice effect on the top. Peach season can be short, so if sweet and juicy peaches aren't available, use nectarines instead.

SERVES 8

TO MAKE THE CRUST: Whisk together the flour, sugar, and salt in a medium bowl. Blend in the butter with a pastry blender or your fingertips until the butter is the size of small blueberries. Stir in the $\frac{1}{3}$ cup ice water with a fork. The dough will be crumbly, but should hold together when pressed with your fingers. If necessary, add the 2 tablespoons water. Divide the dough in half and shape into two flat rounds. Cover and refrigerate for 1 hour or until chilled.

Preheat the oven to 375°F. On a lightly floured surface, roll out one disk of dough for the bottom crust to a 12-inch round. Transfer to a 9-inch deep-dish glass pie plate and flute the edges. Cover with plastic wrap and refrigerate while making the filling.

TO MAKE THE FILLING: Whisk the sugar and flour together in a small bowl. Beat the eggs and egg yolk together in a large bowl with an electric mixer on low speed until blended and smooth. Add the sugar mixture and beat until smooth. With the mixer running, pour in the buttermilk in a steady stream. Beat in the lemon juice and vanilla and almond extract. Arrange the peaches over the bottom crust. Pour the egg mixture over the peaches.

Roll out the remaining dough into a 12-inch round and cut into six $1\frac{1}{2}$-inch-wide strips, preferably with a fluted pastry cutter. Arrange three of the strips parallel to each other over the filling. Place the remaining three strips crosswise across the first strips to create an unwoven rustic lattice and trim the ends. Brush the lattice top with the beaten egg white and sprinkle with the tablespoon of sugar.

Bake for 60 to 65 minutes or until the crust is brown, the juices are bubbling, and a knife inserted in the center comes out clean. Cover the edge with foil toward the end of baking if the crust is getting too brown. Cool completely on a wire rack.

This pie is best served on the day it is made. Store any leftovers in the refrigerator for up to 2 days

CRUST

$2\frac{1}{4}$ cups all-purpose flour

3 tablespoons sugar

$\frac{1}{4}$ teaspoon salt

$\frac{3}{4}$ cup ($1\frac{1}{2}$ sticks) cold unsalted butter, cut up

$\frac{1}{3}$ cup ice water, plus 2 tablespoons

FILLING

$1\frac{1}{2}$ cups sugar

$\frac{1}{4}$ cup all-purpose flour

3 eggs plus 1 egg yolk

1 cup buttermilk

$1\frac{1}{2}$ tablespoons fresh lemon juice

1 teaspoon vanilla extract

$\frac{1}{4}$ teaspoon almond extract

2 cups chopped peeled peaches (see Note, page 102; about 3 peaches)

1 egg white, lightly beaten

1 tablespoon sugar

CHAPTER • SIX

AUTUMN

HARVEST

I had no idea how much like goats chickens are. Both creatures will eat anything, and they are always hungry. Some people use their chickens as waste disposal units. They scrape their dinner leftovers—liquids as well as solids—into the coop, along with vegetable peelings and other compost, and their chickens happily eat it. The results are healthy, happy, and I presume nicely plump birds. I, on the other hand, ended up raising spoiled fussy eaters. I blamed it on my job.

One of the benefits of creating recipes at home was the abundance of food in the house. My pantry was as well stocked as any upscale grocery store. If I needed Thai green curry paste to spice up a dish, I had it. If I wanted to add a pinch of fenugreek or finish a dish with farmstead cheese, no problem. However, as the bits of leftover ingredients accumulated in my fridge, I was too busy testing new recipes to use them up. Enter the chickens.

As the chickens grew and begged for treats, I started feeding them leftover food from my testing. My chickens began eating better than most people I know. They'd developed a fondness for the finely chopped rind of Parmigiano-Reggiano, crumbled Gorgonzola, and al dente pasta. They'd even eaten sushi rice and nori. Leftover souffléd eggs were consumed with gusto, and they casually munched sunflower seeds as if at a sports game.

What they didn't care for were vegetable peels, unless they were finely chopped, and cauliflower and broccoli, unless they were cooked. Bell peppers and out-of-season tomatoes were looked at with disdain, and old lettuce, or for that matter any wilted greens, were left to decay unless nothing else was at hand. Yes, my chickens were and still are food snobs, but we benefited in the end. The flavor of the eggs and the color of their yolks were directly related to what they ate.

Early on, I decided to feed my girls a vegetarian diet under the mistaken assumption that chickens were herbivores. Because they happily ate grain and greens, I assumed they didn't eat meat. I was wrong. I was also misled by the marketing of the "all-natural vegetarian-fed" chicken I was buying with "no animal by-products" in the feed. These "all-natural" chickens were obviously not allowed to run free and eat their natural diet. Luckily, my chicks ignored my arbitrary dietary directions and easily caught their quota of protein by way of bugs, slugs, moths, and worms. Roxanne was happy to get underfoot when anyone was digging in the garden. When I threw her a worm, she'd slurp it down like a six-year-old boy eating spaghetti. Cleo would shoot like lightning across the yard and swallow a moth in midrun.

Although I quickly learned that chickens are omnivores, it took me awhile before I intentionally fed my chickens meat protein. Their irregular egg laying finally prompted me to supplement their diet with mealworms, which they devoured instantly. I still haven't given them meat yet, but who knows. I'm not ruling anything out—except chicken. Oh, chickens will eat anything, and that includes chicken. Sometimes it's just better to not know some things.

....

A ramshackle chicken coop sits on the property of our family's lake cottage. It's been there since the 1940s, maybe longer. Chickens used to roam the property along with sheep and a goat. I'd love to reclaim the coop as a weekend home for the girls, but nature has taken first dibs, and what's left of the structure is slowly fading back into the earth. Even so, I like seeing it there in the woods. It gives me a feeling of continuity, knowing that what I'm doing echoes what my grandparents did.

Those of us raising chickens in our backyards have much in common with past generations. We're looking to connect with nature and provide a healthful, sustainable source of food for our families. We may want more style in our chicken coops and we may be obsessive in our attention to details, but that's only because that's how we as baby boomers or proud members of Gen X or Gen Y deal with everything we do. We're not that different from the folks who set up victory gardens in their backyards during both World Wars.

My grandparents lived in the city and used the lake cottage on weekends or whenever they could get away. They had a large family to feed, and so they raised chickens, but never as pets. In town, my grandmother would buy live chickens and ducks from the farmers' market, then fatten them up in a small pen by the house. As my uncle tells the story, "Ma learned how to kill chickens and ducks while growing up in her Polish village in the early 1900s. She always said she learned from Jewish residents how to kill chickens the right way. You don't let a chicken run around with its head cut off, as it toughens the meat. You talk to them nicely and gently so they stay calm."

I'm told my grandmother would tuck a chicken under her arm, pet it gently, and talk to it, telling the chicken how good it was and how she was so sorry for what she was going to do. She carefully covered its eyes, and then very quickly slit its neck. The chicken never knew what happened and probably didn't feel any pain as she held its limp body and let the blood drain out. The large kettle with boiling water would be ready, and she would slowly turn toward it and plunge the chicken in the water before plucking its feathers.

....

I laid the flat side of my chef's knife across the garlic, made a fist, and pounded the knife with too much force, crushing the garlic straight into the wood fibers of the cutting board. I grabbed the lemon, squeezed every ounce of juice out of it, and stirred in Greek extra-virgin olive oil, dried Greek oregano, and the garlic. I completed the marinade and tossed the meat into the mixture, threw it all in the fridge, and started on the rest of the menu I was serving that evening.

The day had been busy, so it was especially nice to sit on the deck with a glass of wine after our friends arrived. So much so, that I didn't get up to prepare dinner. It was getting late, and we'd all had too much wine without any food. The grill was hot and the basting sauce was ready. Everyone was starving, but I kept finding things to do instead of putting the meat on the grill.

This was the first time we were going to grill chicken since getting the chicks. I thought it would help if friends were around. It didn't. It's one thing to cook chicken inside, and it's quite another to throw thighs, breasts, and legs on the heat as you're looking out at bobbing heads pecking a few feet away.

A recent article in the *International Herald Tribune/Asahi Shimbun* newspaper reminded me of that evening. The article featured a Japanese high school whose curriculum included raising, slaughtering, and eating farm animals. The purpose of the lesson: "Respect for life and what people eat." The article reported that as the teenaged students stood with tears in their eyes, preparing to kill the animal they had raised from infancy, they remembered their teacher's words, "Averting your eyes is the most inconsiderate thing you can do."

I averted my eyes that evening and made Marty grill the chicken.

It's easy for most of us to give little thought to the food we eat. When it moved into my backyard, it got a little more difficult for me. I have a friend whose son took up hunting. It was very hard for this former vegetarian to see her son become enamored with a sport she considered so repugnant. She didn't forbid him. Instead, she taught him about life. She taught him to remember the animal he killed; thank that animal for its life, its spirit, and its food; and honor the sacrificed life by preparing and eating the meat with gratitude and heartfelt thanks. In one of her most poignant stories, she tells of insisting on this when her then-young son and his friend killed a squirrel. They had to skin, cook, and eat this animal with reverence, because they needed to know right from the start what it meant to take a life.

A member of an online chicken group I belong to once remarked that if she couldn't bring herself to slaughter and eat one of the chickens she raised, then perhaps she shouldn't be eating any meat at all. I pondered her views for quite some time. It was not a choice I could make. Becoming a vegetarian is not right for me. It would be fine if I felt strongly about it, but it would be a decision that would probably affect only me, not, I suspect, the animals that are raised for food.

Food is the medium I work in. Writers use words, artists use paint, and I use food as a way to express myself. The importance of food has always been about taste and then appearance for me. The life of the food source wasn't as important before I got chickens. If a recipe didn't work out, I tossed the meat into the garbage can as easily as an artist crumples a piece of sketch paper. After getting my own backyard flock, things began to change. I no longer tasted just the chicken on my plate or that piece of beef. I began to visualize the animal behind it, the being that gave its life. It became harder to toss my failures into the garbage. But also, more important, what I produced had to be the best it could be. When I was a chef, I would transform three dozen egg yolks into a hollandaise without blinking. But the chickens showed me what it took to create that many eggs—over a month of work by one hen. After their arrival, the life force behind the food became what was important to me; that's what created our pleasures.

Raising chickens has given me a new appreciation for the importance of honoring the bird as a whole, and treating the meat and eggs with the attention they deserve. I try to purchase from farmers who raise their meat by natural means on pasture, and prepare the meat carefully, with little waste. And I eat with consciousness, with my eyes wide open.

SO WHY DO CHICKENS WALK SO FUNNY?

Even if you don't have chickens, you know what I'm talking about. That silly bobbing head thing. The head moves back and forth as if there's a string connecting it to the chicken's feet. An endearing trait, yes, but why all the extra motion?

It turns out we're only seeing part of the picture. Our eyes deceive us as to what's actually going on. A chicken thrusts its head forward as it walks, but its head doesn't bob backward. The backward illusion is created because after the head is thrust forward, the chicken's body follows and walks past the head, while the head remains almost stationary.

Scientists believe that by holding their heads steady while their bodies move, chickens and other birds are better able to observe motion. When the head is held steady, the chickens can see subtle movements in the landscape, such as insects to eat or predators to be aware of. It also allows the birds to judge distances more effectively. A chicken on a treadmill will not use the head-thrust motion because it's not moving relative to its surroundings. Fascinating.

The reason other animals don't do this? Their necks are too short. Most birds, even those such as doves or chickadees that appear to have no neck, have relatively long and flexible necks, enabling the birds to use this technique.

Cinnamon Breakfast Popovers

These huge popovers are like giant cinnamon doughnuts. Actually, they're even better because they're baked, not fried. Crisp on the outside, airy and tender on the inside, they're served hot from the oven, dripping with melted butter and cinnamon sugar.

TO MAKE THE POPOVERS: Whisk the flour, cinnamon, and nutmeg together in a large bowl until the spices are well blended with the flour. Whisk the egg and egg whites together in a medium bowl until smooth. Pour in the milk, melted butter, and vanilla, whisking until combined.

Slowly whisk the egg mixture into the flour mixture until the dry ingredients are moistened and almost smooth. Pour the batter into a large liquid measuring cup or bowl with a spout for easy pouring. Let rest for 30 minutes.

TO MAKE THE TOPPING: Combine the sugar and cinnamon together in a small bowl. Set aside. Preheat the oven to 450°F. Coat five popover cups with nonstick cooking spray (popover pans usually have six cups, but dividing the batter among five cups creates extra-large popovers). Pour the batter into the prepared cups.

Bake for 20 minutes. Reduce the oven temperature to 350°F, without opening the oven, and continue baking for another 20 minutes or until puffed, golden brown, and firm. Using a thin knife, make a small slit in the side of each popover to allow the steam to escape. Turn off the oven and let the popovers remain in the oven for 5 minutes to allow the insides to dry slightly. Remove from the oven and place on a wire cooling rack.

As soon as the popovers come out of the oven, brush the tops with the 2 tablespoons melted butter and remove the popovers from the pan. Sprinkle the cinnamon-sugar mixture generously over the tops, holding the popovers over a plate to catch the excess sugar. Serve immediately.

NOTE The popovers can be made up to 1 day ahead. Store in an airtight container at room temperature. To reheat, place on a baking sheet in a 325°F oven for 3 to 5 minutes or until hot.

MAKES 5 POPOVERS

POPOVERS

1 cup bread flour

½ teaspoon ground cinnamon

¼ teaspoon ground nutmeg

1 egg plus 2 egg whites

1 cup whole milk

1 tablespoon unsalted butter, melted

1 teaspoon vanilla extract

CINNAMON-SUGAR TOPPING

3 tablespoons sugar

1 teaspoon ground cinnamon

2 tablespoons unsalted butter, melted

Morning Eggs on Mushroom-Bacon Hash

If breakfast hash brings to mind memories of something unrecognizable out of a can, this recipe will redefine this quintessential American food for you. Fried eggs top a jumble of crisp bacon, fried potatoes, and mushrooms, creating the perfect breakfast for a crisp fall morning. You may want to start the potatoes the night before, for less prep time in the morning.

SERVES 4

8 slices bacon (about 6 ounces), coarsely chopped

1 small onion, chopped

2 cups cooked peeled russet potatoes cut into $\frac{1}{2}$ inch dice (see Note)

Kosher salt

3 tablespoons unsalted butter

8 ounces cremini (baby bella) mushrooms, sliced (2 cups)

$\frac{1}{4}$ teaspoon freshly ground pepper

4 eggs

Heat a large nonstick skillet over medium-high heat until hot. Add the bacon and cook for 2 minutes, stirring. Stir in the onion and cook for 5 to 8 minutes, or until the bacon is brown and crisp and the onion is lightly browned, reducing the heat to medium if the mixture is cooking too fast. Remove the bacon and onion with a slotted spoon and drain on paper towels. Leave the bacon drippings in the skillet (there should be about 2 tablespoons).

Add the potatoes to the skillet and spread out in a single layer if possible. Sprinkle with $\frac{1}{4}$ teaspoon of salt. Cook over medium to medium-high heat for 5 to 8 minutes, carefully stirring and turning the potatoes occasionally until lightly browned. Put the potatoes in a medium bowl, top with the bacon and onion, and keep warm.

Melt 2 tablespoons of the butter in the same skillet and add the mushrooms. Sprinkle with $\frac{1}{4}$ teaspoon of salt and $\frac{1}{8}$ teaspoon of the pepper. Cook for 4 to 6 minutes over medium-high heat, until the mushrooms are lightly browned and tender. Stir the mushrooms into the potato mixture.

While the mushrooms are cooking, melt the remaining tablespoon of butter in another large nonstick skillet. Add the eggs and lightly season with salt and the remaining $\frac{1}{8}$ teaspoon of pepper. Cover and cook over medium to medium-low heat for 3 minutes, or until the whites are set but the yolks are soft. To use the same skillet, put the potato and mushroom mixture in a shallow baking dish and keep warm in a 300°F oven. Serve the eggs over the hash.

NOTE — To cook potatoes, gently boil 1 pound of diced potatoes in a medium saucepan of salted water over medium heat until tender, 5 to 8 minutes. Drain, cool under cold running water, and pat dry.

Sage Frittata with Charred Tomatoes and Curly Parmesan

Frittatas, Italian open-faced omelets, often pose a dilemma. By the time the top and middle of the frittata are cooked through, the eggs on the bottom are usually overcooked. For a moist frittata, shake the eggs up a bit by stirring them, gently allowing the heat to reach all of the eggs at once. Stop stirring when curds begin to form—you don't want scrambled eggs. Toppings are sprinkled on top like a pizza, and the frittata is placed under the broiler to heat the toppings and set the top.

2 tomatoes, seeded (see Note) and cut into 1½- to 2-inch pieces (about 2 cups)

8 eggs

¼ cup half-and-half

¼ teaspoon coarse sea salt

⅛ teaspoon freshly ground pepper

3 tablespoons unsalted butter, cut up

1 tablespoon chopped fresh sage

1 garlic clove, minced

3 ounces Parmigiano-Reggiano cheese, shaved into large curls using a vegetable peeler

Preheat the broiler. Lightly brush a large, rimmed baking sheet with olive oil or coat with nonstick cooking spray. Arrange the tomatoes in one layer, skin-side up, if possible. Broil for 3 to 6 minutes or until the tomatoes are lightly charred.

Meanwhile, whisk the eggs, half-and-half, salt, and pepper in a large bowl for 1½ minutes or until the eggs are well blended and very frothy.

Melt the butter in a medium, nonstick ovenproof skillet over medium-high heat. Add the sage and garlic and sauté, stirring with a heat-resistant rubber spatula until the butter just begins to turn pale brown.

Immediately pour in the eggs and stir, scraping the bottom and sides with the spatula. Cook, stirring, for 2 minutes or until the eggs begin to form curds but are still very moist. Remove from the heat and top with the charred tomatoes.

Place the frittata under the broiler and broil for 1½ to 3 minutes or until the top is dry and set but the center is still moist. Run the spatula under the frittata to release and slide onto a large plate. Pile the Parmesan curls over the frittata and cut into wedges to serve.

NOTE To seed the tomatoes, cut each in half crosswise and gently but firmly squeeze each half until the seeds pop out. Cut the tomatoes into large enough pieces so they will char slightly but still retain some of their shape during cooking.

Golden Spinach Strata

The secret ingredient in this breakfast casserole is butternut squash. The shredded squash blends into this egg puff and looks almost like cheese. It lends a slightly sweet, nutty flavor to this fall dish. I like to use a challah loaf here because the rich egg bread is firm enough to hold its shape during baking, but is light enough to complement the other ingredients. Look for an aged Gouda cheese, such as Mona Lisa. It lends a buttery, caramel note to the dish. If you can't find it, Gruyère is also good. You'll need to assemble this dish the night before.

SERVES 12

Lightly butter a 13-by-9-inch glass baking dish or coat with non-stick cooking spray. Melt the butter in a medium skillet over medium heat. Add the onion and cook for 8 to 10 minutes or until the onion is golden brown, stirring occasionally.

Meanwhile, toss the challah and squash together in a large bowl and arrange in the baking dish. Scatter the browned onion and the spinach over the bread mixture. Whisk the eggs in a large bowl until blended and smooth. Whisk in the half-and-half, salt, and pepper until combined. Pour the egg mixture over the bread and vegetables. Make sure all of the bread mixture is moistened, pressing on the bread cubes if necessary to coat with the egg mixture. Sprinkle the cheese over the top. Cover with plastic wrap and refrigerate overnight.

When ready to bake, preheat the oven to 350°F. Remove the plastic and let the strata sit at room temperature while heating the oven. Bake for 50 to 60 minutes or until the strata is puffed, the top is golden brown, the center is set, and a knife inserted in the center comes out moist but with no milky reside. Let sit for 5 minutes before serving.

2 tablespoons unsalted butter

1 medium onion, sliced

5 cups lightly packed cubed ($^3/_4$- to 1-inch cubes) challah or another egg bread

2 cups lightly packed shredded butternut squash (from about $^3/_4$ pound squash)

One 9- to 10-ounce package frozen chopped spinach, thawed and squeezed dry

9 eggs

$3^1/_2$ cups half-and-half

1 teaspoon kosher salt

$^1/_4$ teaspoon freshly ground pepper

2 cups lightly packed shredded aged Gouda cheese (6 ounces)

Cannellini-Sage Chicken Soup

Loaded with chicken and Italian white kidney beans, this soup makes a hearty main-course supper. Sage is used in several ways in this soup to add distinct layers of flavor. Fresh sage sprigs and dried sage leaves release their flavors slowly as they permeate the broth. Chopped fresh leaves are added for a quick burst of flavor toward the end of cooking, and whole sage leaves floating in each bowl add their aroma as the hot soup is poured over them.

Cook the salt pork in a large pot over medium heat for 5 minutes or until lightly browned. Add the chicken and cover with the water. Bring to a boil over medium-high heat, skimming off the foam that rises to the surface.

Add 2 cups of the onions, the sage sprigs, dried sage, and garlic and cook over medium to medium-low heat to maintain a slow and steady boil for 1 hour, or until the chicken is very tender and the broth is flavorful.

Remove the chicken to a shallow pan and let sit until cool enough to handle. Shred or chop the meat into bite-size pieces. Discard the bones and skin. Remove and discard the sage sprigs. Skim any fat from the top of the broth.

Add the remaining 1/2 cup onions, the chopped fresh sage, celery, carrots, salt, and pepper to the broth. Bring to a boil over medium-high heat, reduce the heat, and simmer, partially covered, for 15 minutes or until the vegetables are tender. Add the chicken, beans, and parsley and cook for 10 minutes or until warm.

To serve, place 1 sage leave in the bottom of each bowl. Spoon the hot soup over the sage. Float 1 sage leaf on the top of the soup and sprinkle the soup with Parmesan cheese.

SERVES 6

6 ounces salt pork, cut into 1/2-inch pieces

One 3 1/2- to 3 3/4-pound chicken, cut up

10 cups water

2 1/2 cups coarsely chopped onions

6 sprigs fresh sage (4 to 6 inches long), stems and all, plus 2 tablespoons chopped fresh sage and 12 fresh sage leaves

1 tablespoon dried sage

3 garlic cloves, chopped

1 1/2 cups sliced celery

1 cup sliced carrots

1/2 teaspoon kosher salt

1/4 teaspoon freshly ground pepper

One 15- to 19-ounce can cannellini beans, rinsed and drained

1/4 cup chopped fresh flat-leaf parsley

1/2 cup shredded Parmesan cheese

Red Lentil Chicken Soup

Red lentils look like salmon-colored split peas and cook to a creamy consistency. Spiked with cinnamon, cumin, and allspice, this soup lends a warm, spicy glow to a cool fall evening. The chicken thighs add lots of flavor and remain moist during cooking, making them the perfect choice for soup making. If you can't find red lentils, you can use brown lentils or split peas instead.

Toss the chicken in a medium bowl with the cumin, cinnamon, and allspice until coated. Heat a large pot over medium-high heat and heat the olive oil. Sauté the chicken for 3 to 5 minutes or until lightly browned. Add the onions and celery and cook for 3 minutes or until slightly softened. Stir in the garlic and cook for 30 seconds or until fragrant.

Pour in the chicken broth and stir in the tomatoes, lentils, salt, pepper, and red pepper flakes. Bring to a boil, reduce the heat, and simmer, partially covered, for 45 minutes, or until the lentils are tender and the soup is slightly thickened, stirring occasionally. Stir in the cilantro before serving.

SERVES 8

6 boneless, skinless chicken thighs ($1\frac{1}{4}$ to $1\frac{1}{2}$ pounds), cut into 1-inch pieces

2 tablespoons ground cumin

1 teaspoon ground cinnamon

$\frac{3}{4}$ teaspoon ground allspice

1 tablespoon extra-virgin olive oil

2 large onions, chopped

2 celery ribs, sliced

4 garlic cloves, minced

Two 32-ounce containers reduced-sodium chicken broth

One 28-ounce can diced tomatoes

$1\frac{1}{2}$ cups red lentils

1 teaspoon kosher salt

$\frac{1}{2}$ teaspoon freshly ground black pepper

$\frac{1}{4}$ teaspoon red pepper flakes

$\frac{1}{2}$ cup chopped fresh cilantro

Fried Egg Sandwich with Avocado, Tomato, and Garlic Mayonnaise

This colorful double-fisted sandwich is one of my favorite quick meals. I always warn everyone to eat it over their plates with a stack of napkins handy and forks nearby to scoop up anything that lands on the plate. If you've never attempted homemade mayonnaise you'll love this recipe. It's made in a couple of minutes in the blender and tastes fabulous. You may never go back to purchased mayonnaise again.

TO MAKE THE MAYONNAISE: Combine the egg, lemon juice, garlic, and salt in a blender container and blend for 30 seconds or until the mixture is smooth. Combine the canola oil and olive oil in a liquid measuring cup with a pour spout.

Remove the center cover of the blender and, with the blender running, pour the oil in a thin stream very slowly. Don't be in a hurry; take your time. If the oil is added too quickly, the egg can't absorb it and the mixture curdles or breaks. The trick is to pour slowly; it should take 2 to 3 minutes to add all of the oil. The mayonnaise will begin to thicken after about 1/2 cup of the oil has been added. Reserve 1/4 cup of mayonnaise for the sandwiches. (Cover and refrigerate the rest; it will keep for up to 1 week.)

TO MAKE THE SANDWICHES: Spread 1 1/2 teaspoons of the mayonnaise on each toasted bread slice. Top four of the bread slices with the mashed avocado and place the tomato slices over the avocado.

Heat the olive oil in a large nonstick skillet over medium heat. Add the eggs, one at a time, being careful not to break the yolks. Cover and cook over medium to medium-low heat for 2 to 3 minutes, or until the whites are set but the yolks are still soft. Gently and carefully remove the eggs from the skillet and place over the tomatoes. Top each egg with a slice of bread and cut the sandwiches in half to serve.

NOTE: The mayonnaise contains a raw egg. If you prefer, you may substitute 1 pasteurized egg and follow the recipe as directed. If the mayonnaise curdles, save the mixture and add 1 egg to a clean blender. Blend until smooth. With the blender running, very slowly add the curdled egg and oil mixture to the new egg until all of the curdled mixture is absorbed.

SERVES 4

GARLIC MAYONNAISE

1 egg (see Note)

2 teaspoons fresh lemon juice

1/4 teaspoon minced garlic

1/4 teaspoon salt

1/2 cup canola oil

1/4 cup extra-virgin olive oil

SANDWICHES

8 slices artisan bread (from an oval loaf, cut 1/2 inch thick), toasted

1 avocado, peeled, pitted, and mashed with a fork

4 thin slices tomato, halved

2 teaspoons extra-virgin olive oil

4 eggs

LOST IN TRANSLATION

If clucks, chirps, squawks, and crowing sound like gibberish to you, you've completely missed the point. Studies have shown that each chicken sound means something specific. Chickens broadcast food calls to indicate that food is present, alerting others of their group, who immediately begin searching the area. It is known that roosters locate and save food for their hens, calling their ladies when treats are present.

Predators elicit different calls. An alarm is sounded when a predator is observed, but the sound will be different, depending on where the predator is coming from. A flying predator, such as a hawk, will bring forth a series of calls by an observant chicken, indicating the size, speed, and shape of the predator. Chickens within listening range will immediately crouch and look up to identify the danger.

A ground predator provokes a different response with a different alarm call, indicating the danger is coming from the ground. Chickens have been observed to stand upright, look for intruders, and run for safety while sounding the ground-predator alarm.

Spicy Chicken and Artichoke Pizza

This pizza is the real thing. Take the time to make your own dough and cook it on a pizza stone for a crackling-crisp, chewy crust. You'll be surprised at to how easy it is to make. I love the fact that the chicken is seasoned like Italian sausage in this recipe. You get the spicy flavor of fennel, basil, oregano, and red pepper without the greasy taste of sausage. Feel free to vary the toppings; just use a light hand for the best results.

TO MAKE THE DOUGH: Pour the water into a large bowl and sprinkle with the yeast. Let sit for 10 minutes or until foamy. Beat in the whole-wheat flour with an electric mixer at low speed, using the flat paddle if available. Add the oil and salt, mixing until blended. Slowly beat in enough of the bread flour so that a dough forms and begins to pull away from the sides of the bowl (the dough will be sticky, but resist the urge to add more flour). Beat for 5 minutes on medium speed to knead. (Alternatively, you can mix and knead the dough entirely by hand.) Lightly oil a large bowl, put in the dough, cover, and let rise in a warm place for 1 hour or until doubled in size.

Meanwhile, place an oven rack in the bottom position of the oven. Place a pizza stone on the rack and preheat the oven to 475°F. The oven should preheat for at least 45 minutes for the best results. Sprinkle a pizza paddle or large baking sheet with cornmeal and set aside.

Toss the chicken in a small bowl with 1 tablespoon of the oil and the fennel, dried basil, red pepper flakes, and oregano. Combine the remaining 1½ tablespoons of oil with the garlic in a cup.

When the dough has doubled in size, gently deflate and roll out on a lightly floured surface to a 15-inch round. Place the pizza dough on the cornmeal-strewn pizza paddle. Shake the pizza to make sure it doesn't stick, and add more cornmeal if necessary. Brush the dough with the garlic oil mixture and spread the pizza sauce over the surface of the dough. Top with the seasoned chicken, artichoke hearts, tomatoes, red onion, and fresh basil. Sprinkle with the mozzarella.

Slide the pizza directly onto the pizza stone and bake for 9 to 11 minutes or until the crust is light golden brown on the edges and the bottom. Cut into wedges and serve.

SERVES 4

DOUGH

³⁄₄ cup warm water (110° to 115°F)

1¹⁄₄ teaspoons active dry yeast

¹⁄₄ cup whole-wheat flour

1 tablespoon extra-virgin olive oil

1 teaspoon kosher salt

1³⁄₄ to 2 cups bread flour

Cornmeal for sprinkling

¹⁄₂ cup diced (¹⁄₂-inch dice) cooked chicken (see pages 13 to 14)

2¹⁄₂ tablespoons extra-virgin olive oil

¹⁄₂ teaspoon fennel seeds, crushed (see Note, page 175)

¹⁄₂ teaspoon dried basil

¹⁄₂ teaspoon red pepper flakes

¹⁄₄ teaspoon dried oregano

1 garlic clove, minced

¹⁄₂ cup prepared pizza sauce

³⁄₄ cup quartered canned artichoke hearts

¹⁄₂ cup diced plum tomatoes

¹⁄₄ cup chopped red onion

2 tablespoons chopped fresh basil

1¹⁄₄ cups shredded mozzarella cheese (5 ounces)

Sesame Chicken with Edamame-Coconut Rice

This colorful stir-fry is flavored with an orange-spiked sauce and served with creamy coconut rice dotted with soybeans, which are called edamame. The chicken tender, or tenderloin, is the long piece of muscle that runs under the chicken breast, close to the bone. The meat is extremely tender and delicate, making it a perfect choice for stir-fries.

TO MAKE THE RICE: Put the rice in a medium saucepan. Stir the coconut milk until smooth and pour it over the rice, along with the water and salt. Cover and bring to a gentle boil over medium heat. Reduce the heat to low and simmer for 15 minutes. Stir in the edamame and continue cooking for 5 minutes or until the liquid is absorbed and the rice and edamame are tender.

TO MAKE THE SAUCE: While the rice is simmering, stir together the ingredients for the sauce in a small bowl. Set aside.

Heat a wok or large skillet over high heat, and heat 1 tablespoon of the canola oil. Stir-fry the chicken for 3 to 5 minutes or until lightly browned and no longer pink in the center. Remove to a plate.

Add the remaining tablespoon of oil to the wok and heat. Add the broccoli, onion, and bell pepper and cook for 2 to 3 minutes or until the vegetables are just beginning to soften. Move the vegetables to the edge of the pan to create a well in the center. Add the garlic and ginger to the center and top with the mushrooms. Stir-fry briefly, about 10 seconds, before combining with the rest of the vegetables in the wok. Stir-fry for 1 minute or until the vegetables are crisp-tender.

Return the chicken to the wok, add the sauce, and bring to a boil, stirring to coat everything. Stir in the cilantro. Sprinkle with the tablespoon of sesame seeds, and serve with the coconut rice.

SERVES 4

RICE

1 cup jasmine rice

One 14-ounce can coconut milk

$1/4$ cup water

$3/4$ teaspoon kosher salt

1 cup frozen edamame, baby peas, or lima beans

SAUCE

$1/4$ cup plus 2 tablespoons hoisin sauce

$1/4$ cup plus 2 tablespoons orange juice

1 tablespoon sesame seeds

2 tablespoons soy sauce

$1/2$ teaspoon dark sesame oil

$1/4$ teaspoon Asian hot chili sauce

2 tablespoons canola oil

1 pound chicken breast tenders, cut into 1-inch pieces

2 cups cut-up broccoli ($1^{1}/_{2}$-inch pieces)

1 large onion, cut into $3/4$-inch wedges

1 red bell pepper, cut into 1-inch pieces

3 garlic cloves, minced

1 tablespoon minced fresh ginger

2 cups sliced mushrooms

$1/4$ cup coarsely chopped fresh cilantro

1 tablespoon sesame seeds

Walnut-Pesto Chicken Breasts

This pesto was originally developed for pasta, but I've found that its unique flavor also blends well with chicken, so I use it often. Lemon and arugula lend the pesto a tangy note. Don't be put off by the small amount of anchovy paste. It takes the place of salt and lifts the flavors of the other ingredients; once you've mixed it in, you won't know it's there.

Preheat the oven to 400°F. Line a small, rimmed baking sheet with foil. Drop the garlic into a food processor with the motor running and process until finely chopped. Add the arugula and basil and pulse until finely chopped. Add the walnuts and pulse until finely chopped. Add the lemon juice, anchovy paste, and pepper. With the processor running, slowly pour in 2 tablespoons of the olive oil. Stir in the cheese.

Slip your fingers under the skin of each chicken breast to create a pocket. Spread 2 tablespoons of the pesto under the skin of each breast. Secure the skin with toothpicks.

Heat a large nonstick skillet over medium-high heat and heat the remaining tablespoon of olive oil. Add the breasts, skin-side down, and cook for 3 to 5 minutes or until browned. Transfer, skin-side up, to the baking sheet.

Bake the chicken for 15 minutes or until no longer pink in the center. Remove the toothpicks before serving.

NOTES When purchasing the chicken for this dish, look for breasts that are well covered with skin, without any tears. It will make it easier to stuff the pesto mixture under the skin.

The chicken breasts can be stuffed with the pesto, covered, and refrigerated for up to 4 hours before baking.

SERVES 4

1 garlic clove

1½ cups packed baby arugula or spinach

¼ cup packed fresh basil leaves

⅓ cup chopped walnuts

1½ teaspoons fresh lemon juice

1½ teaspoons anchovy paste

⅛ teaspoon freshly ground pepper

3 tablespoons extra-virgin olive oil

¼ cup shredded Parmigiano-Reggiano cheese

4 bone-in, skin-on chicken breast halves (about 3 pounds; see Note)

Pot-Roasted Chicken with Lemon and Olives

Use a heavy soup pot or Dutch oven that can go from the stove top to the oven for this homey dish. Browning the chicken on top of the stove and baking it in the same pot not only saves dishes but also concentrates the flavors, adding depth to the dish. The browned and roasted lemon lends a piquant taste to the chicken. Both Kalamata and green olives are added halfway through roasting, not at the beginning, so they don't become bitter. The mouth-puckering pan juices that remain after roasting are only for true lemon lovers, who enjoy them immensely.

Preheat the oven to 425°F. Sprinkle the chicken thighs and drumsticks with the salt and pepper. Heat a large, heavy nonreactive ovenproof pot or Dutch oven over medium-high heat. Heat the oil. Brown the chicken in two batches for 4 to 8 minutes or until golden brown, turning once. Remove the chicken to a plate.

Pour off and discard the excess drippings, leaving a light film of oil on the bottom of the pot. Return the pot to medium-high heat. Add the lemons and cook for 3 to 5 minutes or until lightly browned. Stir in the rosemary and garlic and cook for 30 seconds or until fragrant. Return the chicken to the pan, nestling the pieces among the lemon, rosemary, and garlic. Cover the pot.

Bake the chicken for 25 minutes. Remove from the oven and stir in the Kalamata olives and green olives. Continue baking for another 20 to 25 minutes or until the chicken is no longer pink in the center. Remove the chicken and arrange on a serving platter. Remove the olives with a slotted spoon and scatter over and around the chicken. Garnish with the browned lemon wedges, if desired before serving.

SERVES 4

4 bone-in, skin-on chicken thighs (about 1¼ pounds)

4 chicken drumsticks (about 1 pound)

½ teaspoon kosher salt

½ teaspoon freshly ground pepper

1 tablespoon extra-virgin olive oil

2 lemons, each cut into 6 wedges

4 rosemary sprigs (5 to 7 inches), stems and all

3 garlic cloves, coarsely chopped

¾ cup pitted Kalamata olives

¾ cup almond-stuffed green olives

Chicken Piled with Eggplant, Tomatoes, Peppers, and Garbanzo Beans

My favorite time of the year to make this dish is in early fall, when the vegetable bins at the market are piled high with local tomatoes, eggplants, and bell peppers. Here, they're cooked with the chicken, becoming sweet and silky during roasting. Bathed in garlic oil and chicken juices, they literally melt in your mouth.

Preheat the oven to 425°F. Lightly oil a large, rimmed baking sheet or coat with nonstick cooking spray. Arrange the chicken on the baking sheet. Sprinkle with ½ teaspoon of the salt and ¼ teaspoon of the pepper. Toss the eggplant, three-fourths of the minced garlic, the tomatoes, onions, and bell pepper together in a large bowl.

Stir together the oil, oregano, and the remaining minced garlic in a small cup. Brush half of the seasoned oil mixture over the chicken. Pour the remaining half over the vegetables, sprinkle with the remaining ½ teaspoon salt and ¼ teaspoon pepper, and toss to coat. Arrange the vegetables around the chicken.

Roast the chicken and vegetables for 30 minutes. Remove from the oven and brush the chicken with the pan juices. Stir in the chickpeas. Return to the oven and continue roasting for 20 to 25 minutes or until the chicken is no longer pink in the center and the vegetables are tender.

Serve immediately.

SERVES 4

One 3½- to 4-pound chicken, cut into 8 pieces

1 teaspoon kosher salt

½ teaspoon freshly ground pepper

1 small to medium unpeeled eggplant (8 ounces) cut into 1½-inch pieces (3 cups)

4 garlic cloves, minced

3 plum tomatoes, cut lengthwise into 1-inch wedges (1¼ cups)

2 large onions, cut into 1-inch wedges

1 yellow bell pepper, seeded, deveined, and cut into 1½-inch pieces

¼ cup extra-virgin olive oil

2 teaspoons dried oregano, preferably Greek

¾ cup canned chickpeas (garbanzo beans), rinsed and drained

Harvest Vegetables and Roast Chicken

While roast chicken with vegetables sounds like a complicated fuss-in-the-kitchen-for-several-hours type of recipe, it's really quite simple to make. Just chop the vegetables and pile them in the pan, plop the chicken on top, and it's ready to bake. An hour later, dinner is served. Turning the chicken a couple of times as it roasts helps brown the entire bird, but you can forgo this step if you prefer. The end result is a beautiful browned and crispy chicken accompanied by colorful vegetables, which have been slowly basted with flavorful chicken drippings. You'll be glad you tried it.

SERVES 4

8 garlic cloves

4 unpeeled small red new potatoes (12 ounces), quartered

3 long carrots, halved cross-wise on the diagonal

2 medium onions, cut into 1-inch wedges

1 orange sweet potato (about 8 ounces; see Note), cut crosswise into $3/4$-inch slices

$2^{1}/_{2}$ tablespoons extra-virgin olive oil

2 teaspoons chopped fresh thyme

1 teaspoon kosher salt

$^{1}/_{2}$ teaspoon freshly ground pepper

One $3^{1}/_{2}$- to 4-pound chicken

Preheat the oven to 425°F. Lightly coat a 13-by-9-inch baking pan with olive oil or nonstick cooking spray. Pile the vegetables, including the garlic, into the pan and toss with $1^{1}/_{2}$ tablespoons of the olive oil, 1 teaspoon of the thyme, $^{1}/_{2}$ teaspoon of the salt, and $^{1}/_{4}$ teaspoon of the pepper.

Tuck the wings behind the chicken. Arrange the chicken, breast-side up, on top of the vegetables. Brush the chicken with the remaining 1 tablespoon olive oil and sprinkle with the remaining 1 teaspoon thyme, $^{1}/_{2}$ teaspoon salt, and $^{1}/_{4}$ teaspoon pepper.

Roast the chicken for 20 minutes. Remove from the oven and, using tongs, turn the chicken breast-side down over the vegetables (silicone hot pads or mitts are helpful, too). Roast for an additional 20 minutes. Remove from the oven, stir the vegetables, and turn the chicken breast-side up again. Continue roasting for 15 to 20 minutes or until the chicken and vegetables are lightly browned and the internal temperature of the chicken reaches 175°F at the thickest part of the thigh, without touching a bone.

Cover loosely with foil and let sit for 10 minutes before carving and serving.

NOTE Look for deep-orange sweet potatoes, which are often (mistakenly) labeled yams.

Chocolate Mousse Bars

Chocolate mousse takes on a whole new look when baked in a cake pan and served as a bar. Eggs are the crucial ingredient, keeping the chocolate light and airy. The bars are best served chilled, directly from the refrigerator.

MAKES 16 BARS

10 ounces semisweet chocolate, chopped

$^3/_4$ cup sugar

3 eggs, separated

$^1/_2$ teaspoon vanilla extract

1 cup heavy (whipping) cream

$^1/_3$ cup all-purpose flour

$^1/_8$ teaspoon salt

Preheat the oven to 325°F. Butter an 8-inch square baking pan or coat with nonstick cooking spray. Melt 8 ounces of the chocolate in a small bowl set over a pan of gently simmering water (do not let the bowl touch the water), stirring occasionally until smooth. Remove the bowl and cool slightly until the chocolate is still warm but not hot.

Meanwhile, beat the sugar, egg yolks, and vanilla in a large bowl with an electric mixer at medium speed for 3 minutes or until light and thick. Pour in $^1/_2$ cup of the cream and continue beating for another 2 minutes, or until slightly thickened (the mixture will not whip up). Reduce the speed to low and add the flour and salt. Add the melted chocolate and beat until thoroughly blended.

Beat the egg whites in a medium bowl with an electric mixer at medium-high speed just until soft peaks form; do not overbeat. Stir one-fourth of the egg whites into the chocolate mixture to lighten it. Fold in the remaining egg whites and pour into the baking pan.

Bake for 30 minutes or until the edges are puffed and a toothpick inserted about $1^1/_2$ inches from the edge comes out with just a few crumbs. (A toothpick inserted in the center will come out with some moist batter.) The center may sink slightly as it cools. Cool to room temperature in the pan on a wire rack.

Meanwhile, microwave the remaining $^1/_2$ cup of cream and 2 ounces of chocolate in a medium microwave-safe bowl for 40 to 60 seconds, or until the chocolate is soft but not melted. Stir until the chocolate is melted and smooth. Refrigerate for 30 minutes or until cool but liquid, stirring occasionally.

Beat the cooled chocolate and cream mixture with an electric mixer at medium speed until lighter in color and of a spreadable consistency. Spread the topping over the bars and refrigerate for about 2 hours or until set. Cut into 16 bars and serve chilled. Store in the refrigerator for up to 4 days.

Brown Sugar–Apple Custard Pie

A single egg mixed with a little cream creates a delicate, velvety filling for this pie, transforming it from ordinary into something special. The combination of two types of apples—tart and crisp Granny Smith and sweet and tender Golden Delicious—enhances the flavor of this pie.

TO MAKE THE CRUST: Combine the flour, brown sugar, cinnamon, and salt in a large bowl. Beat with an electric mixer at low speed until mixed, using the paddle attachment if available. Add the butter and beat until the butter is the size of large blueberries with some smaller pieces. With the mixer running, add the water by tablespoons until the dough is moist and just beginning to stick together. You want to stop mixing before a ball forms. (The dough can also be made by hand.)

Gather the dough together with your hands and divide in half. Press each half into a disk, cover, and refrigerate until firm, about 1 hour or overnight. (If you're in a hurry, you can freeze the dough for 15 to 20 minutes or until firm.)

Place the oven rack in the bottom position and preheat the oven to 375°F. Roll out one of the disks on a lightly floured surface to a 12-inch round. Line a 9-inch glass deep-dish pie plate with the dough, trimming the edges evenly with the edge of the pie plate. Refrigerate while preparing the filling.

TO MAKE THE FILLING: Toss all of the apples in a large bowl with the lemon juice, flour, brown sugar, cinnamon, nutmeg, and salt. Whisk the egg and cream together in a small bowl. Pile the apple mixture into the pie shell, mounding it in the center. Pour the egg mixture over the apples.

Roll out the remaining dough to a 12-inch round and place it over the apples. Fold the edges under and flute them. Cut six steam vents in the top. Lightly brush the top crust with the egg white and sprinkle with sugar. Loosely cover the edges of the crust with foil.

SERVES 8

CINNAMON-BROWN SUGAR CRUST

2 cups all-purpose flour

2 tablespoons packed light brown sugar

1/2 teaspoon ground cinnamon

1/8 teaspoon salt

3/4 cup (1 1/2 sticks) cold unsalted butter, cut up

3 to 4 tablespoons ice water

FILLING

3 cups sliced peeled Granny Smith apples (1/4 to 3/8 inch thick; about 1 pound)

3 cups sliced peeled Golden Delicious apples (1/4 to 3/8 inch thick; about 1 pound)

1 tablespoon fresh lemon juice

2 tablespoons all-purpose flour (use 3 tablespoons if apples are extra juicy)

3/4 cup packed light brown sugar

1 teaspoon ground cinnamon

1/2 teaspoon ground nutmeg

1/8 teaspoon salt

1 egg

1/2 cup heavy (whipping) cream

1 egg white, lightly beaten until frothy

1 tablespoon sugar

Bake the pie for 25 minutes. Remove the foil and bake for an additional 25 to 30 minutes, or until the crust is golden brown on the top and the apples are tender (stick the tip of a thin knife through a steam vent to check the apples). Cool on a wire rack.

Serve slightly warm or at room temperature. Store leftovers in the refrigerator for up to 3 days.

NOTE An electric mixer with a paddle attachment makes a perfect pie crust. The paddle quickly breaks up the butter into small pieces while keeping it cold, thereby creating flaky pastry. It's also easy to control the amount of water by slowly adding it while the mixer is running.

FEEL PRETTY

Chickens spend a lot of time grooming themselves throughout the day (and you thought you'd left those teenage years behind). To keep their feathers looking shiny and pretty, they use their beak to transfer oil from a gland near their tail to their feathers and skin. This process is called preening. They like to find a perch and work every part of their feathers and skin, keeping them shiny and beautiful.

They also bathe in the dust. The fine dirt settles on their feathers and filters through to their skin. They'll usually roll around, rubbing the dirt into their pores before shaking like a wet dog, scattering the dirt and debris away. It's their way of keeping parasites from attaching to their skin. When they're done, they walk away looking as clean as if they'd bathed in water (aren't you dog owners jealous?).

Cranberry-Pear Bread Pudding with Bourbon Sauce

A bread pudding is simply a delicate egg custard to which bread is added. Originally developed as a way to use up leftover bread, today's bread puddings are light, creamy, and rich and there's no need to wait for leftover bread to indulge. Use an egg bread for the best results. This bread pudding is baked in a water bath, allowing the custard to cook slowly and evenly with the help of moist, indirect heat. It yields a silkier custard and helps prevent overbaking and curdling.

SERVES 12

TO MAKE THE BREAD PUDDING: Preheat the oven to 350°F. Butter an 11-by-7-inch glass baking dish or coat with nonstick cooking spray. Whisk the eggs, $^3/_4$ cup sugar, vanilla, and nutmeg together in a large bowl until smooth. Add the half-and-half and whisk until blended.

Spread half of the bread in the baking dish and sprinkle with $^1/_2$ cup of the cranberries. Top with the remaining bread. Scatter the pears over the bread and sprinkle with the remaining $^3/_4$ cup of cranberries and the walnuts. Pour the cream mixture over the bread and fruit, pressing with a spatula to moisten all of the bread. Let sit for 15 minutes. Sprinkle with the 2 tablespoons sugar. Place the baking dish in a shallow roasting pan or broiler pan and fill the pan with enough hot water to come about 1 inch up the sides of the dish.

Bake for 50 to 55 minutes, or until a knife inserted in the center comes out moist but with no milky residue. Remove from the water bath and cool on a wire rack.

TO MAKE THE SAUCE: While the bread pudding is baking, melt the butter in a small saucepan over low heat. Whisk in the sugar, half-and-half, and egg yolk and whisk constantly over medium-low heat until slightly thickened and just beginning to simmer. The sauce should coat the back of a spoon. (Do not let the sauce boil or it may curdle.) Remove immediately from the heat and pour into a bowl. Stir in the bourbon.

Serve the warm sauce over the warm or room-temperature bread pudding. Store any leftovers in the refrigerator for up to 3 days.

NOTE Toast the walnuts at 350°F for 6 to 8 minutes or until pale brown and fragrant.

BREAD PUDDING

4 eggs

$^3/_4$ cup sugar, plus 2 tablespoons

$1^1/_2$ teaspoons vanilla extract

$^1/_2$ teaspoon ground nutmeg

3 cups half-and-half

$3^1/_2$ cups cubed challah, brioche, or another rich egg bread or firm white bread ($^3/_4$-inch cubes)

$1^1/_4$ cups dried cranberries

2 Bartlett, Anjou, or Bosc pears, peeled and cut into 1-inch pieces

$^1/_3$ cup coarsely chopped walnuts, toasted (see Note)

BOURBON SAUCE

6 tablespoons unsalted butter

$^3/_4$ cup sugar

$^1/_4$ cup half-and-half

1 egg yolk, beaten

1 tablespoon bourbon, or 2 teaspoons vanilla extract

Pumpkin Spice Cake with Salted Caramel Sauce

There's so much to like about this cake, from the fragrant warm spices and moist pumpkin flavor to the velvety-rich sauce. But maybe the best part is that the cake is actually better the day after it's baked. The flavors mellow and blend more completely while the cake stays moist throughout, making it perfect for do-ahead entertaining.

TO MAKE THE CAKE: Preheat the oven to 350°F. Generously grease a 12-cup Bundt pan with shortening or coat with nonstick cooking spray. Lightly flour, tapping out the excess. (Or coat with a baking spray with flour.)

Whisk together the flour, cinnamon, baking powder, cloves, nutmeg, allspice, baking soda, and salt in a large bowl.

Combine the granulated sugar and oil in a large bowl with an electric mixer at low speed, using the paddle attachment if available, until the sugar is moistened. Add the eggs, one at a time, beating well after adding each egg. Beat in the pumpkin. Slowly beat in the flour mixture, beating just until blended and smooth. Pour into the Bundt pan.

Bake for 55 to 60 minutes or until a wooden skewer inserted in the center of the cake comes out clean. Cool in the pan on a wire rack for 10 minutes. Invert the cake onto the wire rack and remove the pan. Cool completely.

TO MAKE THE SAUCE: Melt the butter in a medium saucepan over medium heat. Stir in the brown sugar, cream, and corn syrup. Bring to a boil over medium-high heat and boil for 3 minutes or until slightly thickened, stirring occasionally. Stir in the salt.

Sprinkle the cake with powdered sugar before serving, and spoon some of the warm sauce over each slice.

NOTE The sauce can be made up to 3 days ahead and stored, covered, in the refrigerator. To serve, heat over low heat or in the microwave until warm.

SERVES 16

CAKE

3¼ cups all-purpose flour

2 teaspoons ground cinnamon

2 teaspoons baking powder

1½ teaspoons ground cloves

1 teaspoon ground nutmeg

1 teaspoon ground allspice

½ teaspoon baking soda

½ teaspoon salt

2¾ cups granulated sugar

1 cup canola oil

4 eggs

One 15-ounce can solid-pack pumpkin

SAUCE

6 tablespoons unsalted butter

1 cup packed dark brown sugar

1 cup heavy (whipping) cream

2 tablespoons light corn syrup

¼ teaspoon coarse sea salt

Powdered sugar for sprinkling

CHAPTER • SEVEN

End of
AUTUMN

How do farmers take vacations? Our trip to South America, to visit our son who was studying in Chile, had been in the planning stages for a long time. Everything was finally taken care of, except for what we were going to do with the chickens. It's not like I could take them to the local chicken kennel. Many friends and neighbors who had come to see the newly arrived chicks offered their help. "Just let us know," they'd volunteer as they were walking out the door. But it was said in that "Let's meet for lunch sometime" kind of voice. They weren't saying "I'd love to get up early and run over to your house in the dark before work to let your chickens out and put out fresh food and clean their droppings tray each morning." I could tell. All the kids in our area, including my own, had left for college, leaving no poor students wanting extra spending money. I was running out of options. So I called my sister. What else is family for?

My sister is not what you would call an animal lover. She's not keen on cats and has stood her ground for almost two decades, repeatedly turning down her two boys' requests for a dog ever since they could talk. She does tolerate Boris, a Russian box turtle, because he eats infrequently and disappears for days at a time in his summer home in the garden. I figured chickens might be just the thing for her.

I'm still not sure why she agreed. The grown-up in me believed it was out of the goodness of her heart. The inner kid in me was sure she was going to add it to the long tally of things she'd done for me, and some day I was going to have to pay up. Or, even worse, she would lord it over me for the rest of my days. Who knows what I'd have to do to make it even. I could see us in our eighties. She'd be saying in a reedy little elderly voice, "Remember when I took care of your chickens?" I was willing to risk even that. I was desperate.

My sister lives across town. This means the chickens had to come to her. The unfortunate part about having a portable coop is you actually believe the advertising and make plans to cart said coop around town. I was going to dismantle both the coop and the run, borrow a large SUV, and load the coop into it. The run would go into our smaller car, and the chickens would be in a traveling cage for the drive across town. After setting up the coop and the run, I was going to run through a list of instructions with my sister that were detailed enough to open a chicken franchise operation, settle the chicks, and drive back.

It was a sunny October morning, and I naively let the chickens out as usual. They always came back for a good treat, so I wasn't worried. After lunch, I easily swooped up Cleo and Roxanne and led them both into the traveling cage. Lulu, however, probably sensing that something was up, avoided the treats as if they were poison. No amount of coaxing, cajoling, or trickery worked. So I tried catching her. What was I thinking?

A chicken on the run is an impressive sight. Lulu, my crazy one, has perfected the chase scene to an art. Her pirouettes rival the top ballerinas as she rises, spins 180 degrees, then runs with outstretched wings toward the back fence. She'll leap in a zigzag pattern from one tree to the next, making me dizzy.

I soon realized I was outmatched and recruited Marty to help. It seemed so simple. With two of us, one could block Lulu's path of escape, while the other stood in her running trajectory ready to grab her or shoo her into the coop. Looking back, I now mutter "What an idiot." A chicken never has just one avenue of escape. It can squeeze through the slightest opening, dodge left or right, and, of course, fly. As soon as we'd get near Lulu, she'd turn 90 degrees and cut a new path through the trees or fly over the coop. I think she was having fun.

Thank goodness it wasn't captured on film, for it quickly became more Keystone Kops than action flick. Don't believe it when someone tells you chickens are dumb. They're cunning, and they'll outsmart you every time. They size up your weaknesses and exploit them. When Lulu was near my end of the yard, she quickly grasped that speed was not my strong suit, but I could zigzag, bend, and follow her

into the brush. So she would zip past me in a whirl, avoiding the bushes. Marty, on the other hand, was fast but less agile through the brush, so when Lulu got anywhere near him, into the bushes she went. We tried to outsmart her by leaving her be and just sitting as if we had no interest in her at all. She knew better. As we rested she rested, and the next time we came near she ran at top speed again with twists and turns that left us dizzy. We kept at it for several hours.

I was getting angrier by the minute. Chasing Lulu wasn't fun, she was no longer cute, and we were both sick and tired of it. We hadn't even disassembled the coop, and we needed to begin packing when we were done with the chickens.

Finally, we had no choice but to get going. We began taking apart the coop and run, as Lulu watched from a hiding place. I must have sounded like a sick Mommy Dearest as I kept up a running commentary while we worked. In my loudest voice, to make sure she heard, I tried scaring her. "You'll get caught by a raccoon, or a hawk, or a fox and you know what, Lulu? It will be your own damn fault and I really don't care." How sad is that? A grown woman trying to scare a chicken; I should have been ashamed. But I wasn't. At that point I really didn't care what happened to her. The days were getting shorter and it would be quite dark before we got back. Lulu would have no place to hide from predators. A chicken alone in the dark with no place to hide is an easy target. But we'd done all we could. We'd been patient and caring. If she was attacked, so be it. I felt a bit guilty, but there was no option. We drove off and left her.

This chicken business was getting more complicated than I had wanted. A few chickens running around the backyard are one thing. Hauling chickens and their coop across town is quite another. So much for chickens providing a calming influence in your life.

I breathed deeply, but couldn't let go of my fear. I was mad but also worried about her. Cleo and Roxanne settled into their transported coop like retired seniors in their new RV. They got busy checking out the dirt in their new location, seemingly oblivious to the fact that Lulu was not with them.

It was dark when we arrived back home. The yard was empty without the coop, and I saw no sign of Lulu. I thought of her beautiful bronze feathers and her perky tail, but saw nothing.

We had lots to do inside, but I kept an ear tuned to the backyard. As we headed outside one last time, flashlights in hand, she suddenly shot from the brush and landed like a thud on the railing of the deck, daring us to catch her. This was our last chance. We devised a plan involving brooms, rakes, and a two-sided attack to force her into the garage. We were like commandos as we plotted and snuck noiselessly around the corner of the garage getting into position. She ran, but her only means of escape was into the garage and we shut the door, trapping her.

We still had another long session of chase-the-chicken as she flew from one corner of the garage to the other, but eventually she seemed to realize the futility of her situation and landed on a garbage can, allowing me to close my hands around her.

I was so happy to have my wayward chick back, I didn't mind driving the forty miles to my sister's house and back that night. The girls, renamed the Chickie-la-la-Ladies by my sister's family, enjoyed their sojourn across town, and we vacationed in peace.

Since that time, I have found the number for a livestock sitter. I had no idea they existed. You can bet that'll be my first call the next time we contemplate a vacation.

END OF AUTUMN

Fried Potatoes and Eggs with Spicy Pepper Sauce

There's something comforting about eating fried potatoes and eggs. It brings back memories of classic diner fare at its best or breakfast at Grandma's. This recipe will remind you of those times, but with an updated twist: In place of the ubiquitous ketchup bottle, there is a spicy red bell pepper sauce that enhances both the eggs and the potatoes. However, if it's a walk down memory lane you crave, feel free to plunk down a red squeeze bottle. To save time, use any type of leftover potatoes, from mashed to baked.

SERVES 4

TO MAKE THE SAUCE: Pulse the roasted red peppers in a food processor until almost smooth, but with a little texture. Sprinkle with the salt and pepper. Heat the oil in a small saucepan over medium heat. Cook the garlic and red pepper flakes for 30 seconds or until fragrant. Add the roasted red peppers and cook over medium to medium-low heat for 2 to 3 minutes to blend the flavors. The sauce will be thick. Set aside.

Heat a large nonstick skillet over medium-high heat until hot. Add 2 tablespoons of the oil and heat until hot. Add the potatoes and onion, and sprinkle with 1/4 teaspoon each of the salt and pepper. Cook, stirring, for 8 to 10 minutes or until golden brown, lowering the heat to medium if cooking too fast. Spoon into a large, shallow bowl and cover loosely with foil to keep warm.

Add the remaining 1/2 tablespoon of oil to the skillet and heat over medium heat. Pour in the eggs and sprinkle with the remaining 1/4 teaspoon each of salt and pepper. Cook for 1 to 2 minutes, stirring constantly, until curds form but the eggs are still moist.

Pile the eggs into the center of the potatoes. Garnish with the avocado, if desired, and serve with the sauce.

NOTE To cook the potatoes, put them in a medium pot and cover with water. Bring to a boil over medium-high heat and cook for 8 minutes or until tender. Drain and pat dry.

SAUCE

4 roasted red bell peppers, drained, patted dry, and chopped (1 cup)

Pinch of kosher salt

Pinch of freshly ground pepper

1 1/2 tablespoons extra-virgin olive oil

2 garlic cloves

1/2 teaspoon red pepper flakes

2 1/2 tablespoons extra-virgin olive oil

4 new red potatoes, cooked (see Note), patted dry, and cut into 6 wedges each

1 medium onion, halved and thinly sliced

1/2 teaspoon kosher salt

1/2 teaspoon freshly ground pepper

8 eggs, beaten

1 avocado, peeled, pitted, and chopped (optional)

DON'T COUNT YOUR EGGS BEFORE THEY'RE LAID

You're anxious to eat breakfast from the eggs of your own backyard hens, but how many omelets can you whip up each week? You should expect to get five or six eggs per chicken each week. The problem, however, is that chickens are not automatons. Their laying schedule will fluctuate according to the breed of chicken, the time of year, the temperature outside, and the amount of daylight. Spring and summer are the peak laying periods, with time off for molting in the fall and a lighter schedule of laying in the winter due to the cold and the reduced daylight.

If you want to increase the number of eggs your chickens lay in the winter, you'll have to add artificial light. That's because light stimulates the pituitary gland of the hens to produce the hormones that start the egg-laying process. Hens need about fourteen hours of daylight for the best egg production. Once you add light, however, don't stop until the natural daylight is back to about fourteen hours per day. Otherwise, the hens may molt and stop laying.

You may prefer to forgo the additional light and let your hens follow their own natural body rhythm. They'll jump back into gear once spring arrives, and you'll soon have more eggs than you know what to do with.

Southwest Skillet Eggs over Tostadas

For a Southwestern-style breakfast, try these chile-scrambled eggs piled over crispy corn tostadas and topped with black beans, tomatoes, and melted cheese. Spoon some of your favorite salsa, Mexican crema, or sour cream on top.

Preheat the oven to 350°F. Line a baking sheet with foil. Arrange the tostadas on the baking sheet. Beat the eggs with the serrano, $\frac{1}{2}$ teaspoon salt, and the pepper.

Heat 1 tablespoon of the olive oil in a medium nonstick skillet over medium-high heat. Add the onion and cook for 4 to 5 minutes or until golden brown, stirring occasionally. Pour in the eggs, reduce the heat to medium, and cook, stirring, for $1\frac{1}{2}$ to 2 minutes, or until curds begin to form but the eggs are still moist. Spoon the eggs over the tostadas.

In a clean medium skillet, add the remaining tablespoon of oil and heat over medium-high heat. Add the cumin and cook for 30 seconds or until fragrant, stirring constantly. Stir in the tomatoes, beans, and remaining $\frac{1}{8}$ teaspoon salt and cook for 2 minutes, stirring occasionally, until the tomatoes are slightly softened and the beans are hot. Stir in the $\frac{1}{4}$ cup cilantro. Spoon the tomatoes and beans over the eggs and sprinkle with the cheese.

Bake for 3 to 5 minutes or until the cheese is melted. Garnish with the 2 tablespoons cilantro and serve.

SERVES 4

4 corn tostadas (5 to 6 inches in diameter)

6 eggs

1 serrano chile, chopped (seeded and deveined, if desired, for less heat)

$\frac{1}{2}$ teaspoon kosher salt, plus $\frac{1}{8}$ teaspoon

$\frac{1}{4}$ teaspoon freshly ground pepper

2 tablespoons extra-virgin olive oil

$\frac{3}{4}$ cup chopped onion

$\frac{1}{2}$ teaspoon ground cumin

1 cup grape tomatoes, halved

$\frac{1}{2}$ cup canned black beans, rinsed and drained

$\frac{1}{4}$ cup chopped fresh cilantro, plus 2 tablespoons

1 cup shredded pepper Jack cheese

Deep-Dish Mushroom Egg Bake with Applewood-Smoked Bacon

Look for extra-smoky bacon for this breakfast egg dish, such as Nueske's bacon. The smokiness complements the earthy mushrooms and nutty Gruyère cheese for a hearty start to the day. It's also perfect for serving a crowd at brunch because it can be completely assembled the day before (see Note).

SERVES 12

- 7 slices (about 6 ounces) applewood-smoked bacon, coarsely chopped
- ³/₄ cup finely chopped shallots (3 large shallots)
- 12 ounces assorted mushrooms, such as oysters, cremini (baby bellas), chanterelles, stemmed shiitakes, and/or button mushrooms, sliced
- ¹/₂ teaspoon kosher salt
- ¹/₄ teaspoon freshly ground pepper
- 4 cups cubed ciabatta bread (³/₄-inch cubes)
- 8 eggs
- 2 cups whole milk
- 2 cups shredded Gruyère cheese (8 ounces)

Fry the bacon in a large skillet over medium-high to medium heat for 4 to 6 minutes or until beginning to brown, stirring often and adjusting the heat as necessary. Add the shallots and continue cooking for 3 minutes or until the bacon is golden brown and the shallots are tender. Remove the bacon and shallots with a slotted spoon and drain on paper towels.

There should be about 2 tablespoons of bacon drippings in the skillet. If necessary, add a small amount of butter or olive oil and heat. Add the mushrooms and season with ¼ teaspoon of the salt and ⅛ teaspoon of the pepper. Cook, stirring frequently, over medium-high heat for 6 to 8 minutes, or until the mushrooms are tender and the mixture is dry. (The mushrooms will release their moisture during cooking but as they continue to cook the moisture will evaporate, leaving the mixture dry.)

Preheat the oven to 350°F. Butter an 11-by-7-inch glass baking dish or coat with nonstick cooking spray. Spread the bread over the bottom of the dish. Top with the mushrooms and sprinkle with the bacon.

Whisk the eggs with the remaining ¼ teaspoon of salt and ⅛ teaspoon of pepper in a large bowl until frothy and thoroughly blended. Whisk in the milk. Pour over the bread mixture in the baking dish and sprinkle with the cheese. Let sit for 15 minutes.

Bake for 45 to 55 minutes or until golden brown, puffed, and a knife inserted in the center comes out moist, but with no milky residue. Let sit for 10 minutes before serving.

NOTE — If making ahead, cover and refrigerate overnight. Bake as directed, adding an additional 5 to 10 minutes of baking time if necessary.

Fruit-Filled Souffléd Pancake

Like a giant popover, this pancake rises spectacularly in the oven because of the magic of eggs. While the sides stay high and firm, the center deflates, creating the perfect place to pile the cinnamon-flavored caramelized fruit. This pancake is often called a German or Dutch pancake, a reference to its Germanic Pennsylvania Dutch origins. I like to accompany it with a light drizzle of real maple syrup.

SERVES 6

TO MAKE THE PANCAKE: Preheat the oven to 450°F. Beat the eggs, sugar, vanilla, and orange zest in a large bowl with an electric mixer at medium speed until blended. Reduce the speed to low and beat in the milk. Beat in the flour and cinnamon until almost smooth.

Heat a medium nonstick ovenproof skillet over medium-high heat. Add the butter, swirl to melt, and heat until the butter stops sizzling. Immediately pour in the batter and put the pan in the oven. Bake for 10 minutes. Reduce the oven temperature to 400°F and bake an additional 10 minutes or until puffed, dark golden brown on the edges, and golden brown in the center.

TO MAKE THE FILLING: While the pancake is baking, melt the butter in a large skillet over medium-high heat. Add the apples and cook for 2 to 3 minutes. Reduce the heat to medium, add the bananas and cranberries and sprinkle with the brown sugar and cinnamon. Stir to coat the fruit. Cook, stirring, for 4 to 5 minutes or until the sugar has dissolved and the fruit is tender, reducing the heat to medium-low if the fruit is cooking too fast.

Remove the pancake from the oven, slide onto a large platter, and sprinkle with powdered sugar. Fill the center with the warm fruit mixture. Cut into wedges to serve. Drizzle with maple syrup, if desired.

NOTE The higher gluten in the bread flour contributes to the spectacular rise of this pancake. All-purpose flour will work, but the pancake will not rise as high.

PANCAKE

4 eggs

2 tablespoons sugar

1 teaspoon vanilla extract

1 teaspoon grated orange zest

3/4 cup milk

3/4 cup bread flour (see Note)

1/2 teaspoon ground cinnamon

2 tablespoons unsalted butter, cut up

FILLING

4 tablespoons unsalted butter, cut up

1 1/2 cups sliced unpeeled apples, such as Braeburn or Honeycrisp (1/4 inch thick)

1 1/2 cups sliced bananas (2 to 3)

3/4 cup dried orange-flavored cranberries

3/4 cup packed light brown sugar

3/4 teaspoon ground cinnamon

Powdered sugar for sprinkling

Maple syrup for drizzling (optional)

Warm Village Salad

Toss the creamy four-minute eggs with fresh spinach, warm croutons, flash-cooked garlicky tomatoes, and a warm vinaigrette. Then finish with the classic combination of feta cheese and Kalamata olives in this quickly assembled version of a Greek salad. It will warm you on the coldest days.

SERVES 2

6 teaspoons extra-virgin olive oil

³/₄ cup cubed (¹/₂-inch cubes) artisan whole-grain bread

8 large cherry tomatoes, quartered

1 garlic clove, minced

2 teaspoons rice vinegar (see Note)

4 eggs

4 cups lightly packed spinach

¹/₂ cup crumbled feta cheese

12 Kalamata olives

¹/₄ teaspoon coarse sea salt

¹/₄ teaspoon freshly ground pepper

Heat 2 teaspoons of the olive oil in a medium nonstick skillet over medium heat. Sauté the bread in the oil for 3 to 4 minutes or until lightly toasted; remove the bread and set aside.

Add the tomatoes and cook, stirring, for 30 seconds or until warm. Add the garlic and cook for 10 seconds or until fragrant. Pour the vinegar into the skillet and bring to a boil. Remove from the heat and stir in the remaining 4 teaspoons of oil; keep the mixture in the skillet and set aside.

Put the eggs in a small saucepan and add enough hot water to cover the eggs by 1 inch. Bring to a boil over medium heat. Boil gently for 4 minutes, reducing the heat if necessary to keep the water at a gentle boil. Pour off the hot water and run the eggs under cold water until they are cool enough to handle. Peel and quarter the eggs. The yolks should be slightly runny but basically hold their shape. The whites should be firm enough to peel.

While the eggs are cooking, toss the spinach in a large bowl with the feta cheese, olives, salt, and pepper. Reheat the tomatoes over medium-high heat until hot. Add the tomatoes, croutons, and half of the eggs to the spinach mixture and toss gently. Top with the remaining eggs and serve.

NOTE   I use rice vinegar in this salad instead of the more traditional red or white wine vinegar because the rice vinegar is milder and doesn't overpower the eggs.

Hearty Tomato Soup with Chicken

Sit down to a hearty bowl of chunky tomato soup with diced chicken, bell pepper, and onion. Redolent with Mediterranean seasonings like anise-flavored fennel and saffron (a spice that's made for tomatoes), the soup's aroma will fill your kitchen. Top it off with toasted garlic croutons for a satisfying meal.

SERVES 6

Preheat the oven to 400°F. Heat a large pot over medium-high heat. Heat 2 tablespoons of the olive oil. Cook the chicken for 3 to 4 minutes or until lightly browned. Transfer to a plate. Add the remaining tablespoon of oil to the pot, reduce the heat to medium, and cook the onion and carrot for 5 minutes or until starting to soften. Stir in the bell pepper and cook for 2 minutes. Stir in the garlic and cook for 30 seconds or until fragrant.

Stir in the chicken broth, tomatoes, fennel, salt, pepper, and saffron. Bring to a boil, reduce the heat to medium-low, and simmer for 20 minutes. Return the chicken to the pot and continue cooking for 8 to 10 minutes, or until the chicken is no longer pink in the center and the vegetables are tender.

TO MAKE THE CROUTONS: Stir together the olive oil and garlic in a cup. Brush over the baguette slices and place on a baking sheet. Bake for 5 to 8 minutes or until lightly toasted.

To serve, top each bowl of soup with a crouton.

NOTE You can crush the fennel seeds with a mortar and pestle or the side of your chef's knife for a coarse texture, or grind them in a spice grinder if you want them ground finer.

For the best results, buy saffron threads, not ground saffron, and crush them between your fingers.

3 tablespoons extra-virgin olive oil

2 boneless, skinless chicken breast halves (about 12 ounces), cut into 1-inch pieces

1 large onion, chopped

1 carrot, chopped

1 green bell pepper, seeded, deveined, and chopped

4 garlic cloves, minced

2³/₄ cups reduced-sodium chicken broth

One 28-ounce can diced tomatoes

1 teaspoon fennel seeds, crushed (see Note)

¹/₂ teaspoon kosher salt

¹/₂ teaspoon freshly ground pepper

¹/₄ teaspoon crushed saffron threads (see Note)

TOASTED GARLIC CROUTONS

1 tablespoon extra-virgin olive oil

1 garlic clove, minced

6 slices baguette (³/₈ inch thick)

Chicken and Vegetable Stew over Parmesan Polenta

Stews are cold-weather food, and this is the type of dish you want to hurry home for. It's as warming as a down comforter in the middle of the night. Chicken thighs are the best choice for stewing because they can cook long and slow without becoming dry. While the stew is simmering, cook the polenta so the two dishes are ready at the same time.

Sprinkle the chicken with the salt and pepper. Put the flour in a shallow dish and dip the chicken into the flour to coat all sides. Reserve 1 tablespoon of the leftover flour. Heat a large pot over medium-high heat. Heat the olive oil. Cook the chicken for 5 to 7 minutes or until brown on all sides. Remove to a plate.

Reduce the heat to medium, stir the onion into the pot, and cook for 2 minutes. Add the garlic and cook for 30 seconds. Whisk in the reserved 1 tablespoon flour and cook for 1 minute. Stir in the carrots, mushrooms, and rosemary and nestle the chicken into the vegetables. Pour the chicken broth over the chicken and vegetables and bring to a boil. Partly cover and simmer over medium-low heat for 25 to 30 minutes, or until the chicken is no longer pink in the center and the vegetables are tender.

TO MAKE THE POLENTA: Pour the water into a medium saucepan and slowly whisk in the polenta. Add the salt and bring to a boil over medium heat, whisking constantly so no lumps form. Reduce the heat to medium-low and boil gently for 15 to 20 minutes or until very thick, stirring frequently. (Be careful because, as it thickens, the mixture will pop and spit as it cooks.) Stir in the butter and cheese.

Remove the chicken and vegetables from the pot and whisk in the tomato paste. If the sauce is thin, bring the sauce to a boil over high heat and boil for 3 to 5 minutes or until slightly thickened. Return the chicken and vegetables to the pot.

Serve the vegetables and sauce over the polenta and top each serving with a piece of chicken.

4 bone-in chicken thighs, skin removed (about 1¼ pounds)

¼ teaspoon kosher salt

¼ teaspoon freshly ground pepper

¼ cup all-purpose flour

1 tablespoon extra-virgin olive oil

1 large onion, cut into 1-inch wedges

3 garlic cloves, minced

2 large carrots, sliced

8-ounces cremini (baby bella) mushrooms, halved

2 teaspoons chopped fresh rosemary, or 1 teaspoon dried

1½ cups reduced-sodium chicken broth

PARMESAN POLENTA

3 cups water

1 cup finely ground polenta, yellow cornmeal, or corn grits

½ teaspoon kosher salt

2 tablespoons unsalted butter

¼ cup grated Parmigiano-Reggiano cheese

1 tablespoon tomato paste

CHILL OUT

You have your own hens and their eggs are gorgeous. You're tempted to show off the chicks' handiwork by displaying the eggs on your counter. As beautiful as the eggs look, and as proud as you feel, it's not a smart move. Eggs are best kept chilled in the refrigerator, not set out as objets d'art to blend with your decorating scheme. It's a matter of quality and food safety; they'll stay fresher and keep seven times longer in the refrigerator—for up to five weeks. Store them in an egg carton to preserve the moisture in the egg and prevent odors from entering the porous shell. Place the eggs in the carton with the pointed side down. It keeps the yolk centered and protects the air sac at the wide end of the egg.

Freshly laid eggs have a protective coating on the outside called the cuticle, or bloom. This seals the pores, keeping in moisture and keeping out bacteria. To protect the bloom, avoid washing the eggs. If you must wash some of the eggs, use those first, as they will not last as long. The commercial egg industry washes the eggs and coats them with a light spray of mineral oil to reseal the eggshell pores. Provide a clean nesting area each day and collect the eggs often and your eggs should remain clean and blemish free.

Tagliatelle with Saffron Chicken

This is a special-occasion pasta dish that is creamy, luscious, and full of flavor. The tagliatelle, a thin egg pasta, mimics the golden color of the saffron. Saffron is an exquisite spice, but a little goes a long way in flavoring the chicken and pasta.

SERVES 4

Cook the tagliatelle in a large pot of boiling salted water for 4 to 6 minutes, or according to the package directions, and drain.

Meanwhile, heat a large skillet over medium-high heat and heat the olive oil. Cook the chicken for 3 to 4 minutes or until browned, stirring occasionally. Remove to a plate. Stir in the celery and cook for 1 minute. Add the garlic and cook, stirring, for 30 seconds.

Increase the heat to high. Pour in the wine and bring to a boil, scraping up the browned bits from the bottom of the pan. Boil until the wine is reduced by about half. Pour in the tomatoes and stir in the rosemary, saffron, salt, and pepper. Bring to a boil, reduce the heat to medium, and cook for 1 minute.

Add the cream and bring to a boil over medium-high heat. Return the chicken to the skillet and cook for 2 minutes or until the chicken is no longer pink in the center and the sauce has thickened slightly. Add the pasta to the sauce and heat until hot. Stir in the parsley.

Serve immediately.

8 ounces tagliatelle or fettuccine

1 tablespoon extra-virgin olive oil

2 boneless, skinless chicken breast halves (about 12 ounces), cut into ³/₄-inch pieces

1 celery rib, diced

3 garlic cloves, minced

¹/₂ cup white wine or ¹/₂ cup reduced-sodium chicken broth plus 1 teaspoon fresh lemon juice

One 14¹/₂-ounce can diced tomatoes

1 teaspoon chopped fresh rosemary

¹/₈ teaspoon crushed saffron threads

¹/₄ teaspoon kosher salt

¹/₄ teaspoon freshly ground pepper

¹/₂ cup heavy (whipping) cream

¹/₄ cup chopped fresh flat-leaf parsley

Chicken and Spinach Pie

This pie makes a stunning presentation. The crisp, golden-brown, layered phyllo crust surrounds a creamy chicken, spinach, and feta filling. Serve it for a casual supper or as part of a brunch. It's a versatile dish that can be made ahead.

SERVES 8

5 tablespoons extra-virgin olive oil

1 large onion, chopped

3 garlic cloves, chopped

One 9- to 10-ounce package frozen chopped spinach, thawed and squeezed dry

1½ cups chopped (1-inch pieces) cooked chicken (see pages 13 to 14)

3 eggs

3 tablespoons all-purpose flour

1 cup cottage cheese

5 ounces feta cheese, crumbled (1 cup)

½ teaspoon dried oregano, preferably Greek

¼ teaspoon kosher salt

¼ teaspoon freshly ground pepper

16 sheets frozen phyllo dough (from a 16-ounce box), thawed (see Note)

Preheat the oven to 375°F. Heat 1 tablespoon of the oil in a medium skillet over medium heat. Cook the onion for 3 minutes or until it begins to soften. Add the garlic and cook for 30 seconds or until fragrant. Stir in the spinach, and then add the chicken. Remove from the heat and cool in the pan.

Whisk the eggs in a large bowl until blended. Whisk in the flour until smooth. Stir in the spinach mixture, cottage cheese, feta cheese, oregano, salt, and pepper.

Lightly oil a 10-inch deep-dish glass pie plate. Place 1 sheet of phyllo in the dish, letting the phyllo hang over the edges. Lightly brush with some of the remaining oil. Place a second sheet over the first so that they are crisscross, and lightly brush with oil. Add 6 more sheets of phyllo, alternating the direction of each sheet around the pie plate so that they crisscross each other and cover the dish completely, brushing each sheet with oil.

Spread the filling over the phyllo. Top with the remaining 8 sheets of phyllo, oiling and crisscrossing them as you did the bottom layers. Brush the top layer with oil and scrunch the overhanging phyllo onto the rim of the pie plate to create a free-form edge. Brush any remaining oil on top. Score the top of the pie into eight wedges by lightly cutting into the phyllo with a small serrated knife.

Bake for 35 to 40 minutes or until golden brown and a knife inserted into the middle comes out clean.

NOTES Thaw the phyllo in the refrigerator overnight for the best results. When working with phyllo, lay the sheets on the work surface and cover with a dry towel to keep them from drying out.

The pie can be assembled up to 8 hours ahead of time. Cover and refrigerate until ready to bake.

Golden Chicken with Caramelized Sweet Potatoes

This recipe was inspired by the luscious candied sweet potatoes served at Monell's in Nashville. The sweet potatoes caramelize as the brown sugar mingles with the chicken juices during baking. Using bone-in chicken breasts, rather than boneless, increases the flavor and allows the chicken and potatoes to cook in the same amount of time.

SERVES 4

Preheat the oven to 425°F. If the back rib bones are attached to the chicken breasts, remove them with kitchen shears. Lightly oil a large, rimmed baking sheet or coat with nonstick cooking spray. Arrange the chicken breasts on the pan. Season with ¼ teaspoon each of the salt and pepper.

Mix together the thyme, sage, allspice, and the remaining ¼ teaspoon each of the salt and pepper in a small cup. Brush the chicken with 1 tablespoon of the melted butter and sprinkle with the spice mixture.

Arrange the sweet potatoes in a single layer, if possible, around the chicken. Brush both sides of the potatoes with 2 tablespoons of the butter. Stir the brown sugar into the remaining 2 tablespoons of butter.

Bake the chicken for 20 minutes, and remove from the oven. Turn the sweet potatoes and lightly brush with the brown sugar mixture. Brush the rest over the chicken breasts.

Return to the oven and continue baking for another 10 to 15 minutes, or until the chicken is no longer pink in the center and the sweet potatoes are lightly browned and tender.

Serve immediately.

NOTE Look for deep-orange sweet potatoes, often labeled as yams.

4 bone-in, skin-on chicken breast halves (about 3 pounds)

½ teaspoon kosher salt

½ teaspoon freshly ground pepper

1 teaspoon dried thyme

1 teaspoon dried sage

¼ teaspoon ground allspice

5 tablespoons unsalted butter, melted

1½ pounds orange sweet potatoes (see Note), sliced ⅝ inch thick (about 20 slices)

2 tablespoons packed light brown sugar

Chicken with Pomegranate-Orange Sauce

When looking for a festive dish, what could be better than a crispy-skinned roast chicken served with an elegant, silky sauce? The sauce relies on the juices that form during roasting, which in turn are flavored by the orange and onion stuffing and pomegranate baste. Garnish the dish with fresh pomegranate seeds for a special touch.

SERVES 4

1 medium onion, cut into 8 wedges

1 medium orange, cut into 8 wedges

One 3½- to 4-pound chicken

2 sprigs fresh thyme, plus 2 teaspoons chopped fresh thyme

½ teaspoon kosher salt, plus ⅛ teaspoon

¼ teaspoon freshly ground pepper, plus ⅛ teaspoon

3 tablespoons unsalted butter, softened

1 cup pomegranate juice (see Note)

½ cup reduced-sodium chicken broth, plus additional if necessary

2 tablespoons all-purpose flour

2 tablespoons orange juice

½ teaspoon balsamic vinegar

Preheat the oven to 400°F. Tuck 3 wedges each of the onion and orange into the chicken cavity along with the 2 sprigs of thyme. Sprinkle the outside of the chicken with the remaining 2 teaspoons of thyme, ½ teaspoon salt, and ¼ teaspoon pepper. Slather the butter over the chicken, massaging it into the skin. Place in a shallow roasting pan slightly larger than the chicken. Tuck the wing tips behind the chicken.

Squeeze the orange juice from the remaining 5 orange wedges over the chicken and place the wedges around the bird along with the remaining 5 wedges of onion. Pour ¼ cup of the pomegranate juice around the chicken.

Bake the chicken for 20 minutes. Remove from the oven, reduce the oven temperature to 375°F, and baste the chicken with the pan juices. Pour ¼ cup of the pomegranate juice over the chicken. Continue baking for 40 to 50 minutes or until the temperature at the thickest point of the thigh registers 175°F, basting the chicken every 20 minutes.

Remove the chicken from the oven and let sit while making the sauce. Remove the onion and orange wedges from the chicken cavity and put in the roasting pan. Strain the juices from the pan into a small bowl, pressing on the orange and onion to extract their flavor. Discard the solids.

Skim the fat that rises to the surface of the bowl. Return 2 tablespoons of the fat to the roasting pan and discard the rest. Add enough chicken broth (about ½ cup) to the juices in the bowl to equal ¾ cup.

Heat the roasting pan with the 2 tablespoons of fat over medium heat. Whisk in the flour and cook for 1 minute. Whisk in the broth mixture, the remaining $\frac{1}{2}$ cup of pomegranate juice, the orange juice, balsamic vinegar, and the $\frac{1}{8}$ teaspoon each of salt and pepper. Bring to a boil and cook, whisking and scraping up the browned bits at the bottom of the roasting pan, for 1 to 2 minutes or until it reaches the desired consistency.

Carve the chicken and serve the sauce over the chicken.

NOTE   Cranberry juice can be substituted for the pomegranate juice.

RAINBOW EGGS AND YOLKS

Hens produce eggs in a wide range of colors, from shades of deep chocolate brown to light brown, green, blue, pink, and white. My birds' olive green eggs and blue eggs even have a beautiful light-blue lining. The color of the egg shell is determined by the breed of the hen. Everyone's question is, "Do colored eggs (other than brown) taste different?" The answer is no. The hen's diet has the greatest impact on flavor.

The color of an egg yolk will vary from deep orange to pale yellow. Certain plants are high in natural pigments called carotenoids, and when chickens consume them, they produce brightly colored yolks. Eggs from free-range hens often have bright-orange yolks because the hens have access to a wider variety of plants containing the pigments. While commercially raised caged hens cannot be fed artificial colors, the color of their yolks will be affected by the type of feed they eat. And their feed can be enhanced by natural colors such as marigold petals to deepen the color of their yolks. But don't be fooled; commercial eggs with orange yolks won't taste as good as the free-range eggs they mimic.

Flat-Roasted Chicken Stuffed with Herbed Goat Cheese

Roasting a flat, butterflied chicken has several benefits. It's easy to carve, it roasts faster because the inside of the chicken gets direct heat, and it also roasts more evenly because the meat is all the same thickness. There are no high areas, like the breast, cooking faster and becoming over-done. Stuffing the chicken under the skin not only flavors the meat but also keeps it moist.

6 ounces fresh goat cheese

2 tablespoons chopped mixed fresh herbs, such as rosemary, thyme, and sage

3 teaspoons extra-virgin olive oil

2 teaspoons grated lemon zest

$3/4$ teaspoon kosher salt

$1/2$ teaspoon freshly ground pepper

One $3^{1}/_{2}$- to 4-pound chicken, backbone removed (see Note, page 39)

Preheat the oven to 400°F. Lightly oil a large, rimmed baking sheet or coat with nonstick cooking spray. Stir together the cheese, 1 tablespoon of the herbs, 1 teaspoon of the oil, 1 teaspoon of the lemon zest, and $1/4$ teaspoon each of the salt and pepper in a small bowl until blended.

Loosen the skin of the chicken over the breast and all the way to the tops of the thighs by gently slipping your hand between the skin and the meat to create a pocket, being careful not to tear the skin. Spoon the cheese mixture under the skin and press the skin to spread out the stuffing evenly.

Spread out the chicken on the baking sheet so it's as flat as possible, skin-side up. Position the legs so they are knock-kneed, with the legs facing each other. Tuck the wing tips behind the chicken. Brush the chicken with the remaining 2 teaspoons olive oil. Sprinkle with the remaining 1 tablespoon herbs, 1 teaspoon lemon zest, $1/2$ tea-spoon salt, and $1/4$ teaspoon pepper, rubbing the herbs and lemon zest lightly into the skin.

Bake the chicken for 30 minutes. Remove from the oven and brush the chicken with the pan juices. Bake for an additional 10 to 15 minutes or until the internal temperature in the thickest part of the thigh reaches 175°F. Let sit for 10 minutes before carving and serving.

NOTE When purchasing the chicken, look for one that is well cov-ered with skin, without any tears. It will make it easier to stuff the cheese mixture under the skin.

Poached Pears and Apricots with Marsala Cream Sauce

Poached pears always add a fresh and elegant finish to a meal. But they are truly impressive when served with this creamy variation of zabaglione, a warm, custard-like sauce made with egg yolks and wine, which hails from Italy. Sweet Marsala, an Italian dessert wine traditionally used to make zabaglione, adds caramel overtones to this rich sauce.

SERVES 4

PEARS

4 cups water

2 cups sugar

4 cinnamon sticks

1 vanilla bean, split lengthwise

4 firm but ripe Bosc pears (see Note)

½ cup dried apricots

SAUCE

4 egg yolks

½ cup sugar

½ cup heavy (whipping) cream

⅓ cup sweet Marsala

TO MAKE THE PEARS: Stir together the water, sugar, cinnamon sticks, and vanilla bean in a large pot. Bring to a boil over medium-high heat. Meanwhile, peel the pears and cut a flat base so they stand upright. Working from the bottom of the pear, remove the core with a melon baller or grapefruit spoon and discard. Add the pears and apricots to the liquid, reduce the heat to medium or medium-low, partially cover, and boil gently for 25 to 35 minutes or until very tender when pierced with a skewer, turning the pears occasionally. Carefully remove the pears with a slotted spoon and set upright on a plate; place the apricots next to the pears. The poaching liquid can be discarded or stored in the refrigerator for another use.

TO MAKE THE SAUCE: Whisk the egg yolks and sugar in a heavy, medium saucepan until the sugar is dissolved and the eggs yolks are lighter in color. Whisk in the cream and Marsala. Cook the sauce over medium to medium-low heat, whisking constantly, until the sauce thickens and almost comes to a boil, 4 to 6 minutes. The sauce should coat the back of a spoon. Remove from the heat before it comes to a boil. Immediately pour into a small bowl to avoid overcooking.

To serve, spoon 3 tablespoons of the warm sauce on each dessert plate and place a pear in the center. Arrange the apricots around the pears.

NOTES

To judge the ripeness of a pear, press it near the stem; the flesh should yield slightly. Pears that are soft at the center are overripe. Bosc pears are perfect for poaching, as they keep their long, elegant shape during cooking.

Pears can be cooked up to 1 day ahead. Bring to room temperature before serving.

Bittersweet-Espresso Crème Brûlée

Crème brûlée is nothing more than a fancy pudding, and it's probably much easier to make than you think. This version is rich in egg yolks, chocolate, and espresso. It's baked in a water bath to keep the custard silky smooth. Allow enough time for the custard to chill and set before caramelizing the top. A kitchen torch is handy for that purpose, but it's not essential (see Note).

Preheat the oven to 300°F. Heat the cream, chocolate, and espresso powder together in a medium saucepan over medium to medium-low heat, stirring frequently, until the chocolate is melted and the cream is steamy hot, but not simmering. Remove from the heat and whisk until smooth.

Meanwhile, whisk the egg yolks, ¼ cup of the sugar, the vanilla, and salt together in a medium bowl until smooth. Slowly pour the hot cream mixture into the egg yolks while whisking constantly. Pour through a strainer into a liquid measuring cup or bowl with a pourable spout.

Arrange six 8- to 12-ounce ramekins or custard cups in a shallow roasting pan or broiler pan. Pour the chocolate cream mixture into the ramekins. Fill the pan with enough hot water to come halfway up the sides of the ramekins (being careful not to get any water in the custard).

Bake for 30 to 35 minutes or until the custard is set and a toothpick inserted into the center comes out clean. Remove the ramekins from the water, and cool to room temperature on a wire rack. Refrigerate until chilled, about 4 hours or overnight.

Sprinkle the tops of the custards with the remaining ¼ cup of sugar. Using a kitchen torch, heat the sugar until melted and golden brown, being careful not to warm the custard too much (see Note). Cool to room temperature, and refrigerate until ready to serve.

SERVES 6

2¼ cups heavy (whipping) cream

3 ounces bittersweet chocolate (60% cacao), chopped

2 tablespoons espresso powder

4 egg yolks

½ cup sugar

1 teaspoon vanilla extract

Pinch of salt

Crème brûlée can also be caramelized under the broiler. Place the ramekins in a shallow roasting pan and surround with ice cubes (to keep the custard cool). Broil for 3 to 6 minutes or until the sugar melts and caramelizes to golden brown, watching carefully to prevent them from browning too much.

Instead of a small kitchen torch you can also use a larger handyman's blow torch. Just be careful to move the torch in a circular pattern, keeping it far enough away from the sugar so that it melts but doesn't burn the sugar or melt the custard below.

CRACKED UP

You've cracked your egg, but what's that on it? If it's white and stringy, it's a chalaza. Strands of thick egg white are attached to both sides of the yolk to hold the yolk in the middle of the egg. They are part of the egg white and safe to eat. The thicker the chalazae, the fresher the egg.

Occasionally, a spot of blood will appear on the yolk. This occurs when a small blood vessel is ruptured during the formation of the egg. It does not indicate a fertilized egg. There's nothing wrong with the egg and it's safe to eat. However, the spot can be easily removed with the tip of a knife.

Toasted Pecan–Apple Pie

Can't decide between pecan or apple pie? This pecan pie holds a hidden surprise below the nuts. Both the pecans and apples are baked in a lush brown sugar–egg custard, while the egg yolk crust bakes up golden brown and extra-crisp.

TO MAKE THE CRUST: Whisk together the flour, granulated sugar, and salt in medium bowl. Blend in the butter with a pastry blender or your fingertips until the butter is the size of blueberries, with some smaller pieces. Whisk together the egg yolk and 2 tablespoons of the ice water. Toss with the flour mixture, adding additional water if necessary, to form a dough. Gather the dough together and press into a disk. Cover with plastic wrap and refrigerate until firm, at least 1 hour or overnight.

Place the oven rack in the bottom position and preheat the oven to 350°F. Roll out the dough to a 13-inch round. Line a 10-inch deep-dish glass pie plate. Trim the overhanging dough to $\frac{1}{2}$ inch, turn the edge under, and flute. Beat the egg white until loose and frothy. Brush over the bottom and sides of the dough. Refrigerate while preparing the filling.

TO MAKE THE FILLING: Beat together the eggs, egg yolk, and flour in a large bowl with an electric mixer at medium speed until blended and smooth. Beat in the brown sugar, corn syrup, melted butter, vanilla, and salt. Stir in the pecans. Arrange the apples over the bottom of the pie shell. Pour the pecan mixture over the apples.

Bake the pie on the bottom oven rack for 45 minutes. Cover the edge of the crust with foil and continue baking for 20 to 25 minutes, or until puffed and a knife inserted into the center comes out moist but clean. Cool completely on a wire rack. Serve at room temperature. Store leftovers in the refrigerator for up to 2 days.

NOTES Toast the pecans in a 350°F oven for 6 to 8 minutes or until slightly darker in color.

Use tart apples for contrast with the sweet brown sugar custard.

EGG YOLK CRUST

$1\frac{1}{4}$ cups all-purpose flour

1 tablespoon granulated sugar

Pinch of salt

$\frac{1}{2}$ cup (1 stick) cold unsalted butter, cut up

1 egg, separated

2 to 3 tablespoons ice water

FILLING

3 eggs plus 1 egg yolk

3 tablespoons all-purpose flour

1 cup packed dark brown sugar

1 cup dark corn syrup

1 tablespoon unsalted butter, melted

1 teaspoon vanilla extract

$\frac{1}{8}$ teaspoon salt

2 cups pecan halves, toasted (see Note)

$1\frac{1}{2}$ cups chopped ($\frac{3}{4}$-inch pieces) peeled tart apples, such as Granny Smith, Rome, Sweetango or Braeburn (see Note)

Ginger-Caramel Cheesecake

The soft and chewy ginger caramels that I make during the holidays are a big favorite of family and friends, so the combination naturally occurred to me when I was developing this cheesecake. The sweet and spicy ginger mellows as it bakes, creating a luxuriously rich dessert with caramel notes, followed by the mild taste of ginger. Topped with a caramel sauce, it's pure indulgence.

TO MAKE THE CRUST: Preheat the oven to 350°F. Line the outside of a 9-inch springform pan with heavy-duty foil, securing the foil firmly around the top edge. Stir together the cookie crumbs and brown sugar in a small bowl. Stir in the butter until the crumbs are moistened. Press firmly into the bottom of the pan.

Bake for 10 minutes or until set. Cool slightly on a wire rack while assembling the filling.

TO MAKE THE FILLING: In a large bowl, beat the cream cheese with an electric mixer at low speed, using the paddle attachment if available, until smooth. Beat in the brown sugar and flour until mixed. Add the sour cream, whipping cream, ginger, and vanilla, beating until combined. Add the eggs, one at a time, beating just until each one is blended. Pour the batter over the crust. Place the springform pan in a large, shallow pan or broiler pan. Add hot water to come 1 inch up the sides of the springform.

Bake for 50 to 55 minutes or until the top is light brown and the edges are slightly puffed. The center will jiggle when tapped (the cheesecake will set up firmly as it cools). Remove from the pan of water, remove the foil, and cool completely in the pan on a wire rack. Refrigerate, uncovered, overnight.

SERVES 12

CRUST

1½ cups gingersnap cookie crumbs (see Note)

2 tablespoons packed dark brown sugar

4 tablespoons unsalted butter, melted

FILLING

Three 8-ounce packages cream cheese, softened

1¼ cups packed dark brown sugar

2 tablespoons all-purpose flour

½ cup sour cream

⅓ cup heavy (whipping) cream

1½ tablespoons minced fresh ginger

½ teaspoon vanilla extract

3 eggs

CARAMEL SAUCE

½ cup heavy (whipping) cream

⅓ cup dark brown sugar

1 tablespoon light corn syrup

TO MAKE THE CARAMEL SAUCE: Bring the cream, brown sugar, and corn syrup to a rapid boil in a medium saucepan over medium-high heat, stirring. Boil for $2\frac{1}{2}$ to 3 minutes, stirring, or until the mixture thickens enough that you can glimpse the bottom of the pan while you're stirring. Cool to room temperature.

To serve, spoon some of the caramel sauce over each slice of cheesecake. (Refrigerate any leftover cake and sauce.)

NOTE To make gingersnap cookie crumbs, crush about twenty-six $1\frac{3}{4}$-inch gingersnap cookies by pulsing in a food processor or crushing with a rolling pin in a resealable bag until finely ground.

CHICKEN BREEDS

Chickens come in all sorts of colors, shapes, and sizes; there are more than 175 varieties. The type you choose depends in part on whether you want chickens for meat, eggs, or both (which are called dual purpose). If appearance interests you, you have a wide choice: the poofy-topped Polish, which appears to be wearing the latest in haute couture head-pieces; the lace-trimmed Wyandotte; the tiny Silkie, with its soft-as-silk coat; and the exotic naked-neck Turken, with its turkeylike neck. The chicken world is full of interesting speci-mens. Decide what you're looking for, whether it be lots of eggs, striking additions to your lawn ornaments, colorful eggs, or a heavy meat bird. Don't forget to do some research to find breeds that do well in your climate.

CHAPTER · EIGHT

MIDWINTER

As winter settled in the first year, the chicks were not adapting. I liked the fact that they were no longer up at 5:30 A.M., but it was often still dark at 7:30, or later, when I let them out of their coop on days I had an early-morning meeting or job to go to. I'd lost my zeal for running out and greeting the girls in the morning, I realized as I pulled on the Sorels; grabbed my parka that had been rechristened the chicken coat because of the food, feathers, and unmentionables it had been baptized with; and jammed a fleece hat over my ears. My husband grinned smugly as he took another sip of warm coffee. I thoroughly regretted my agreement to undertake all chicken duties by myself.

I trudged through the high-pitched creaking snow to open the coop and let the chicks out into the frigid morning. You can tell the morning temperature by the sound the snow makes as you step on it: When it's warm, the snow is quiet; when it's cold, the snow crunches; and when it's frigid, the snow squeaks loudly. Every morning my three sweet girls acted surprised, as if overnight they'd forgotten they live in this chilly wasteland. When I reassured them spring would come again, their beady eyes accusingly blinked "It's all lies!"

Food was their salvation; it not only provided nourishment but also kept them warm, and they ate greedily. As the self-proclaimed Godfather, Roxanne hip-checked the other two out of the way. She righteously marched to the front of the food queue. When I had extra time, I made them hot oatmeal and brought it out with their morning food to ease my conscience. At night they got cracked corn, which they digested more slowly, helping them to keep warm through the extra-cold nights.

The chicks seemed toasty in their heated chicken coop with their special heating pad, so I didn't worry as we headed into January and February. Our winters had been getting progressively milder, so I assumed the chicks would be fine. As it turned out, it was the chicks' luck that year that we were hit with one of the coldest winters in recent memory. I began to worry. I spent countless hours on the Internet trying to determine how cold it could get before chickens' health would begin to suffer. What I found was that most people in this country didn't know what real cold was. I saw lots of entries for people who were worried about temperatures getting down to freezing! Ha, freezing is 32 degrees Fahrenheit, a virtual heat wave during a Minnesota winter. My one saving thought was that farmers had raised chickens in Minnesota since frontier days; the chickens must somehow have survived.

I read that Vaseline is good for protecting chicken combs from freezing. Each breed has a different type of comb. Some are large and showy, others are small and petite. Roxanne has a single large, showy comb (naturally), while Cleo and Lulu have small petite pea combs. There are various evolutionary explanations as to why chickens developed combs, but the usual ones have to do with sexual attraction and regulating body temperature. I certainly didn't want to take any chances that my ladies wouldn't be sexually attractive, even though they would never meet a rooster in their lifetimes.

So I dutifully attempted to rub their combs each morning with Vaseline from a large jar I had purchased and labeled in large letters, Chickens Only, in case any of us decided to smear some on our own lips. I quickly found out my girls wanted no part of the Vaseline project, whether it was keeping them pretty or warm or neither. They squawked and squirmed until I finally gave up on the daft idea. For the record, with all the cold we had, none of my chickens' combs froze, and they are all still strutting around alluringly, so I can't tell you how cold it needs to get before a chicken's comb turns white and then black with frost, although it does happen.

I've said I would never eat one of my chickens, but I am ashamed to say I did accidentally almost cook one of them. It happened one night. The girls' sleeping arrangements never changed: Crazy Lulu was always first in at night and grabbed the prime spot under the heat lamp. Cleo was next and cozied in as much as she could. Our lady of the night Roxanne was always the last to bed, but she used her weight to push her way into a prime location in the coop. Cleo got pushed to the back, where she warmed herself on the heating pad. Crazy Lulu refused to budge, so Roxanne planted herself on top of Lulu and as close to the heat lamp as possible. As the temperature kept dropping, I turned up the heat lamp, trying to keep the coop cozy and warm. I was able to maintain a temperature of between forty-five and fifty degrees Fahrenheit, even with zero degree temps outside, and the chicks seemed happy. Until Black Sunday.

That morning, I let the chicks out into their run as normal, but I smelled something strange and I worried that somehow some of the electrical wiring had gone bad. I double-checked all my outdoor safety cords, and everything seemed fine. I came back outside with a breakfast treat for the girls, and as I set it down, I shrieked in horror: Roxanne had a huge black burnt spot on her back!

As I ran screaming, "Oh my god, I've burnt a hole in Roxanne!" my mind was racing: What should I do? What do you do for a burnt chicken? Can I bring her in to a vet, or would I be arrested for cruelty to chickens? Do I rub her with aloe vera or Bacitracin? Ice is good for burns. No, there's no way she's going to let me hold an ice pack on her in the middle of January!

I ran to my library of chicken manuals. A lot of good they were—none of the books offered any information. I was too embarrassed to call anyone. The Internet is anonymous, so I secretly looked up burnt chicken/chick, afraid of what kinky Web sites might turn up. I can honestly say there was nothing in any of the books or on the Internet on what to do for a burnt chicken. I must be the only one who's ever had to worry about it. My search did come up with recipes for blackened chicken, however. Definitely not what I was looking for.

Afraid of what I'd find when I went back outside, I didn't want to go alone to look at Roxanne. I dragged my husband, who had been doing his best to deal with a hysterical wife and who really didn't want to get involved (remember the agreement?). There she was eating, scratching, and pecking the ground like nothing was wrong. Where was the burnt spot? Gone! My husband looked at me strangely. I stumbled over my words as I rushed to explain, "I didn't imagine it! It was there! Really! A big black spot in the middle of a golden brown chick! Where did it go?" I looked again—she was fine.

Unfortunately, it really happened. But apparently only her outer feathers were burned, and they had either dropped out on their own, or she groomed them out, or one of the other girls helped her. Whatever had happened, the singed feathers were gone, and she seemed none the worse for it. I watched the heat lamp carefully from then on, and joined the chicks in wondering if spring would ever come.

Instead, it continued to get colder. I watched the weather forecasts hourly like a captain about to set sail. Zero degrees tonight? No problem, I relaxed. Ten below? I started getting nervous. Twenty below? I was worried. Minnesota weather forecasters are notorious for predicting worst-case scenarios every day. Thus it seemed that we either had biblical floods, Saharan heat, or hell-freezing cold. I therefore tried not to overreact.

One night we arrived home after ten with the outside temperature dropping toward twenty below, and I had to react. I could not in good conscience leave my tiny hens outside. I didn't want to be responsible for three frozen chicksicles. My original plan had been to move the chicks into the garage if the outside temps became too severe, but with an uninsulated garage facing into the wind, it was almost as cold in there as it was outside.

I'd purchased a medium-size wire dog kennel with a solid removable floor to transport the chicks, and we hauled it into the house that night. Putting the chicks on the lower level, where the cats slept at night, didn't seem smart. So I set up the back hall for their use. (My husband wisely didn't want to deal with the consequence if the hens froze, so he didn't say a word.) I quickly covered the floor with heavy plastic, lined the kennel with lots of paper, and ran out to grab each chick, one by one. Roxanne came first, and I could see her hunched body visibly relax in the warmth. Cleo gladly joined her. Crazy Lulu stood squawking in the coop, calling for her friends and wondering why she'd been abandoned on this cruel night. Even she didn't fight as I scooped her up and carried her into the house. The three birds literally cooed like pigeons, they were so happy. I put a blanket partway over their kennel to block the light, and they comfortably slept the night away.

We tiptoed around the house in the morning, hoping not to wake our guests. Their keen ears easily heard us, however, and since they were warm, they were raring to go. It's a fact that chickens poop all night long, wherever they roost. Therefore, the kennel floor had to be cleaned before I could feed them. It was still dark and extremely cold, and I didn't want to let them outside. So into the bathroom they went while I cleaned the cage. Bad move! Real bad! Chickens poop wherever they are. I now also had to clean the bathroom. Clean, fed, and watered, the chickens felt ready to roam. No way was I going to let them run through the house. "Forget it," I told them.

The outside temperature didn't rise much, and I couldn't bring myself to throw them back into the cold. So in the house they stayed. I was surprised to find a couple of eggs in the corner of the kennel; they'd created their own nesting spot. The pecking, cooing, and little squabbles kept me company as I worked at my desk. But cleaning up after they spilled their food and water bowl prevented me from finishing my work. I listened to the doomsayer's daily forecast, and learned the nighttime temps would not be any better than the previous night's. I couldn't let them back outside.

I rigged up a more stable food and water dispenser that benefited all of us. As I sat down at the desk, the girls decided they were bored. When they got bored, they got loud. They began clucking at the tops of their voices, each outdoing the next. I considered heaving them outside. But I had one more idea.

I hooked up our portable speakers and turned on the radio. A startled look came over their faces; they were mesmerized. They looked around furtively, wondering where the orchestra was hidden. They soon understood the sound was coming from the little black boxes as I fiddled with the volume. They loved it. My three hyper chicks almost swayed in unison as they listened to a Mozart concerto. The afternoon was actually peaceful, and I reminded myself to give an extra donation to Minnesota Public Radio.

One day stretched into four before the cold spell broke. In place of the bathroom, I put them in the garage while I cleaned their indoor coop twice a day. But that meant I also had to clean the freezing garage floor. By the last couple days of the freeze, I was tired of scraping up frozen poop from the garage, so I put them outside while I cleaned the coop. They hovered on the doorstep, jumping up and down on one foot until I carried them back in. I figured at least they'd be reminded just how good they had it. Next year I'd have to investigate better options. How much would it cost to heat the garage?

CHICKEN MAGIC

Amaze your friends by predicting the color of a chicken's egg just by looking at her ears. First step? Find the ears. Flat and unobtrusive, a chicken's ears lie slightly behind and below the eyes, and are sometimes hidden by a tuft of feathers. Around the ear is a soft tissue of skin, the ear lobe, so to speak. The color of this delicate skin indicates the color of the eggs.

Chickens with white or pale skin produce white eggs, while chickens with red or pink skin produce brown eggs. My Easter Egg chick Cleo has iridescent green ears, and her eggs are a lovely, olive-toned green, while Crazy Lulu's blue eggs are reflected in the blue tone of her ears.

Nutmeg-Coated Creamy French Toast

Golden crisp on the outside yet tender on the inside, here is the ultimate in French toast. The additional egg yolks give extra richness, body, and color to this twist on the classic. This recipe is perfect for entertaining because it's made the day before. Simply fry and serve in the morning.

Cut the bread into thick slices a little shy of 1 inch (see Note). Arrange the bread in a single layer in a 13-by-9-inch pan, using an additional 8-inch square pan if necessary.

Whisk the eggs, egg yolks, and salt together in a medium bowl for 1 to 2 minutes, or until they are light, frothy, and completely smooth. (There should be no bits of egg or stringiness remaining, or you will have pieces of cooked egg on the toast.) Whisk in the half-and-half, yogurt, granulated sugar, and 2 teaspoons nutmeg until well blended. Pour the egg mixture over the bread. Cover with plastic wrap and refrigerate overnight, carefully turning the bread once or twice if possible.

When ready to cook, preheat an electric nonstick griddle to 350°F or heat a nonstick skillet over medium heat. Lightly brush the griddle or skillet with some butter and cook the bread in batches for 6 to 8 minutes or until golden brown on the outside but still soft in the center, turning once. Adjust the heat as necessary.

While the bread is frying, stir together the powdered sugar and 1/8 teaspoon nutmeg and put in a fine-mesh strainer. Sprinkle the hot French toast with the powdered sugar mixture and serve topped with maple syrup or preserves.

NOTE The bread is thickly sliced so the center of each slice will stay creamy, but if the slices are too thick, the center will not cook in the time it takes to cook the outside.

One 1-pound loaf unsliced bread, preferably challah, brioche, or another rich egg bread, or a firm, fine-textured white bread

5 eggs plus 3 egg yolks

1/4 teaspoon salt

1 cup half-and-half or milk

1/2 cup plain yogurt, preferably Greek

3 tablespoons granulated sugar

2 teaspoons ground nutmeg, plus 1/8 teaspoon

Butter or canola oil for frying

2 tablespoons powdered sugar

Maple syrup or fruit preserves for serving

Bacon and Egg Breakfast Tarts

Individual breakfast tarts sound impressive, but they are deceptively easy to make, especially since most of the preparation can be done ahead of time (see Note). Use your freshest eggs, and they'll spread less as you crack them into the tart shells. And ask your butcher for slab bacon. It's the whole side, or slab, of bacon before it's been sliced. The advantage is that you can cut the bacon as thick as you like.

Thaw the puff pastry according to the package directions. Line a baking sheet with parchment paper. Roll out the pastry on a lightly floured surface to a 12-inch square. Cut into four squares. Trim each square to about 5½ inches. Place on the baking sheet.

Fold over and press ½ inch on each edge of the squares to form a rim. Using a fork, prick each pastry square inside the rim every ½ inch to keep the center of the pastry from puffing up. Whisk 1 of the eggs in a small bowl until frothy. Brush the pastry squares with the egg. Cover and refrigerate for 15 minutes.

Meanwhile, preheat the oven to 425°F. Cook the bacon in a medium skillet over medium heat for 6 to 8 minutes or until browned, stirring frequently. Drain on a paper towel–lined plate. Stir together the cream, 6 tablespoons of the cheese, the mustard, and pepper. Spread over the center of the puff pastry squares.

Bake for 8 to 10 minutes or until light golden brown. If the center has puffed, prick with a fork to deflate. Crack the remaining 4 eggs into small cups and pour one into the center of each tart shell. Sprinkle the eggs with the salt. Scatter the bacon over the eggs and arrange the tomatoes over the egg whites. Sprinkle the remaining 2 tablespoons of cheese over the egg whites and tomatoes. Top with green onion.

Bake for an additional 5 to 7 minutes or until the tart is golden brown, the egg whites are firm, and the egg yolks are soft.

Serve immediately.

NOTE   Much of the assembly of these tarts can be done the day before. The puff pastry squares can be prepared and refrigerated overnight. The bacon can be browned the day before and stored in the refrigerator, and the cream mixture can be prepared and refrigerated overnight, too.

SERVES 4

1 sheet frozen puff pastry

5 eggs

4 ounces slab bacon or thickly sliced bacon, cut into ½-inch pieces

¼ cup heavy (whipping) cream

8 tablespoons shredded Parmesan cheese

½ teaspoon Dijon mustard

⅛ teaspoon freshly ground pepper

⅛ teaspoon kosher salt

¼ cup grape tomatoes, halved lengthwise

¼ cup sliced green onion (green part only)

Scrambled Eggs over Crisp Polenta with Maple-Balsamic Drizzle

This sophisticated dish is really just an uptown version of eggs and grits. Ground cornmeal, known as grits, cornmeal mush, or polenta, is paired with eggs in many cultures. This dish forms a perfect circle, from the cracked corn that's added to the chickens' winter diet to keep them warm to the resulting corn-fed eggs and the fried triangles of polenta the eggs are served with.

SERVES 4

1½ cups cold water

½ cup finely ground polenta, yellow cornmeal, or corn grits

Pinch of kosher salt, plus ⅛ teaspoon

2½ tablespoons unsalted butter

¼ cup pure maple syrup, preferably dark amber or Grade B

2 teaspoons balsamic vinegar

6 eggs

⅛ teaspoon freshly ground pepper

Pour the water into a medium saucepan and slowly whisk in the polenta and a pinch of salt until smooth. Bring to a boil over medium heat, whisking constantly so no lumps form. Reduce the heat to medium-low and boil gently for 15 to 20 minutes or until very thick, whisking frequently. Be careful—the polenta will pop in large spitting bubbles as it begins to thicken. Remove from the heat and stir in ½ tablespoon of the butter. Line an 8-inch square pan with plastic wrap and pour the polenta into the pan. Cover and refrigerate until chilled and firm, about 1 hour or overnight.

Preheat the oven to 250°F and line a baking sheet with foil. Remove the polenta from the pan and transfer to a cutting board. Cut into four squares (the polenta will be about ½ inch thick). Cut each square in half diagonally to make triangles. Melt 1 tablespoon of the butter in a large nonstick skillet over medium-high heat. Add the polenta and cook for 10 to 12 minutes or until lightly browned on both sides, turning once. Place the polenta on the baking sheet and keep warm in the oven.

Add the maple syrup and balsamic vinegar to the skillet and bring to a boil over high heat. Boil for 30 to 60 seconds or until syrupy. Pour into a small cup or pitcher.

Whisk the eggs with the ⅛ teaspoon salt and the pepper in a large bowl until frothy. Melt the remaining 1 tablespoon of butter in a medium nonstick skillet over medium heat. Add the eggs and cook for 1 to 2 minutes, stirring constantly, until moist curds form. Remove from the heat.

To serve, arrange two polenta triangles on each plate. Drizzle with the syrup and spoon the eggs partially over the polenta.

Balsamic Chicken Liver Pâté

This velvety, mild pâté is accented with the sweet tang of balsamic vinegar. It's a hit at parties, even with those who think they don't like chicken livers. The secret to its creamy and mellow taste is soaking the chicken livers in milk before cooking. For those who prefer a bolder, more pronounced flavor, feel free to shorten or eliminate this step.

Put the livers in a small bowl and pour in enough milk to cover them. Cover with plastic wrap and refrigerate for at least 12 hours or up to 24 hours. Drain the chicken livers and discard the milk. Rinse the livers under running water and drain well. Remove and discard all of the connective tissue and pat the livers dry with paper towels.

Melt 3 tablespoons of the butter in a medium nonstick skillet over medium heat. Cook the shallots and garlic for 1 minute or until slightly soft. Add the chicken livers and cook over medium heat for 5 to 7 minutes, or until almost cooked through but still slightly pink in the center, stirring and turning them frequently. Remove the chicken livers to a plate and cool to room temperature.

Add the balsamic vinegar to the skillet and bring to a boil over medium heat. Boil for 10 to 20 seconds, stirring and scraping up any bits on the bottom of the pan. Remove from the heat and cool until warm, rather than hot. Pour into the bowl of a food processor.

Add the chicken livers and pulse until finely chopped. Add the remaining 5 tablespoons of butter and the salt and pepper and pulse until combined. Process until the mixture is light and smooth.

Spoon the puréed livers into a small serving dish, cover with plastic wrap, and refrigerate for 3 hours or until set. To garnish, press the hard-cooked egg yolk through a strainer to finely crumble. Sprinkle over the top of the pâté and lightly sprinkle with chopped parsley.

Serve with the baguette, apples, or crackers.

Ingredients

8 ounces chicken livers, rinsed and drained

$\frac{1}{2}$ cup milk, or as needed

$\frac{1}{2}$ cup (1 stick) unsalted butter, softened

$\frac{1}{3}$ cup minced shallots

1 garlic clove, minced

$1\frac{1}{2}$ tablespoons balsamic vinegar

$\frac{1}{2}$ teaspoon kosher salt

$\frac{1}{4}$ teaspoon freshly ground pepper

1 hard-cooked egg yolk (see Note, page 31)

1 to 2 teaspoons chopped fresh flat-leaf parsley

Thinly sliced baguette, apples, or crackers for serving

Double-Garlic Chicken Noodle Soup

There's nothing more comforting than a pot of soup simmering on the back burner when snowflakes are falling. This old-fashioned chicken noodle soup ups the ante with roasted garlic noodles. Their mellow taste belies the full head of garlic they contain.

TO MAKE THE SOUP: Put the chicken in a large soup pot and pour in the water. Bring to a boil over medium-high heat, skimming off the foam as it rises to the surface. Add all of the remaining ingredients and return to the boil. Reduce the heat and gently simmer for 1 hour or until the chicken is very tender and the broth is flavorful. Remove the chicken from the broth and let sit until cool enough to handle.

TO MAKE THE NOODLES: While the soup is cooking, preheat the oven to 400°F. Slice off the top third of the head of garlic (leave the papery skin on). Put the garlic on a square of foil and drizzle the exposed cloves with the olive oil. Wrap in the foil.

Bake the garlic for 45 to 60 minutes or until it feels very soft when squeezed. Cool to room temperature. Squeeze the garlic cloves out of the garlic skin onto a cutting board and mash with the side of a chef's knife to a paste. (There should be about 3 tablespoons.)

When the chicken is cool, remove the chicken meat from the bones and shred or coarsely chop (there will be about 4 cups of meat). Skim off any fat that has risen to the surface of the soup and return the meat to the soup.

Cook the noodles in a large pot of boiling salted water for 8 minutes or until al dente. Drain and toss with the melted butter and garlic paste in a large bowl. Toss with the parsley.

To serve, ladle the soup into bowls and top with the noodles.

SERVES 6

CHICKEN SOUP

One 3-pound chicken, cut up

8 cups water

4 garlic cloves, minced

3 large sprigs fresh thyme

2 large onions, coarsely chopped

2 carrots, chopped

2 celery ribs, chopped

1 bay leaf

1 teaspoon kosher salt

$\frac{1}{2}$ teaspoon freshly ground pepper

ROASTED GARLIC NOODLES

1 head garlic

1 teaspoon extra-virgin olive oil

8 ounces extra-wide egg noodles

2 tablespoons unsalted butter, melted

$\frac{1}{4}$ cup chopped fresh flat-leaf parsley

Chipotle-Spiced Three-Bean Chili

Dried smoked jalapeños, known as chipotle chiles, turn up the heat on this chili. Made with three different types of beans and boneless chicken, it's a hearty one-dish meal that's low in fat and good for you. Top with all your favorite chili toppings or just a simple squeeze of lime.

SERVES 6

Heat a large pot over medium-high heat. Heat the oil. Brown the chicken for 6 to 8 minutes or until browned on all sides, stirring frequently. Stir in the onion, reduce the heat to medium, and cook for 3 minutes or until slightly softened. Add the garlic and cook for 30 seconds or until fragrant, stirring constantly.

Stir in all of the remaining ingredients except the cilantro. Bring to a boil, reduce the heat, and simmer for 35 to 45 minutes or until slightly thickened, stirring occasionally. Stir in the cilantro and serve.

NOTES The black beans, chili beans, and kidney beans in this recipe are added directly to the chili without rinsing or draining. The additional liquid from the beans adds extra flavor and body to the chili.

Chipotle chiles in adobo sauce can be found canned in the Latino section of the grocery store or in Latin markets.

1 tablespoon extra-virgin olive oil

1 pound boneless, skinless chicken breast halves or thighs, cut into 3/4- to 1-inch pieces, or 1 pound ground chicken

1 large onion, chopped

3 garlic cloves, minced

One 28-ounce can diced roasted tomatoes

One 15-ounce can black beans (see Note)

One 16-ounce can chili beans (see Note)

One 16-ounce can kidney beans (see Note)

1 cup reduced-sodium chicken broth

1 tablespoon ground cumin

2 teaspoons chili powder

1 to 2 teaspoons finely chopped chipotle chiles in adobo sauce, veins and seeds removed for less heat, if desired (see Note)

3/4 teaspoon kosher salt

1/2 teaspoon freshly ground pepper

1/4 cup chopped fresh cilantro

Burmese Fried Rice with Eggs

I feel fortunate to have learned something about the Karen people of Burma through a family that recently immigrated to our area. They have carried their food traditions with them and prepare delightful fresh, spicy meals. This fried rice was inspired by a casual dish they prepared: colorful vegetable fried rice crowned with a gently fried egg. It is easily adapted to whatever vegetables are in season or in your refrigerator.

Stir together the soy sauce, sesame oil, hoisin, and chili sauce in a small bowl and set aside.

Heat a large wok or nonstick skillet over high heat, and heat 1 tablespoon of the oil. Stir-fry the coleslaw mix, carrots, and onion for 45 seconds, or until the carrots and cabbage become brighter in color. Toss in the peas and garlic and cook for 15 seconds. Stir in the rice and cook for 2 to 3 minutes or until the rice is hot and the vegetables are crisp-tender. Stir in the soy mixture and remove from the heat.

Heat the remaining 1 tablespoon oil in a medium nonstick skillet over medium heat. Add the eggs, and cook for 3 to 4 minutes or until the whites are set and the yolks are still soft.

When the eggs are almost ready, reheat the rice mixture over medium heat for 1 to 2 minutes or until hot. Stir in the cilantro.

Serve the rice topped with the eggs.

NOTES

The secret to good fried rice is to plan ahead. Cook the rice the day before or use leftover rice.

This dish goes together very quickly when all of the ingredients are assembled and ready to cook. Because the eggs should be prepared as soon as the rice and vegetable stir-fry is completed, have the nonstick skillet with the oil ready to heat, and the eggs cracked into individual cups before you begin.

SERVES 4

2 tablespoons soy sauce

2 teaspoons dark sesame oil

1 teaspoon hoisin sauce

$\frac{1}{2}$ teaspoon Asian chili sauce, such as Sriracha, or more to taste

2 tablespoons canola oil

$1\frac{1}{2}$ cups cabbage coleslaw mix

$\frac{3}{4}$ cup shredded carrots

1 medium onion, halved lengthwise and halves cut lengthwise into slivers

$\frac{1}{2}$ cup frozen baby peas, thawed

2 garlic cloves, minced

3 cups cold cooked basmati rice (see Note)

4 eggs (see Note)

$\frac{1}{2}$ cup coarsely chopped fresh cilantro

Chicken Couscous with Pistachios

This quick one-pot meal can be prepared in 6 minutes of hands-on time. The key is to prep all of the ingredients before you start cooking. The enticing sweet-savory background note in this dish comes from the addition of cinnamon. This recipe was developed with chicken breasts, but boneless, skinless chicken thighs or chicken tenders would be equally good.

Heat a large skillet over medium-high heat. Heat the oil. Add the chicken and onion, sprinkle with the salt and pepper, and cook for 3 minutes or until lightly browned, stirring frequently. Add the carrot, garlic, and cinnamon and cook for 30 seconds or until aromatic.

Stir in the broth and raisins. Bring to a boil, reduce the heat to medium-low, and simmer for 1 to 2 minutes, or until the chicken is no longer pink in the center. Stir in the couscous. Cover and remove from the heat. Let sit for 5 minutes or until the liquid is absorbed. Stir in the pistachios and green onions.

Serve immediately.

SERVES 4

1½ tablespoons extra-virgin olive oil

1 pound boneless, skinless chicken breast halves, cut into ¾-inch pieces

1 small onion, halved and sliced

½ teaspoon kosher salt

¼ teaspoon freshly ground pepper

1 carrot, finely chopped

2 garlic cloves, minced

1 tablespoon ground cinnamon

1¾ cups reduced-sodium chicken broth

½ cup raisins

1 cup couscous

½ cup salted roasted pistachios or almonds

½ cup sliced green onions (green part only)

Cheddar-Dill Chicken Cobbler

Create a heartland farmhouse supper with this savory version of a traditional cobbler. The dill-flavored chicken and vegetable stew is topped with cheddar drop biscuits for a warming meal that's perfect after you've trudged through the snow to gather the eggs in your chicken coop.

SERVES 8

TO MAKE THE COBBLER: Melt the butter in a large saucepan over medium heat. Add the onion and cook for 3 minutes or until it begins to soften, stirring occasionally. Add the carrots and cook for 2 minutes. Stir in the garlic and cook for 30 seconds or until aromatic. Stir in the flour and cook for 1 minute. Whisk in the broth, half-and-half, lemon juice, salt, and pepper. Bring to a boil, reduce the heat, and simmer for 5 minutes or until the vegetables are crisp-tender, stirring occasionally. Stir in the chicken and dill, and set aside.

TO MAKE THE BISCUITS: Preheat the oven to 400°F. Butter an 11-by-7-inch glass baking dish or coat with nonstick cooking spray. Pulse the flour, baking powder, and salt in the food processor until blended. Add the butter and pulse until the butter is the size of blueberries. Pour in the milk and pulse until a moist dough forms. Stir in the cheese and dill.

Bring the chicken and vegetables to a boil over medium heat. Pour into the baking dish. Drop the biscuit dough in six mounds over the chicken mixture.

Bake for 30 to 35 minutes or until golden brown and bubbly and a toothpick inserted in the center of the biscuits comes out clean.

Serve immediately.

NOTES The chicken and vegetable mixture can be prepared and refrigerated up to 1 day ahead.

The biscuits can be made by hand using a pastry blender or your fingers to blend the butter into the flour.

COBBLER

4 tablespoons unsalted butter

1 large onion, coarsely chopped

2 medium carrots, sliced 1/4 inch thick

3 garlic cloves, minced

1/3 cup all-purpose flour

1 1/2 cups reduced-sodium chicken broth

1/2 cup half-and-half or milk

2 teaspoons fresh lemon juice

1 teaspoon kosher salt

1/2 teaspoon freshly ground pepper

2 cups shredded or chopped poached chicken (see Note, page 33)

2 tablespoons chopped fresh dill

BISCUITS

1 cup all-purpose flour

1 teaspoon baking powder

1/4 teaspoon salt

4 tablespoons cold unsalted butter, cut up

1/2 cup milk

1/2 cup shredded sharp cheddar cheese

1 tablespoon chopped fresh dill

Chicken Lasagna with Greens

This lasagna is a refreshing change from the traditional classic made with red sauce. The delicate cream sauce allows the special flavor of pasture-raised chicken to shine through, and the greens provide color and garden-fresh taste.

SERVES 8

Preheat the oven to 350°F. Oil an 11-by-7-inch glass baking dish with extra-virgin olive oil or coat with nonstick cooking spray. Heat 3 tablespoons of the oil in a medium saucepan over medium heat. Add 3 of the garlic cloves and cook for 30 to 60 seconds or until fragrant. Whisk in the flour and cook for 1 minute, whisking constantly. Whisk in the broth, cream, 1/2 teaspoon of the salt, and 1/4 teaspoon of the pepper. Bring to a boil over medium-high heat, whisking constantly. Reduce the heat and simmer for 3 minutes, stirring occasionally. Stir in the tarragon and set aside.

Cut off the chard leaves from the stems. Slice the leaves about 1/2 inch wide (there will be about 8 firmly packed cups). Thinly slice the stems (about 1 cup).

Heat the remaining 1 tablespoon oil in a large skillet over medium heat, add the chard stems, and cook for 3 minutes, stirring constantly. Increase the heat to medium-high and add the chard leaves. Cook, stirring and turning with tongs for 3 to 4 minutes or until wilted, and add the remaining 2 garlic cloves and 1/4 teaspoon each of salt and pepper. Transfer to a large bowl and cool slightly, pressing on the chard and pouring out any accumulated liquid.

Spoon a light coating of sauce over the bottom of the pan. Lay 3 noodles in the pan, overlapping as necessary. Layer one-third of the chard, chicken, sauce, and cheese. Repeat the layers two more times. Bake for 55 to 60 minutes or until golden brown, hot, and bubbly. Let sit for 10 minutes before serving.

NOTE The lasagna can be assembled up to 8 hours ahead. Cover with plastic wrap and refrigerate until ready to bake. Let sit at room temperature while the oven preheats. Add 5 to 10 minutes to the baking time, if necessary.

4 tablespoons extra-virgin olive oil

5 garlic cloves, minced

1/3 cup all-purpose flour

1 1/2 cups reduced-sodium chicken broth

1 cup heavy (whipping) cream

3/4 teaspoon kosher salt

1/2 teaspoon freshly ground pepper

2 tablespoons chopped fresh tarragon

14 to 16 ounces rainbow or red chard (about 2 bunches)

9 no-boil lasagna noodles

3 cups shredded poached chicken (see Note, page 33)

3 cups shredded Gruyère cheese (12 ounces)

Tuscan Chicken with Bacon and Italian Beans

As the chicken slowly braises, it picks up the surrounding flavors of onion, garlic, sweet bell pepper, tomato, and smoky bacon. Creamy cannellini beans—white kidney beans popular in Tuscany—are added toward the end.

SERVES 4

Preheat the oven to 325°F. Cook the bacon in a large ovenproof pot over medium heat until brown and crisp, stirring occasionally. Remove the bacon with a slotted spoon. Brown the chicken in batches in the bacon drippings, 6 to 8 minutes, turning as needed to brown all sides. Remove the chicken, and then remove and discard all but 1 tablespoon of the drippings from the pot.

Sauté the onions and bell pepper over medium heat for 3 minutes or until they just begin to soften. Add the garlic and stir until fragrant, about 30 seconds. Return the chicken to the pot and nestle the pieces in the onions and bell pepper. Season the chicken with rosemary, salt, pepper, and cinnamon. Sprinkle the bacon over the chicken, top with the tomatoes, and pour in the chicken broth. Bring to a boil over medium-high heat and partially cover.

Transfer to the oven and bake for 30 minutes, keeping the lid ajar so that the liquid barely simmers. Stir in the beans. Continue baking for another 15 minutes or until the chicken is tender and no longer pink in the center. Arrange the chicken on a serving platter and cover loosely with foil. Place the pot over high heat and boil for 5 to 8 minutes or until slightly thickened.

Spoon the vegetable mixture over the chicken and serve.

NOTES I like to use an extra-smoky bacon like Neuske's for more flavor.

Braising—the technique of slowly cooking browned meat in a small amount of liquid—is used to tenderize tough cuts of meat. Although it's the perfect method for cooking tough stewing hens, they have become difficult to find. This recipe has been adapted for a younger hen, and the cooking time is much shorter.

5 slices (about 4 ounces) applewood-smoked bacon, chopped (see Note)

One 3½-pound chicken, cut into 8 pieces

2 medium onions, coarsely chopped

1 yellow bell pepper, seeded, deveined, and coarsely chopped

4 garlic cloves, sliced

1 tablespoon chopped fresh rosemary

¾ teaspoon coarse sea salt

¼ teaspoon freshly ground pepper

½ teaspoon ground cinnamon

One 14½-ounce can diced tomatoes

½ cup reduced-sodium chicken broth

One 15- to 19-ounce can cannellini beans, rinsed and drained

Pan-Roasted Stilton Chicken with Apples

A chicken that's allowed to run will provide the full flavor necessary to support the tangy Stilton cheese and tart sweetness of the apples in this dish. Talk to the purveyors at the farmers' market or your butcher, and they'll be happy to tell you about the chickens they sell.

SERVES 4

Preheat the oven to 425°F. Lightly oil a small, rimmed baking sheet with extra-virgin olive oil or coat with nonstick cooking spray. Season the chicken breasts with the salt and pepper and sprinkle with the rosemary.

Melt the butter with the oil in a large nonstick skillet over medium-high heat. Cook the chicken for 6 minutes or until browned on both sides, turning once. Transfer to the baking sheet. Add the apple slices to the skillet and cook over medium-high heat for 3 to 4 minutes, or until slightly softened and lightly browned. Spoon the apples around the chicken, placing a couple of slices over each breast.

Bake for 6 minutes or until the chicken feels slightly firm when pressed. Scatter the cheese over the chicken and apples. Continue baking another 2 minutes, or until the cheese is melted and the chicken is no longer pink in the center.

Serve the chicken with the apples.

4 boneless, skinless chicken breast halves (about 1½ pounds)

¼ teaspoon kosher salt

¼ teaspoon freshly ground pepper

1 tablespoon chopped fresh rosemary

1 tablespoon unsalted butter

1½ teaspoons extra-virgin olive oil

2 unpeeled Honeycrisp or Fuji apples, cored and sliced ¼ inch thick (about 2¼ cups)

2 ounces Stilton cheese, crumbled (about ⅓ cup)

A DAY IN THE LIFE OF A CHICKEN

Sunrise, and it's time to get up and greet the day. The chickens are hungry and usually eat the bulk of their food in the morning, so make sure it's nutritious. The time for snacks and treats is in the afternoon, after they've already eaten their fill of the important food.

Once they're feeling full, they're ready to preen and look beautiful. Around mid-morning it's time for a dust bath, and by late morning they're ready to doze in the sun by spreading their bodies and upper wings in a Jayne Mansfield–style pose. Noon brings more eating and drinking, followed by increased activity—scratching for bugs and other interesting items.

By the middle of the afternoon, the hens are ready for another nap, followed by a thorough preening. Mine like to do this on the deck railing, where they can survey their kingdom. Then they come running for treats, ready to fill up for the long night.

When twilight appears, like clockwork, the chickens head back to the coop, where they perch on the roosting bars, tuck their head under their wings, close their eyes, and fall asleep.

Holiday Roast Chicken with Cranberry-Fig Stuffing

For small holiday celebrations, a roast chicken is as celebratory as turkey, but much easier to handle and quicker to prepare. The traditional bread stuffing is accented with fruits of the season, for a colorful side dish.

SERVES 6

4 cups cubed (³/₄-inch cubes) baguette

3 tablespoons unsalted butter, softened

¹/₂ cup minced shallots

¹/₂ cup dried cranberries

¹/₂ cup chopped dried figs, preferably Calimyrna, or dried apricots

¹/₂ cup reduced-sodium chicken broth

1 egg, beaten

¹/₄ cup chopped fresh flat-leaf parsley

2 tablespoons chopped fresh thyme

³/₄ teaspoon kosher salt

¹/₂ teaspoon freshly ground pepper

One 4¹/₂- to 5-pound chicken

Preheat the oven to 400°F. Butter an 8-inch square glass or ceramic baking dish or coat with nonstick cooking spray. Spread out the bread cubes in a single layer on a large, rimmed baking sheet and bake for 5 minutes or until slightly dry. Cool and transfer to a large bowl (see Note).

Meanwhile, melt 2 tablespoons of the butter in a small skillet and cook the shallots for 1 minute, stirring frequently. Pour over the bread. Toss in the cranberries and figs. Moisten the bread with the broth. Stir in the egg, sprinkle with the parsley, 1 tablespoon of the thyme, and ¹/₄ teaspoon each of the salt and pepper, and toss until well blended. Reserve 1¹/₂ cups of the stuffing for the chicken and place the rest in the baking dish. Cover with foil (see Note).

Place a roasting rack in a shallow roasting pan. Oil the roasting rack or coat with nonstick cooking spray. Tuck the chicken wing tips behind the chicken. Spread the remaining 1 tablespoon of butter over the chicken. Sprinkle with the remaining 1 tablespoon of thyme, ¹/₂ teaspoon of salt, and ¹/₄ teaspoon of pepper. Spoon the reserved stuffing into the chicken cavity so that it's filled loosely. If the chicken cavity will not hold all of the reserved stuffing, add any remaining to the baking dish.

Bake the chicken for 60 to 70 minutes or until the internal temperature of the chicken at the thickest point of the thigh (without touching a bone) registers 175°F and the temperature of the stuffing inside the chicken registers at least 165°F.
(continued)

About 15 minutes before the chicken is ready to come out of the oven, bake the dish of stuffing alongside until the stuffing is hot and the internal temperature registers at least 165°F, 20 to 25 minutes.

Remove the chicken from the oven and loosely cover with foil for 10 minutes before serving. Spoon out the stuffing and carve.

NOTES The bread for the stuffing can be prepared up to 3 days in advance and kept in an airtight bag.

The stuffing can be prepared up to 8 hours ahead of time, covered, and stored in the refrigerator. Do not spoon the stuffing into the chicken until right before baking. An additional 5 to 10 minutes of baking time may be necessary.

A MORE NUTRITIOUS EGG

Still not convinced that the taste of home- or farmer-raised eggs is worth it? Then think of your health. There is growing evidence that eggs from hens that are allowed to graze on pasture not only taste better, but are better for you. A number of studies have showed that pasture-raised eggs have less cholesterol; less saturated fat; more omega-3s; and more vitamins A, D, and E than conventionally raised eggs from confined hens.

Black-Bottom Raspberry Meringues

These meringues offer a tender, sweet, but fleeting guilt-free pleasure. They are crisp but airy, and melt instantly in your mouth. The dipped chocolate bottoms make them irresistible.

2 egg whites

$1/4$ teaspoon cream of tartar

$1/2$ cup powdered sugar

$1/4$ teaspoon raspberry extract

2 drops red food coloring

2 ounces bittersweet or semisweet chocolate, chopped (optional)

Preheat the oven to 225°F. Line a baking sheet with parchment paper. Beat the egg whites in a large bowl with an electric mixer at medium-low speed until frothy. Add the cream of tartar, increase the speed to medium, and beat until soft peaks form, about 1 minute. Slowly sprinkle in the powdered sugar and beat at medium-high speed for 1 to 2 minutes or until stiff peaks form. Beat in the raspberry extract. Add the food coloring and stir gently a couple of times until it is swirled through the egg whites.

On the baking sheet, pipe the meringues using a pastry bag with a $1/2$-inch star tip into thirty-six swirled rounds 1 inch in diameter. Or use a teaspoon to dollop the meringues. Make sure you leave long, loopy ends as you pull your piping tip or spoon away from the meringue. It will give the meringues a delicate, playful look.

Bake for 1 hour and 15 minutes. The meringues will still be slightly soft but will firm as they cool. Keeping the meringues in the oven, turn off the oven, and place a wooden spoon in the oven door to prop it open slightly. Let the meringues sit for 15 minutes. Transfer to a wire cooling rack to cool completely. (You can store the meringues in an airtight container for up to a week at room temperature.)

If desired, microwave the chocolate in a small microwave-safe bowl for 25 to 30 seconds, until soft but not melted. Stir until the chocolate is melted and smooth. Line a baking sheet with foil, shiny-side up. Dip the bottom of each cooled meringue into the melted chocolate and place on the foil-lined baking sheet. Refrigerate for 5 minutes or until the chocolate is set. Serve immediately, or store in an airtight container for up to 2 days at room temperature.

NOTE For best results, bake the meringues on a day when the humidity is low. High humidity will cause the meringues to become soft and sticky instead of crisp.

Miniature Almond-Filled Cream Puffs

These classic profiteroles, or miniature cream puffs, never go out of style. They puff magically in the oven due to the combination of eggs, steam, and heat. Bread flour provides a little extra gluten, resulting in a bigger puff without sacrificing tenderness. The dough is easy to make, but be sure you bring the water to a full boil before adding the flour.

TO MAKE THE CREAM PUFFS: Preheat the oven to 400°F. Line a baking sheet with parchment paper. Bring the water, butter, granulated sugar, and salt to a boil in a medium saucepan over medium heat, stirring occasionally. The butter should be melted by the time the water comes to a full boil. While the pan is still on the heat, dump the flour in all at once and immediately begin stirring vigorously with a wooden spoon for 30 to 60 seconds, or until the dough forms into a smooth ball and pulls away from the sides of the pan, leaving only a light film.

Remove from the heat and let sit for 1 minute to cool slightly. Add the eggs, one at a time, quickly stirring each egg until blended (see Note). The dough should be golden, shiny, and very smooth. It should plop lazily from the spoon when you hold it up.

Put the dough into a large pastry bag fitted with a 1/2-inch star tip and pipe twenty-four mounds about the size of a ping-pong ball onto the prepared pan, or drop by teaspoonfuls, using two spoons.

Bake for 20 minutes or until puffed and light golden brown. Remove from the oven and make a small slit in the side of each puff with the tip of a knife. This will allow excess moisture in the center to escape. Bake for an additional 5 minutes or until firm and golden brown. Cool completely on a wire rack.

TO MAKE THE ALMOND FILLING: Pulse the egg yolks, granulated sugar, and almond paste in a food processor until blended and smooth. Add the flour and pulse until blended.

SERVES 8
MAKES 24 CREAM PUFFS

CREAM PUFFS

1/2 cup water

4 tablespoons cold unsalted butter, cut up

1 tablespoon granulated sugar

1/4 teaspoon salt

1/2 cup bread flour

2 eggs, at room temperature

ALMOND FILLING

3 egg yolks

1/3 cup granulated sugar

2 tablespoons almond paste, crumbled

1/4 cup all-purpose flour

1 cup half-and-half

2 tablespoons unsalted butter

1/2 teaspoon vanilla extract

CHOCOLATE SAUCE

8 ounces semisweet chocolate, chopped

1 cup whole milk

2 tablespoons packed light brown sugar

1/2 cup sliced almonds, toasted (see Note)

Heat the half-and-half in a small saucepan over medium heat until small bubbles appear on the edges. With the food processor running, pour in a slow steady stream into the egg yolk mixture, processing until incorporated. Return the egg yolk mixture to the same saucepan and cook over medium heat, whisking constantly, until it thickens and comes to a boil. Cook for 1 minute, whisking briskly. Remove from the heat. Whisk in the butter and vanilla. Pour into a small bowl, place plastic wrap directly on the surface of the filling, and refrigerate until cold.

TO MAKE THE SAUCE: Combine the ingredients in a medium saucepan. Bring to a simmer over medium heat and cook, stirring constantly, until the chocolate is melted and smooth.

Spoon or pipe the filling into the cream puffs. Serve in a pool of chocolate sauce and sprinkle with the almonds.

NOTES Toast the almonds at 400°F for 3 to 5 minutes or until lightly browned.

When you add the first egg to the cream puff dough, the dough will become very slippery, and you will feel like the egg is not going to blend in. Keep stirring quickly, and all of a sudden the dough will catch and pull together into a very thick mass. That's when you want to add your second egg. The same thing will happen, but this egg will become incorporated more quickly.

Deep Chocolate Tart with Chocolate Chip Crust

Eggs perform their magic in this elegant tart by transforming a simple chocolate sauce into a decadent filling. The addition of eggs to the chocolate mixture causes the filling to thicken and set when heated, resulting in a smooth, silky dessert. A melt-in-your-mouth cookie dough crust sweetens every bite.

SERVES 8

TO MAKE THE CRUST: Preheat the oven to 375°F. Liberally coat an 8-inch tart pan with a removable bottom with nonstick cooking spray. Beat the butter with the sugar and salt in a large bowl with an electric mixer at medium speed until blended, using the paddle attachment, if available. Beat in the egg yolk until smooth. With the mixer on low, slowly beat in the flour just until combined. Stir in the chocolate chips. With lightly floured fingers, press the dough into the bottom and up the sides of the tart pan to form the crust.

Bake the crust for 15 to 20 minutes or until golden brown. Let sit on a wire rack until the filling is ready.

TO MAKE THE FILLING: While the crust is baking, put the chocolate in a medium bowl with the cream and butter. Place the bowl over a saucepan of gently simmering water over low heat and let sit, stirring occasionally, until the chocolate is melted and smooth. Remove the bowl from the saucepan, and cool slightly.

Beat the eggs and egg yolk in a large bowl with an electric mixer at medium speed until blended. Pour in the sugar and salt and beat for 2 to 3 minutes or until light and fluffy. Pour in the chocolate mixture and beat on low speed just until blended. Pour into the baked crust.

Bake the tart for 15 to 20 minutes or until the filling is set and does not jiggle when the pan is tapped. Cool in the pan on a wire rack for 10 minutes. Remove the sides of the pan. Cool completely before serving.

Serve with sweetened whipped cream, if desired.

CRUST

1/2 cup (1 stick) unsalted butter, softened

1/3 cup sugar

1/4 teaspoon salt

1 egg yolk

1 1/3 cups all-purpose flour

1/4 cup miniature semisweet chocolate chips

FILLING

8 ounces semisweet chocolate, chopped

1/2 cup heavy (whipping) cream

4 tablespoons unsalted butter, cut up

2 eggs plus 1 egg yolk

1/4 cup sugar

1/8 teaspoon salt

Sweetened whipped cream for serving (optional)

HOW LONG DO CHICKENS LIVE?

Raising chickens is a commitment—some can live to be fifteen years old. Often chickens don't make it past five or six years due to predators, disease, or other problems. However, most chickens will live past the one or two years that laying facilities keep their chickens before culling them and getting younger birds. Well-cared-for birds can produce eggs for many years, although not as consistently as young layers.

CHAPTER · NINE

LATE

Winter

I grabbed a pale green egg laid by Cleo from the pottery bowl and tapped it firmly on the kitchen counter. Then I aggressively whisked three eggs for an omelet, keeping them whirling until they were very frothy. As I whisked, I thought back to the finest omelet I'd ever tasted. Although it was years ago, I remembered it well.

Our transatlantic flight arrived in Paris, and we took the high-speed rail to Lyon, where Marty was taking a class that summer. Our tired first glimpse of the city was from under the edge of a soggy umbrella as a cold rain poured down that chilly June day, giving everything a gloomy look. Hungry, we stopped at a simple bistro and ordered a light lunch. The omelets arrived golden and glistening. The eggs were so delicate and tender, they quivered as I stuck my fork into them. The plump omelet formed a perfect rectangle on the plate as though loving hands had tucked the stray frilly edges under, while bright flecks of green herbs flowed from the inside as my fork pierced the filling. We ate the omelets and a crisp baguette while sipping glasses of local white wine. The rain had stopped and the sun began to appear, and it seemed like nothing could taste so good or be so perfect again.

As the butter sizzled in the pan, I prepared to duplicate that meal by making an omelet with eggs from my own chicks. I waited until the butter had stopped sizzling and was just starting to turn lightly brown before pouring the eggs in the pan, fork at the ready. As soon as I poured in the eggs I swung into action, shaking the pan and stirring the eggs at the same time. In less than a minute, the omelet was ready. My omelet might not have been as beautiful, but it was as close as I'd come to duplicating the flavor. I now knew the French secret: freshly laid eggs.

....

The girls' sporadic egg laying forced me to think more seriously about the reasons I was keeping chickens. Their egg laying had gone on the blink. Lulu was the only bird making deposits to the nest. What would happen when they all stopped laying and I wasn't getting any more eggs? It seemed I had an obligation to provide for them as I would for any pet as it aged. On the other hand, they were a food source, and that's why they were in our backyard. The conflict was a modern dilemma; my grandparents would never have been bothered by it.

The notice that had appeared in my e-mail in-box gave me pause. A Dressing Class would be held if there was enough interest. Euphemisms make it all so easy. Attending a dressing class sounded like something I did in junior high school, learning about the latest in fashion and makeup. A later announcement called it a

Processing Workshop. I liked that, maybe canning tomatoes or jams and jellies. Of course it was really a slaughtering and butchering class, a BYOC event—bring your own chicken. As soon as the notice appeared, I sent a message saying I was interested. Then I started to think about it.

I had signed up out of a sense of obligation—to my chickens and to my profession. No, I hadn't decided to offer up one of the girls; they were very young, and I was sure they had many good laying years to come. And I wasn't planning on writing an exposé on how food travels to your plate. However, I did feel that because I earned my living from food, it might behoove me to find out what happens during the one part of the food process I rarely acknowledged.

Several suggestions were offered to those who didn't want to bring their own chicken to the class. We could purchase a chicken from a feed store or take one of the chickens that others in the group had volunteered for the event. I was having a hard time dealing with this. I tried to envision driving to the feed store to choose a bird, knowing I was bringing it to its death. I couldn't do it. Using one of the chickens that were volunteered seemed slightly better; supposedly they'd lived out their natural lives and were now in their final stage. Not knowing the chicken would make it easier. Or would it?

I'd signed up so quickly that when I actually took time to think about it, I couldn't envision doing the deed. Perhaps I could simply watch. That would accomplish my goal, and I wouldn't have to do the killing myself. Someone else would still be doing the deed that I couldn't bring myself to do, but taking the life of an animal simply out of a hunger for knowledge, not food, seemed wrong. I kept playing out the scene in my mind. I felt guilty killing bugs in the house; how could I kill a chicken? I wasn't sure I had my grandmother's strength.

As the date of the class came closer, I was given a reprieve. They were holding it on a day I had to be out of town for business. My emotions were mixed. I was glad to postpone having to make the final decision, but sorry I wasn't forced to make that decision. Sometimes strength rises with adversity. I was left with thoughts and feelings that hadn't been resolved. I told the organizers I'd be interested the next time they offered the class.

I know I'm typical of most people. We're happier not looking behind the curtain to see the reality backstage. Imagining the process of dressing a chicken did resolve one issue for me: I couldn't slaughter my girls any more than I could slaughter my cats. They're my pets. I'm still open on the question of whether I could kill another chicken. The issue won't disappear, and I know that sometime in the future I will have the opportunity to test my own strength of character. In the meantime, a big thank-you to all the farmers and small meat producers who daily do what I have a hard time even thinking about.

Lemon-Sizzled Eggs

These fried eggs offer contrasting taste sensations with their crispy brown bottoms, tender whites, and velvety yellow yolks, accented with lemon. I was introduced to this technique of cooking eggs in olive oil while I was traveling in Greece. The Greeks seemed truly appalled when I mentioned that most Americans cook eggs in butter. Don't be put off by the amount of oil in this recipe; splurge a bit, as it really makes this dish.

SERVES 2

4 eggs

$1/4$ cup extra-virgin olive oil

$1/4$ teaspoon coarse sea salt

$1/8$ teaspoon freshly ground pepper

1 tablespoon fresh lemon juice

1 tablespoon plus 1 teaspoon finely sliced green onion (green part only)

Crack each egg into its own small cup. Heat a medium nonstick skillet over high heat (see Note). Add the oil and swirl to coat the bottom of the pan. When the oil is hot, immediately add the eggs, sprinkle with salt and pepper, and cook over high heat for 1 to $1\frac{1}{2}$ minutes, or until the whites are almost set, reducing the heat if necessary to avoid burning them. The eggs will bubble up, and the edges will begin to brown.

Pour the lemon juice over the eggs and immediately cover. Cook for an additional minute or until the whites are firm and the yolks are still soft. Scatter the green onion over the eggs before serving.

NOTE: This recipe can be easily multiplied to serve 4 or 6. Use a large nonstick skillet.

SMART CHICKS

Research has shown that chickens are quite intelligent. Their neuron organization is highly structured. They have the capacity for self-control as well as the ability to anticipate the future based on past experiences. That's more intelligence than many teenagers I know—in fact, more than some adults, too. This ability may increase their chances of survival, but it also means they may be capable of such human emotions as worry and stress. Researchers are hoping their studies will not only aid the scientific community but also lead to more humane treatment of chickens.

Sicilian Eggs with Ciabatta and Parmesan

Poached eggs nestled in a hearty tomato sauce are a Sicilian tradition. Their savory taste can be enjoyed at any time of the day, from breakfast through supper. The tomato sauce comes together in a little over 5 minutes, resulting in fresh-from-the-garden flavor. Pancetta, which is Italian bacon, adds a meaty depth to the sauce, while basil adds a fresh, summery flavor. The eggs are topped with cheese, and are accompanied by toast brushed with olive oil.

SERVES 4

Brown the pancetta in a large skillet over medium to medium-high heat, stirring frequently. Add the garlic and cook for 30 seconds or until fragrant. Pour in the tomatoes and add the tomato paste, stirring until mixed. Stir in the basil, salt, and pepper. Bring to a boil, reduce the heat to low, and simmer for 5 minutes (see Note).

Meanwhile, crack each egg into its own small cup. Fill a medium nonstick skillet with water, cover, and bring to a gentle boil over high heat. Remove from the heat and gently slide the eggs into the water. Cover and let sit for 3 minutes or until the whites are set but the yolks are still soft. Remove with a slotted spoon and drain briefly on paper towels (while still in the spoon). While the eggs are cooking, toast the bread and brush with olive oil. Cut the bread in half diagonally.

To serve, arrange the toast halves on opposite sides of individual plates. Spoon about ¾ cup of the tomato sauce down the center of each plate and place a poached egg over the tomato sauce. Sprinkle with the cheese.

NOTES — Pancetta is rolled and cured with salt and spices, but it's not smoked. Bacon can be substituted but will give the sauce a slightly different flavor.

The tomato sauce can be prepared up to 3 days ahead of time and stored, covered, in the refrigerator.

½ cup chopped pancetta or bacon (see Note)

2 garlic cloves, minced

One 28-ounce can diced tomatoes

1 tablespoon tomato paste

3 tablespoons chopped fresh basil

¼ teaspoon kosher salt

¼ teaspoon freshly ground pepper

4 eggs

4 slices ciabatta or Italian bread, cut ½ inch thick

1 tablespoon extra-virgin olive oil

2 tablespoons shredded Parmigiano-Reggiano cheese

Chicken Udon Noodle Soup

The Japanese are masters of noodle soups. While we were in Tokyo, we found ourselves returning often to Restaurant Mozu, a tiny noodle shop with a single counter and humongous pots of steaming broth. We always ordered the udon noodle soup. It came with a variety of meat choices, but it always included a whole hard-cooked egg. This soup is a simpler version. Serve it in deep earthenware bowls with Asian soup spoons and chopsticks.

Put the eggs in a small saucepan and add enough hot water to just cover. Bring to a boil over high heat. Reduce the heat to medium-low and gently boil for 6 minutes, reducing the heat if necessary to maintain a very gentle boil. Put the eggs in a bowl of ice water until cool enough to handle. Peel under running water and quarter the eggs.

Pour the broth into a large saucepan, add the ginger, soy sauce, and mirin and bring to a boil over medium heat. Reduce the heat to medium-low and simmer for 3 minutes. Add the carrot and simmer for 3 minutes. Add the chicken, cabbage, and mushrooms. Return to a simmer and gently simmer for 5 minutes. Stir in the green onions.

Meanwhile, cook the noodles in a large pot of boiling salted water for 8 minutes or until al dente and drain.

To serve, pile the noodles in a mound in the center of each bowl. Pour the soup over the noodles and arrange the eggs around the noodles.

NOTE Udon noodles are thick wheat noodles, which are available dried or fresh in the Asian section of grocery stores or in Asian markets. This recipe is based on dried noodles, but if you are lucky enough to have fresh ones, follow the cooking directions on the package.

SERVES 4

4 eggs

6 cups reduced-sodium chicken broth

3 tablespoons minced fresh ginger

1½ tablespoons soy sauce

2 teaspoons mirin

½ cup finely diced carrot

1¾ cups shredded poached chicken (see Note, page 33)

1 cup sliced napa cabbage (½ inch thick)

8 shiitake mushroom caps, sliced

½ cup diagonally sliced green onions (green part only)

6 ounces udon noodles (see Note)

Toasted Chicken Sandwiches with Caramelized Apples and Smoked Gouda

Looking for sandwiches with flavor and pizzazz? These will bring raves. Starting with golden fried onions nestled on the bottom, they're layered with spiced caramelized apples, succulent chicken, smoky cheese, and a touch of honey mustard. Grill them on the stove top until golden and crisp or with a panini press.

SERVES 4

Heat the oil and 1 tablespoon of the butter in a large nonstick skillet over medium heat. Add the onions and sprinkle with the salt and pepper. Cook the onions, stirring occasionally, for 8 to 10 minutes or until they are wilted and golden brown. Transfer to a plate.

Melt 1 tablespoon of the remaining butter in the same skillet over medium heat and add the apples. Combine the sugar and allspice and sprinkle over the apples, stirring to coat them. Increase the heat to medium-high and cook the apples for 5 to 8 minutes, or until brown but still slightly crisp, increasing the heat to high if necessary.

Spread the mustard over one side of each slice of bread and lightly spread the remaining 2 tablespoons of butter over the other sides. Arrange the cheese over the mustard side of half of the bread slices. Layer with the caramelized onions, chicken, and apples. Top with the remaining bread, mustard-side down.

Grill the sandwiches in a skillet or on a griddle, lightly coated with butter or olive oil, over medium heat for 6 to 8 minutes or until the bread is toasted golden brown and the cheese is melted, turning as needed.

Serve immediately.

NOTE The onions and apples can be cooked (separately) up to 8 hours ahead of time and refrigerated. Bring to room temperature before using.

1 tablespoon extra-virgin olive oil

4 tablespoons unsalted butter, softened

2 large onions, halved and thinly sliced

1/4 teaspoon salt

1/4 teaspoon freshly ground pepper

2 unpeeled apples, such as Honeycrisp or Gala, sliced

2 teaspoons sugar

1/2 teaspoon ground allspice

1/4 cup honey mustard

8 slices country French bread (cut 1/2 inch thick from an oval loaf)

1 cup shredded smoked Gouda cheese (4 ounces)

2 cooked chicken breasts (see pages 13 to 14), thinly sliced (about 2 cups)

Baked Pasta Carbonara

This version of the Italian Roman classic—pasta with bacon, eggs, and cheese—is a homey rendition, similar to American macaroni and cheese. It's easy to make but totally decadent.

SERVES 6

Preheat the oven to 350°F. Butter a 6-cup glass or ceramic baking dish or coat with nonstick cooking spray. Cook the pasta in a large pot of boiling salted water according to package directions. Drain and rinse to cool the pasta. Transfer to a large bowl.

While the pasta is cooking, heat a medium skillet over medium heat. Add the olive oil and cook the pancetta for 5 minutes or until lightly browned, stirring frequently. The pancetta will begin to render its fat and the pieces will begin to separate instead of clumping together. Add the garlic and cook for 30 seconds or until fragrant. Remove from the heat.

Whisk the eggs in a medium bowl until smooth. Whisk in the half-and-half, ½ cup of the Parmesan cheese, the black pepper, salt, and red pepper flakes. Stir in the pancetta mixture, Gruyère cheese, and parsley.

Pour the sauce over the cooked pasta in the bowl and stir until all of the noodles are coated with the sauce. Transfer to the baking dish and sprinkle with the remaining ¼ cup of Parmesan cheese.

Bake for 30 minutes or until lightly browned and slightly puffed but creamy. Let sit for 5 minutes before serving.

8 ounces farfalle (bow-tie) pasta

1 tablespoon extra-virgin olive oil

4 ounces pancetta or bacon (see Note, page 226), chopped

3 garlic cloves, minced

3 eggs

1½ cups half-and-half

¾ cup grated Parmigiano-Reggiano cheese

½ teaspoon freshly ground black pepper

¼ teaspoon kosher salt

¼ teaspoon red pepper flakes

¾ cup shredded Gruyère cheese (13 ounces)

⅓ cup chopped fresh flat-leaf parsley

Chilean Casserole with Caramelized Corn Topping

I was lucky enough to enjoy Chile's national dish, *pastel de choclo*, in the tiny village of Pomaire, where potters make the special clay dishes in which this casserole is traditionally baked. Eating the casserole is like going on a treasure hunt. It's chock-full of ground beef, chicken, eggs, olives, and raisins, and you never know what you're going to find as you dip your fork in. The corn topping is caramelized with a light sprinkling of sugar and tastes like you're eating extra-sweet corn on the cob. While the Chileans serve this dish during the summer to take advantage of the fresh corn, I prefer it in the winter because it's such a warm, cozy dish.

TO MAKE THE CASSEROLE: Trim the chicken thighs of any excess fat. Rub with 1 teaspoon of the minced garlic and sprinkle with ½ teaspoon of the salt and the ¼ teaspoon pepper.

Heat a large nonstick skillet over medium-high heat. Heat the olive oil (the chicken should sizzle when added). Brown the chicken, in batches if necessary, laying the chicken pieces out as flat as possible. Cook for 7 to 10 minutes or until brown on the outside and no longer pink in the center, turning once. Remove the chicken and cut each thigh in half.

Add the onion to the same skillet and cook, stirring frequently, over medium to medium-low heat for 3 minutes. Crumble the ground beef into the skillet, increase the heat to medium-high, and cook for 5 minutes or until no longer pink. Stir in the raisins and cumin and sprinkle with the remaining ¼ teaspoon of salt and the ⅛ teaspoon pepper. Stir in the remaining 2 teaspoons of garlic and cook for 30 seconds or until fragrant.

Preheat the oven to 400°F. Oil an 11-by-7-inch glass baking dish or coat with nonstick cooking spray. Place on a large, rimmed baking sheet. Spoon the ground beef mixture into the baking dish and nestle the chicken, eggs, and olives in the ground beef mixture.

TO MAKE THE TOPPING: Puree the corn in a food processor until smooth. Pour in the milk and puree the mixture until smooth. Add the egg and salt and process until blended. With the processor running, pour in the hot butter and process again until blended.

SERVES 6

CASSEROLE

6 boneless, skinless chicken thighs (1¼ to 1½ pounds)

3 teaspoons minced garlic

¾ teaspoon coarse sea salt

¼ teaspoon freshly ground pepper, plus ⅛ teaspoon

1 tablespoon extra-virgin olive oil

1 large onion, chopped (1 cup)

1 pound ground beef (85% lean)

½ cup raisins

2 teaspoons ground cumin

Six 3-minute eggs, halved (see Note)

½ cup pitted Kalamata olives, halved and rinsed

TOPPING

6 cups fresh or thawed corn kernels (8 ears or three 12-ounce bags)

½ cup milk

1 egg

1 teaspoon coarse salt

5 tablespoons butter, melted and still very hot

¼ cup sugar

Pour the corn topping over the filling, making sure to cover the entire surface. Right before baking, sprinkle the sugar over the corn topping.

Bake the casserole for 40 to 45 minutes or until golden brown and slightly puffed. Let sit for 5 minutes before serving.

NOTES For 3-minute eggs, arrange the eggs in a single layer in a medium pot and fill with just enough water to cover. Bring to a gentle boil, reduce the heat to medium or medium-low, and cook for 3 minutes at a very slow, gentle boil. Put the eggs in a bowl of ice water until cool. Peel and cut the eggs in half.

The casserole can be assembled, covered, and refrigerated for up to 8 hours before baking. Sprinkle the sugar over the corn topping right before baking.

This casserole is traditionally baked and served in individual pottery bowls. To bake in individual bowls, oil or coat with nonstick cooking spray six $1\frac{1}{2}$- to 2-cup ovenproof bowls and place on a rimmed baking sheet. Spoon the filling mixture into the bowls and top with the corn topping. Sprinkle each bowl with 2 teaspoons of the sugar right before baking. Bake for 35 to 40 minutes.

FLYING FEATHERS

Chickens grow a new coat of feathers every year, usually in the fall. The old feathers drop off and new feathers eventually emerge. During this process, called molting, the birds normally stop laying and look quite rough and ragged until their new plumage develops. There are approximately 8,000 feathers on each chicken. While they molt, feathers fly everywhere.

Chicken Potpie in a Blanket of Puff Pastry

Tucked under a flaky golden-brown blanket of puff pastry are large chunks of chicken, potatoes, and mushrooms in a rosemary-scented sauce. This meal is comfort food at its best.

Thaw the puff pastry according to the package directions. Preheat the oven to 400°F. Butter an 11-by-7-inch glass baking dish or coat with nonstick cooking spray.

Melt the butter in a large saucepan over medium heat. Sauté the shallots and garlic for 30 to 40 seconds or until they begin to soften and smell fragrant. Stir in the flour and cook for 1 minute, stirring constantly. Whisk in the broth and bring to a boil. Stir in the mushrooms, potatoes, carrots, rosemary, salt, and pepper and simmer for 5 minutes. Stir in the chicken and peas and simmer for 3 minutes. Spoon the chicken mixture into the baking dish.

On a lightly floured surface, roll the puff pastry to a 13-by-9-inch rectangle. Drape over the baking dish, gently pressing the pastry where it touches the rim of the dish.

Bake for 30 to 35 minutes or until the pastry is golden brown. Remove from the oven and let sit for 5 minutes before serving. Use a spoon to scoop out the chicken mixture, topping each serving with a piece of pastry.

1 sheet frozen puff pastry (from a 17.3-ounce package)

4 tablespoons unsalted butter

½ cup chopped shallots

3 garlic cloves, minced

½ cup all-purpose flour

2 cups reduced-sodium chicken broth

2 cups (5 ounces) sliced mushrooms

12 ounces unpeeled small red potatoes (4 to 5 potatoes), diced (2 cups)

1 cup halved and sliced carrots

1 tablespoon chopped fresh rosemary

½ teaspoon kosher salt

¼ teaspoon freshly ground pepper

3 cups chopped (¾-inch pieces) cooked chicken (see pages 13 to 14)

¾ cup frozen baby peas

Paprika Chicken with Hummus

I first tasted chicken served on a bed of warm hummus at Restaurant Ambrosia in Santiago, Chile. It was a revelation. The hummus was light, creamy, and a delightful counterpoint to the spiced chicken. In this streamlined version, chicken seasoned with two types of paprika—smoked and sweet—sits on a bed of prepared hummus.

Put the chicken between two sheets of parchment paper or plastic wrap. Pound with the flat side of a meat mallet, a heavy pan, or a rolling pin until the chicken is flattened evenly and about $\frac{1}{2}$ inch thick (see Note). Stir together the cumin, smoked paprika, salt, and pepper and rub over both sides of the chicken breasts.

Stir together the hummus, sweet paprika, and turmeric in a small microwave-safe bowl until well mixed. Stir in the water (this helps lighten the mixture).

Heat a large skillet over medium-high heat and heat the oil. Sauté the chicken, in batches if necessary, for 6 to 8 minutes, reducing the heat to medium if cooking too fast, until the chicken is golden brown and no longer pink in the center, turning once.

Meanwhile, cover the hummus mixture and microwave on high for 40 to 90 seconds, or until warm.

To serve, spoon the hummus onto individual plates or a platter. Place the chicken partially over the hummus.

NOTE: To keep the parchment paper or plastic wrap from sticking to the meat while pounding, brush both sides of the chicken lightly with water. Pat the chicken breasts dry before cooking.

SERVES 4

4 boneless, skinless chicken breast halves (about 1½ pounds)

1½ teaspoons ground cumin

1½ teaspoons smoked paprika (*pimentón*)

¼ teaspoon coarse sea salt

¼ teaspoon freshly ground pepper

1 cup prepared hummus

1 teaspoon sweet Hungarian paprika

¼ teaspoon ground turmeric

2 tablespoons water

1 tablespoon extra-virgin olive oil

Chicken Breasts with Sherry Vinaigrette Cream Sauce

It's nice to have a simple dish in your repertoire that exudes elegance. This is such a dish, and it's ready from start to finish in 20 minutes. The chicken is lightly coated with a silky restaurant-quality reduction sauce. Sherry vinegar, used in place of wine, mellows and sweetens as it's reduced, concentrating the flavor. The browned bits on the bottom of the skillet provide the rich foundation for the sauce, while the cream blends the flavors and lightens the texture.

Preheat the oven to 400°F. Season the chicken with the ¼ teaspoon each of salt and pepper. Heat a large skillet over medium-high heat and heat the oil. Cook the chicken for 3 to 4 minutes or until lightly browned, turning once. Place on a small, rimmed baking sheet and bake the chicken breasts for 5 to 7 minutes, or until no longer pink in the center.

While the chicken is baking, sauté the shallots in the same skillet over medium-low heat for 40 seconds, or until they are just beginning to soften. Increase the heat to high and immediately add the vinegar. Bring to a boil and continue boiling over high heat for 30 to 60 seconds or until reduced by half, scraping up the browned bits on the bottom of the skillet. Add the broth and boil 1 minute or until reduced by half. Add the cream and continue boiling over high heat for 1 minute, or until slightly thickened (the bottom of the pan will begin to show as you stir the sauce). Season the sauce with a pinch each of salt and pepper.

Arrange the chicken breasts on a serving platter and spoon the sauce over them.

NOTE Sherry vinegar from Spain is often aged for many years, like balsamic vinegar. The longer it is aged, the higher the quality tends to be. It can be found near other vinegars in most grocery stores. If unavailable, dry sherry can be substituted.

4 boneless, skinless chicken breast halves (about 1½ pounds)

¼ teaspoon of kosher salt, plus a pinch

¼ teaspoon of freshly ground pepper, plus a pinch

1 tablespoon extra-virgin olive oil

¼ cup minced shallots

⅓ cup sherry vinegar (see Note)

½ cup reduced-sodium chicken broth

⅓ cup heavy (whipping) cream

Chicken with Charred Cauliflower and Peppers

High-temperature roasting brings out the best in this cauliflower, red bell pepper, and chicken drumstick combo. The high heat browns and slightly chars the edges of the vegetables, caramelizing them and bringing out the nutty flavor of the cauliflower. The bell peppers sweeten as they roast, and the chicken develops a golden crispy skin. The best part is that it's ready in a little over 30 minutes, making it a perfect dish for a weeknight meal.

Preheat the oven to 450°F. Lightly oil a large, rimmed baking sheet or spray with nonstick cooking spray. Toss the cauliflower and red bell peppers with 2 tablespoons of the oil and the lemon juice in a large bowl. Add 2 of the garlic cloves and ¼ teaspoon each of the salt and pepper and toss the vegetables to mix. Arrange on the baking sheet.

Toss the chicken drumsticks in the same bowl with the remaining oil, garlic, salt, pepper, and the cumin. Nestle the chicken in and around the vegetables.

Bake for 30 to 40 minutes or until the chicken is no longer pink in the center and the vegetables are tender.

Serve immediately.

SERVES 4

1 small head cauliflower (about 1 pound), cut into florets (4 cups)

2 large red bell peppers, seeded, deveined, and cut into 2-inch pieces

3 tablespoons extra-virgin olive oil

1 tablespoon fresh lemon juice

4 garlic cloves, minced

¾ teaspoon coarse sea salt

½ teaspoon freshly ground pepper

8 chicken drumsticks (about 2 pounds)

2 teaspoons ground cumin

Pot-Roast Chicken with Mushrooms

Move over, beef—chicken makes a great pot roast. Braised in a heavy pot and surrounded by potatoes, carrots, and two kinds of mushrooms, this chicken begs to be served with crusty bread to soak up the juices.

Preheat the oven to 350°F. Pour the boiling water over the porcini in a small heat-proof bowl and let soak for 30 minutes. Drain, reserving the soaking liquid. Strain the soaking liquid through a paper coffee filter to remove any sediment and reserve the liquid. Rinse the mushrooms of any sediment and pat dry. Coarsely chop.

While the porcini are soaking, heat a large ovenproof pot, such as a Dutch oven, over medium-high heat and heat the oil. Brown the chicken in batches for 4 to 6 minutes, turning once. Remove the chicken, add the onion, and cook for 3 minutes, stirring occasionally. Add the garlic and cook for 15 seconds, stirring constantly.

Return the chicken to the pot and nestle the potatoes, carrots, and cremini and porcini mushrooms all around. Pour in the soaking liquid from the mushrooms and add enough of the broth to come about halfway up the chicken. Stir in the salt and pepper. Cover and bring to a boil over medium-high heat.

Bake for 45 to 50 minutes or until the chicken is no longer pink in the center and the vegetables are tender. Remove the chicken and vegetables to a platter. Boil the pan juices over high heat for 5 to 8 minutes or until slightly thickened (or the consistency you prefer).

Serve the chicken and vegetables accompanied by the pan juices.

$3/4$ cup boiling water

1 ounce dried porcini mushrooms or other dried mushrooms

2 tablespoons extra-virgin olive oil

One 3-pound chicken, cut into 8 pieces

$1^1/2$ cups coarsely chopped onion (1 to 2 onions)

3 garlic cloves, coarsely chopped

6 unpeeled small red potatoes (about 1 pound), quartered

3 carrots, cut crosswise into 4 pieces each

8-ounces cremini (baby bella) mushrooms, halved

1 cup reduced-sodium chicken broth, or as needed

1 teaspoon kosher salt

$1/2$ teaspoon freshly ground pepper

Roast Chicken with Crispy Smashed Potatoes

As much as I love new ingredients and different flavor combinations, there are times when a meal of meat and potatoes is simply the best. The roast chicken, slathered with butter and seasoned with salt and pepper, shines on its own without competing flavors. Look for a bird that has been well taken care of and allowed pasture time to roam. Its flavor will be fuller, richer, and tastier than a confined bird. You may want to make extra potatoes for the potato lovers in your group. A cross between roasted potatoes and mashed potatoes, they're crisp and dripping with the flavor of the buttery chicken. They may well be the best-tasting potatoes you've ever eaten.

SERVES 4

One 3$\frac{1}{2}$- to 4-pound chicken

1$\frac{1}{4}$ teaspoons coarse sea salt

1 teaspoon freshly ground pepper

6 tablespoons unsalted butter, softened

6 unpeeled small red potatoes

6 unpeeled small fingerling or small white potatoes

6 garlic cloves

2 large onions, cut into 1-inch wedges

1 tablespoon extra-virgin olive oil

Preheat the oven to 425°F. Pat the chicken dry with paper towels so the butter will adhere to the skin, and tuck the wings behind the back. Sprinkle the chicken all over with $\frac{1}{2}$ teaspoon each of the salt and pepper. Coat the chicken with 4 tablespoons of the butter, using your hands to slather the butter all over. Place the chicken, breast-side up, in the center of a shallow roasting pan or large, rimmed baking sheet.

Toss the red potatoes, fingerling potatoes, garlic, and onions with the olive oil in a medium bowl. Sprinkle with $\frac{1}{2}$ teaspoon of the salt and the remaining $\frac{1}{2}$ teaspoon pepper and toss to coat. Arrange the vegetables around the chicken.

Bake for 30 minutes. Meanwhile, melt the remaining 2 tablespoons of butter. Remove the chicken and vegetables from the oven. Transfer one potato at a time to a plate. Using the flat side of a meat pounder, or a potato masher, gently pound or smash the potatoes until they flatten slightly and split open. The potatoes should not completely fall apart. Return the potatoes to the roasting pan, brush with the melted butter, and sprinkle with the remaining $\frac{1}{4}$ teaspoon of salt. Turn the chicken breast-side down (silicone hot pads or mitts are helpful).

Continue baking for another 15 minutes. Remove from the oven and turn the chicken breast-side up. Turn the potatoes. Bake for another 10 to 15 minutes, or until the internal temperature of the chicken at the thickest point of the thigh (without touching a bone) registers 175°F, and the potatoes are golden brown and tender.

Let the chicken rest for 10 minutes before carving. Serve surrounded by the potatoes, onions, and garlic.

Chocolate Mocha Soufflés

Soufflés make the perfect showcase for your backyard eggs. Don't be intimidated. The eggs do all the work as they rise dramatically, producing a spectacular dish that you'll get the credit for. These individual soufflés should be eaten as soon after baking as possible because they will deflate quickly once pulled from the oven.

TO MAKE THE SOUFFLÉS: Preheat the oven to 400°F. Butter six ⅔ cup ramekins and sprinkle with sugar. Place on a baking sheet. Put the chocolate, butter, and the espresso powder in a medium bowl.

Whisk the ¼ cup sugar, the cocoa, cornstarch, and salt together in a small saucepan. Slowly whisk in the half-and-half. Bring to a boil over medium heat, reduce the heat to medium-low, and gently boil for 1 minute, whisking constantly. Pour over the chocolate and let sit for 1 minute. Whisk until smooth. Let sit for 5 minutes to cool slightly, and then whisk in the egg yolks and Kahlúa.

Beat the egg whites in a medium bowl with an electric mixer at medium speed until frothy. Add the cream of tartar and beat for 1 minute or until firm, but not stiff, peaks form. Stir in one-fourth of the egg whites to lighten the chocolate mixture, and then fold in the remaining egg whites. Spoon into the ramekins.

Bake the soufflés for 3 minutes. Reduce the oven temperature to 375°F and bake for another 10 minutes, or until the soufflés have risen and set.

TO MAKE THE COFFEE CREAM: While the soufflés are baking, beat the ingredients together in a medium bowl with an electric mixer at medium-high speed until soft peaks form.

Serve the soufflés immediately, topped with the coffee cream.

NOTE Bittersweet chocolate (60 to 70% cacao) can also be used.

SERVES 6

SOUFFLÉS

4 ounces semisweet chocolate, finely chopped (see Note)

2 tablespoons unsalted butter

2 teaspoons instant espresso powder or instant coffee

1 tablespoon unsweetened cocoa

Sugar for sprinkling, plus ¼ cup

1 tablespoon cornstarch

⅛ teaspoon salt

⅔ cup half-and-half

3 eggs, separated

1 tablespoon Kahlúa or another coffee liqueur, or cold coffee

¼ teaspoon cream of tartar

COFFEE CREAM

¾ cup heavy (whipping) cream

1 tablespoon sugar

½ teaspoon instant espresso powder or instant coffee

Orange Shortbread Bites

These shortbread cookies, made with an egg yolk, are richer and more tender than traditional ones. Paired with an orange-flavored curd, they're transformed into tiny sandwich cookies.

TO MAKE THE SHORTBREAD: Preheat the oven to 375°F. Line two baking sheets with parchment paper. Beat the butter and orange zest in a large bowl with an electric mixer at low speed for 1 minute. Add the granulated sugar and beat for an additional minute. Add the egg yolks and beat until blended.

Whisk together the flour, cornstarch, cardamom, and salt in a small bowl. With the mixer on low, slowly beat the flour mixture into the dough. Shape into a flat disk, cover, and refrigerate for 1 hour or until firm.

Roll 1 teaspoon of dough into a ¾- to 1-inch ball and place on a baking sheet. Repeat with the remaining dough to make 40 cookies. Press each ball, flattening it slightly, until 1¼ inches in diameter.

Bake the cookies for 8 to 10 minutes or until golden brown on the bottom and along the edges. Transfer to a wire rack and cool.

TO MAKE THE FILLING: Whisk the orange juice, granulated sugar, egg yolks, and salt together in a small bowl until blended. Whisk in the orange zest. Melt the butter in a small saucepan and slowly pour into the orange juice mixture, whisking constantly. Pour the orange juice mixture back into the same saucepan and cook over medium heat, whisking constantly, until thickened and bubbles just begin to form on the outside edge. Do not let the orange curd come to a full boil, or the mixture may curdle. Pour into a clean small bowl. Cover and refrigerate for 1 hour or until cooled.

To assemble the cookies, spoon a generous teaspoon of orange curd onto the flat side of a cookie. Repeat until you've covered half of the cookies. Top with the remaining cookies and gently press together. Store in the refrigerator until ready to serve. Sprinkle the tops with the powdered sugar before serving.

MAKES 20
SANDWICH COOKIES
(½ CUP OF CURD)

SHORTBREAD

½ cup (1 stick) unsalted butter, softened and cut up

1½ teaspoons grated orange zest

¾ cup granulated sugar

2 egg yolks

1¼ cups all-purpose flour

2 tablespoons cornstarch

½ teaspoon ground cardamom

¼ teaspoon salt

ORANGE CURD FILLING

¼ cup fresh orange juice

¼ cup granulated sugar

3 egg yolks

Pinch of salt

2 teaspoons grated orange zest

2 tablespoons unsalted butter

Powdered sugar for sprinkling

Banana Cupcakes with Brown Butter Cream Cheese Frosting

When the winter egg supply runs low, I'm particular about where I use my eggs. These cupcakes are worthy of those precious orbs. Moist and luscious with ripe bananas, toasted walnuts, and allspice, they're crowned with a nutty-tasting butter frosting.

TO MAKE THE CUPCAKES: Preheat the oven to 350°F. Line a 12-cup muffin pan with cupcake liners or coat with nonstick cooking spray. Whisk together the flour, baking powder, allspice, baking soda, and salt in a medium bowl.

Beat the butter, granulated sugar, and vanilla in a large bowl with an electric mixer at medium speed for 3 minutes or until light and fluffy. Reduce the speed to low and add the eggs and egg yolk, one at a time, beating well after adding each one. Beat in the flour mixture in three parts alternately with the milk, beginning and ending with the flour. Beat in the bananas and stir in the walnuts. Spoon the batter into the muffin cups (they will be almost full).

Bake the cupcakes for 25 to 30 minutes or until a wooden tooth-pick inserted in the center of a cupcake comes out clean. Remove the cupcakes from the pan and cool completely on a wire rack.

TO MAKE THE FROSTING: While the cupcakes are cooling, melt the butter in a small saucepan over medium heat and cook for 2 to 3 minutes, or until the milk solids in the bottom of the pan turn brown and the butter smells nutty, reducing the heat to medium-low or low if the butter is cooking too fast. Watch carefully so the butter does not burn. Pour into a medium bowl and chill in the refrigerator for 30 minutes, or until the consistency of softened butter, stirring occasionally.

Beat the browned butter with an electric mixer at medium speed until smooth. Beat in the cream cheese and vanilla. Slowly add enough of the powdered sugar to make a spreadable frosting. Pipe the frosting on top of each cupcake using a pastry bag and a star tip, or spread with a spoon, leaving the edges of the cupcake showing.

Serve at room temperature. Store in the refrigerator for up to 3 days.

MAKES 12 CUPCAKES

CUPCAKES

1¾ cups all-purpose flour

1 teaspoon baking powder

1 teaspoon ground allspice

¼ teaspoon baking soda

¼ teaspoon salt

½ cup (1 stick) unsalted butter, softened

1 cup granulated sugar

1 teaspoon vanilla extract

2 eggs plus 1 egg yolk

¼ cup milk

2 very ripe bananas, mashed (1 cup)

½ cup chopped walnuts, toasted (see Note, page 160)

FROSTING

4 tablespoons unsalted butter, cut up

4 ounces cream cheese, softened

¼ teaspoon vanilla extract

1¾ to 2 cups powdered sugar

POSTSCRIPT: IN MEMORIAM

During the editing of this book, one of my three girls, Crazy Lulu, became ill and died suddenly. The necropsy showed an egg had become lodged in her abdomen, resulting in a severe infection. Losing a chicken is as difficult as losing any beloved pet. We all miss her dearly, especially her coop mates, but we're thankful that she shared her life with us.

—JANICE COLE

Index

TABLE OF EQUIVALENTS

Liquid/Dry Measurements

U.S.	Metric
1/4 teaspoon	1.25 milliliters
1/2 teaspoon	2.5 milliliters
1 teaspoon	5 milliliters
1 tablespoon (3 teaspoons)	15 milliliters
1 fluid ounce (2 tablespoons)	30 milliliters
1/4 cup	60 milliliters
1/3 cup	80 milliliters
1/2 cup	120 milliliters
1 cup	240 milliliters
1 pint (2 cups)	480 milliliters
1 quart (4 cups, 32 ounces)	960 milliliters
1 gallon (4 quarts)	3.84 liters
1 ounce (by weight)	28 grams
1 pound	448 grams
2.2 pounds	1 kilogram

Oven Temperatures

Fahrenheit	Celsius	Gas
250	120	1/2
275	140	1
300	150	2
325	160	3
350	180	4
375	190	5
400	200	6
425	220	7
450	230	8
475	240	9
500	260	10

Lengths

U.S.	Metric
1/8 inch	3 millimeters
1/4 inch	6 millimeters
1/2 inch	12 millimeters
1 inch	2.5 centimeters